Wisecracks

∴

Wisecracks

∵

HUMOR AND MORALITY
IN EVERYDAY LIFE

David Shoemaker

THE UNIVERSITY OF CHICAGO PRESS
CHICAGO AND LONDON

The University of Chicago Press, Chicago 60637
The University of Chicago Press, Ltd., London
© 2024 by The University of Chicago
Published 2024
Printed in the United States of America

33 32 31 30 29 28 27 26 25 24   1 2 3 4 5

ISBN-13: 978-0-226-83296-8 (cloth)
ISBN-13: 978-0-226-83298-2 (paper)
ISBN-13: 978-0-226-83297-5 (e-book)
DOI: https://doi.org/10.7208/chicago/9780226832975.001.0001

Library of Congress Cataloging-in-Publication Data

Names: Shoemaker, David, 1964– author.
Title: Wisecracks : humor and morality in everyday life / David Shoemaker.
Description: Chicago : The University of Chicago Press, 2024. | Includes
    bibliographical references and index.
Identifiers: LCCN 2023033210 | ISBN 9780226832968 (cloth) | ISBN
    9780226832982 (paperback) | ISBN 9780226832975 (ebook)
Subjects: LCSH: Wit and humor—Moral and ethical aspects. | Wit and
    humor—Social aspects. | Wit and humor—Therapeutic use.
Classification: LCC PN6147 .S46 2024 | DDC 152.4/3—dc23/eng/20230830
LC record available at https://lccn.loc.gov/2023033210

♾ This paper meets the requirements of ANSI/NISO Z39.48-1992
(Permanence of Paper).

To all of my hilarious friends . . .

. . . if only I had some.

Contents

Part Three
FINDING FUNNY

Introduction

When I told my buddy Mark that I was going to write a book on humor, his immediate response was "But that assumes you know something about it."

Now *that's* what I'm talking about!

No, seriously, that's what I'm talking about!

Nearly every book or article that's been written on humor focuses on canned jokes, those packaged bits of funny that we tell or retell one another, with their familiar setups and punch lines, the ones that may start with, "Did you hear the one about . . . ?" or "A priest, a rabbi, and a duck walk into a bar." This book doesn't have much to say about jokes, which are actually pretty rare in our everyday lives. We may occasionally watch a comedian's new Netflix special on a Friday evening, pass along jokes we've heard to our friends at the bar every once in a while, or act out our favorite bits from a *Saturday Night Live* sketch to our colleagues now and again. These canned materials are certainly one source of amusement in our lives. But by far the more prevalent source comes from the banter, teasing, mockery, prankery, taking the piss, leg-pulling, joshing, and quippery that happen between people in everyday life who know each other, sometimes pretty well. These knockabout humorous exchanges are informal and interpersonal. They are familiar funny features of daily conversations, part of our back-and-forth dialogues with each other, whereas the jokes we tell are monologues, prepared performances that interrupt ordinary conversations. The more informal witty exchanges I want to focus on often involve multiple parties attempting to one up each other, trying to make ever funnier contributions to an ongoing amusement party. They are what I'm calling *wisecracks*, which are made, not told, and they are the main focus of this book.[1] (A quick remark about notes, the first of which has just appeared: They will provide references of work cited, more detailed philosophical exploration of some of the issues raised for those interested, and additional opportunity for more of my dumb wisecracks. Please feel free to ignore them.)

As we'll see, there's not always a hard-and-fast distinction between jokes and wisecracks, but the basic difference I want to emphasize between them has to do with where the funniness is typically located in each. The funniness in jokes is found primarily in their logical or semantic structure. Many writers like to point to the *incongruity* of jokes as the source of their funniness, perhaps involving the introduction of some unexpected mismatch, the exploitation of some ambiguity in the language, or a switcheroo in how ordinary scripts might go. Consider a classic "moron" joke:

> The Space Agency of Moronistan announced today that they would send a manned mission to the sun. When asked how they would withstand the heat, they responded, "Oh, we'll go at night."

The funniness of this joke comes from the incongruous idea of a space agency with such ridiculously stupid engineers. But the funniness is completely contained within the joke itself. It can be fully and equally recognized in hearing someone tell it to you, overhearing someone telling it to someone else, seeing it on TV, reading it on the internet, or receiving it in an email or text message.

Wisecracks, by contrast, are intentional bits of humor whose funniness is found not just in their formal features but also in their interpersonal features. When we tease others, for instance, often what's funny isn't found just in our quips themselves but in the reactions of those we are teasing. When I pull your leg, its funniness isn't going to come simply from the false remarks I make; it will come, in addition, from the fact that I fooled you for a bit with those remarks, that I "got you." When two people of shared ethnicity make a crack that exploits some stereotype about their group, its funniness may come only from their shared disdain for that stereotype or for the people who believe that stereotype. These are all contextual, interpersonal matters.

Sometimes, of course, the difference between prepared jokes and wisecracks may not be all that clear. For example, some professional comedians relay anecdotes in a wisecrack-ish form—informally, spontaneously, and incorporating audience feedback—and some interpersonal teasing takes on a joke-ish form, as when Black teenagers play "the dozens," crafting increasingly outrageous insults of each other (often about their mothers). But there remains a recognizable distinction between jokes and wisecracks, at least of the kind I'm most interested in, and it's one that motivates this book. Wisecracks are the kinds of witticisms we make *with* each other. And it's with that "with" that we arrive at the fundamental problem.

Because the funniness of jokes essentially comes just from their formal features, on their own they don't raise much moral trouble (despite what some people think). Only wisecracks raise genuine moral trouble, precisely because their funniness—or lack thereof!—is so interpersonal. Wise-cracking is a way that people interact with other people, a way of treating other people, and, as such, wisecracks are explicitly subject to the norms of morality. But wisecracks are also subject to the norms of humor. And the overarching aim of this book is to reveal just how intertwined both sets of norms actually are. Whether a wisecrack is funny—or just how funny it is—can sometimes depend on what moral or immoral features it has, just as its moral status can sometimes depend on what funny or unfunny features it has. Further, a good sense of humor actually requires a good sense of moral-ity, just as a good sense of morality requires a good sense of humor.

Working through Mark's wisecrack illustrates and expands on these points, and it also helps introduce the chapters to come. First, Mark's re-mark was funny, but why? After all, on its face it seems to be a kind of insult. He sounds like he's saying that I'm not funny, that I know nothing about humor, so I couldn't possibly write an informed book on humor. But given that I'm implying that I *do* know something about humor by taking on this project, this would be a pretty harsh thing to say. Indeed, were he just to say all that explicitly ("You're not funny, so why think you could write a good book about humor!"), it wouldn't be funny at all. So what's going on?

The answer is that he's not actually insulting me, and I know he's not in-sulting me. Instead, he's merely acting as if he were. But then why is acting like you're insulting someone funny? Imagine a stranger, who, overhearing my announcement that I'm writing a book on humor, pipes up and says, as if he were insulting me, "Well, that assumes you know something about it!" That's not funny; instead, it's just weird. The funniness of Mark's identical comment thus must have something to do with the fact that we know each other.

Faux insults from people we know can be funny. What about real in-sults? They can be funny too. Suppose I've already self-published five books on humor, each of them worse and more unfunny than the previous one. Hardly anyone bought them, and those who did regretted it. Mark knows all this, and when I announce yet another book on humor, he wryly remarks, "I'm sure this will be the one that turns it all around for you!" This is a sar-castic insult, saying the opposite of what he means, which is that I really am unfunny, and this will most definitely not be the one that turns it all around for me. But how he says it is also funny.

Even if I can recognize this wisecrack as an attempt at a funny put-down, however, I may or may not *find* it funny, that is, I may not in fact be amused by it. Indeed, while the funniness of wisecracks comes in part from their interpersonal nature, that same interpersonal nature is what also may give rise to anger, if there's some mistreatment thought to be contained within it. And if Mark's wisecrack were to make me angry, it's going to be psychologically difficult, if not impossible, for me to be amused at the same time.

As it turns out, the funniness of Mark's original faux insult, and my ability to find it funny, depend on a lot of things. He must know and like me, I must know and like him. I have to give him the benefit of the doubt that he's not actually insulting me and that he doesn't have any malice toward me, and he must know that I know and like him and will give him the benefit of the doubt. He must also know that I know that he knows that I know and like him and will give him the benefit of the doubt. We must be friends, in other words, of a familiar sort. All of this information enables me to know that he doesn't mean what he says as an insult, even though he's pretending that he does.

But none of this yet explains why a friend pretending to insult me is funny. Why isn't it instead, like a stranger pretending to insult me, just weird? Answering this question more generally is the aim of chapter 1. Many people are going to come to the table thinking that there's nothing more to what's funny than what different individuals in fact find funny: If I'm amused by something, they think, then it's funny to me, and if you aren't amused by it, then it's not funny to you, and that's that. Put like that, the view is wrong, but it does have a wee bit of truth in it. In order to find out what makes things funny, we do have to make some reference to how people feel about it: things are funny because of their specific way of interacting with our *senses of humor*. It's our humor sensibility that determines what's funny and what's not. But it's not just anyone's actual amused response that determines what's funny, because people can be, and often are, mistaken about what's funny or not. If you think that it's funny when a police interrogator tortures an innocent suspect, say, you're just wrong. People can also be mistaken in declaring some things not funny that are: Mark's faux insult was indeed funny, and those who think otherwise are wrong. How to determine whose responses are right and whose are wrong is a fascinating story that I hope to make clear by the end of chapter 1.

Wisecracking, as we all know, can have many dark sides. First, some wisecracks are exclusionary. Humor among members of in-groups about members of out-groups often seals the borders between them. Private jokes do this by speaking a language deliberately obscure to outsiders. Mockery may do this by presenting those outsiders as lower, as lesser, than insiders.

Second, sometimes there are asymmetrical relationships in which only one side gets to engage in teasing or mockery of the other, and this hardens hierarchy. We see this phenomenon most clearly in studies of organizations in which bosses tease or mock their employees, and the employees (for fear of losing their jobs) have to "take it" and can't tease or mock their bosses back.[2]

Third, some humor just plain hurts. Mockery, in particular, when it's done by insiders to outsiders (to those who are "different," socially excluded, nerds, the disabled, etc.) can reinforce exclusion, difference, and the pain of being an outsider. This is the kind of humor that involves "laughing at" someone, and we all know how painful being laughed at can be.

Fourth, some hurtful humor has "next-generation" bad effects, shaping otherwise innocent people in ways that cause them to become hurtful to others down the line. A study of autistic teenagers in China revealed that several of them engaged in aggressive humor, mercilessly teasing and ridiculing other students, a type of humor that most studies suggest that those with autism typically don't engage in.[3] When the authors investigated more deeply, they found a heartbreaking explanation of why: These kids had been so mercilessly teased for being "different" when they were younger that they saw this kind of humor as the only way to fit in with others, and so that's what they practiced themselves.[4]

Fifth, certain kinds of identity-based humor, wisecracks directed at people that reference their group membership (e.g., their gender, class, ethnicity, or race) can generate what's known as a "social identity threat," where what's communicated to the targeted person is "that they are at risk of being devalued, rejected, or of becoming the target of discrimination because of their group membership."[5] It also just plain hurts, as it reminds people of their oppressed or marginalized status.

Sixth, because of their context dependence, occasional reliance on hard-to-read intentions, or serious subtlety, lots of wisecracks may be easily misunderstood, and that can fracture relationships.

Seventh, some wisecracks are deceptive, involving pulling the wool over someone's eyes, deliberately preventing them from seeing some truth that everyone around them can see. But deliberately deceiving someone is immoral, isn't it, so aren't such wisecracks immoral as well?

This is a lot of darkness. As a result, some people insist that whenever wisecracks have any of these immoral features, they just aren't funny. These people are right that some forms of wisecracking humor do have immoral features. But they are wrong in thinking that those features eliminate all the humor. True, a brutally cruel wisecrack may not be funny at all. But sometimes cruelty in a wisecrack is precisely what makes it funny (or funnier). Once the view of the general relation between humor and morality is set forth in chapter 2, we'll be ready to explore over the following three chapters the specific moral worries raised by deceptive humor, mockery, and stereotyping wisecracks.

First, though, you might well wonder, given all the dark sides and moral risks of wisecracking, why we should bother defending it at all? After all, what are we even defending? A little amusement? Sure, that may be enjoyable for a second, but who cares about such a trivial pleasure when immorality may be at stake?

As it turns out, there are many reasons to engage in the wisecracking life, beyond the enjoyment any individual crack may bring. First, those who make you feel amusement's pleasure are going to be people you're likely to gravitate toward, to want to hang around. Amusing people are likable, they're fun, and they make you feel good. Humor brings people together. Debbie Downer doesn't have any friends.[6]

Second, many wisecracks involve self-deprecating anecdotes. In telling these, you invite listeners' sympathy and protective warmth. A self-deprecating humor style generally also seems to increase one's emotional and psychological well-being, better enabling one to cope with various setbacks.[7] And other people are obviously drawn to emotionally healthy people.

Third, in making wisecracks about your experiences, you create or reinforce enjoyable bonds with those who also have had similar experiences, inviting empathy and identification. Wisecracking between close friends assumes lots of shared background and knowledge, generating or buttressing intimacy between wisecrackers.

Fourth, wisecracking signals, and can bring about, reconciliation. As John Morreall insightfully notes:

When two people are quarreling, one of the first things they stop doing together is laughing; they refuse to laugh at each other's attempts at humor, and refuse to laugh together at something incongruous happening to them. As soon as they begin to laugh once more, we know that the end of the quarrel is at hand.[8]

Fifth, between those who aren't yet in a personal relationship, humor can reduce uncertainty and social distance, increase cooperation, and generate trust.[9] In general, a good sense of humor is strongly correlated with social competence. Humorous people are more cheerful, and so, again, are more likely to attract friends. They are better able to manage their emotions, so they seem far less volatile and more inviting.[10]

Sixth, wisecracks of various kinds also serve to create and reinforce group boundaries. When in-group members make fun of those outside the group, yes, it may exclude those others, but it also makes the insiders feel like special club members. Teasing within the group thus serves to bond its members.[11] Wisecracking is particularly powerful at reinforcing bonds within families. Loving siblings sometimes tease and mock each other mercilessly, and it is in fact an expression of their strong love for each other (especially for family members who have a harder time expressing affection straightforwardly). More generally, though, underdogs together make fun of their bullies, and this too unites them, makes them stronger. Cancer survivors make wisecracks with each other about their ordeals, bringing them closer together. These are all familiar phenomena.

Seventh, wisecracks provide a fascinating way to identify, test, or alter the status of relationships that one is in. Suppose I hadn't known Mark very well: We'd only hung out at the bar a bit and played pool together a few times. Then one day I announce my plans for this humor book and he says, "That assumes you know something about it." On the one hand, I could respond by feeling offended, thinking, "You don't know me well enough to tease me like that!" This thought alone is quite revealing. On the other hand, I might recognize the humor in the remark and see it as a sign that he regards me as in fact a closer friend than I had realized up until that point. We only tease the ones we love, perhaps (at least in certain ways). And I may come to regard him now as a closer friend. That is, the wisecrack serves, in its way, to *make* us closer friends than we had been just one moment before; it bonds us. This is one of the great powers of wisecracking.[12]

Do I need to go on? These should all be familiar points that we don't really need empirical investigation to verify (although there's plenty). These facts generate powerful reasons to appreciate and engage in wisecracking humor, to join in on the amusement party, and so to refine and widen the range of our humor sensibilities so as to be more inclusive in what we find funny, both to increase the range and type of relationships we can enter into and to reap the vast prudential benefits of being in those relationships. Good stuff!

We've thus got excellent reasons to engage in the wisecracking life, but we may also have serious moral qualms about doing so. My title points to a kind of pun: Wisecracks may both bridge cracks and crack bridges, bond people and divide them. Which one occurs depends crucially on what role, if any, empathy plays in the exchange. This is the first of two subthemes running throughout the book. Not enough empathy can lead to callous or cruel wisecrackery of the sort that generates hurt, exclusion, discrimination, or worse. But too much empathy can—surprisingly—be bad as well, breeding overly sensitive people who never want to tread on anyone's feelings, who think kindness is incompatible with the tiniest bit of meanness or deception, and who get morally upset by any wisecracks that incorporate such things. Both types of people—the under- and overempathic—have bad senses of humor *and* morality, and it's not a coincidence why.

Empathy can be extended too much or too little. To get the social benefits of wisecrackery, you have to deploy empathy in moderation. You have to know what people can take and what they can't. You have to know the types of humor they'll enjoy and those they won't. But you also have to know when you ought to sympathize with their misfortunes and when it's OK to emotionally detach from those misfortunes and make fun of them for those misfortunes. Being a successful wisecracker means both that your wisecracks are funny and that they are well-taken. That is, the success of your wisecracks depends in part on what you mean for them to do. This is the second main subtheme of the book: What crucially matters in responding correctly to both the funniness and the moral status of a wisecrack are the wisecracker's intentions and motives, which amount to what the wisecracker means by it and what his or her attitudes are toward others affected or targeted by the wisecrack.

Many people today disagree with this view. They maintain that how we should respond to both jokes and wisecracks is at least sometimes determined independently of what anyone means by it and is instead determined exclusively by how some people take it, that is, by whether some are morally offended by it.

I aim to argue against this view, but it will take some doing. How we ought to respond to wisecracks does depend fundamentally on the intentions and motives of those who make them, as well as on the relationships and contexts within which they are made. These contextual factors are the only way to differentiate between morally innocent and morally heinous wisecracks, for example, that are otherwise identical to each other in terms of their content.

Now back to the outline of the book. From the general relation between humor and morality laid out in chapter 2, chapters 3–5 will focus on three specific moral troubles associated with some kinds of wisecracks. Return to Mark's zinger. It could well have been presented in different ways, and these differences would have translated into differences in both its degree of funniness and how I might have taken the remark. Suppose first that when I told him I was going to write a book on humor, Mark had said, "I'm just kidding here, but that assumes you know something about it." The qualification announcing that he's "just kidding" would squash any humor in his subsequent quip. Suppose, alternatively, that my previous book had been critically trashed and a commercial failure, facts that I'm still very sensitive about, so Mark said: "Oh, I see what your motto is: 'Give the people more of what they don't want.'" This remark, while funny, stings me; indeed, as in the earlier example, I may have a hard time finding it funny. Finally, suppose he'd leaned in and said, "Hmmm, isn't Shoemaker a German name? You're right, the Germans are well known for their humor stylings. I'm sure it'll be a big hit." This remark sarcastically plays with an ethnic stereotype, disparaging Germans for their poor senses of humor. But doesn't morality counsel that we avoid such stereotyping?

Each of these alternatives raises a specific type of moral concern. The first reveals that deception is a component of some humor. His humor-killing "I'm just kidding here" signals that he doesn't really mean what he's about to say (as if he's insulting me), but if he'd left the "just kidding" out, it would indeed be an attempt to deceive me—if only for a second—about his actual beliefs of my humor qualifications, a deception for the sake of amusement. Some may think this isn't "real" deception, but they are wrong. Indeed, a huge swath of wisecracking humor does require actual deception in order to be funny. For me to prank you or pull your leg in a funny way, I have to get you to believe something false, full stop. Perhaps, then, this isn't *immoral* deception? It is, as it turns out, but certain immoralities may often be justifiable nonetheless, as long as there's enough funny in them and there aren't other objectionably immoral elements in play.

The second sarcastic version of Mark's wisecrack—"Give the people more of what they don't want"—is an example of mockery. Mockery aims to sting the mocked person, at least a little bit. I don't build you up in mocking you; I only aim to knock you down to size. So there seems to be a kind of meanness to it. But isn't aiming at meanness immoral? As we'll see in chapter 4, while there's definitely a sting in mockery, it's often nevertheless perfectly OK to engage in and be amused by it. More controversially, the demands of inclusivity may sometimes morally justify, and even morally require, mocking people often thought to be "out of bounds" for such treatment. Defending this point will involve a discussion of the "punching up/punching down" distinction that many are fond of. It's a distinction that doesn't withstand critical investigation very well, as it turns out.

The third version of Mark's wisecrack, about German humor (or the lack thereof), plays with an ethnic stereotype. This is one example of stereotyping humor, and chapter 5 is all about these and others, mostly racial and gendered jokes or wisecracks. Many people think that stereotyping humor is mostly immoral, that it just can't be funny, or, even if it is, that no one should engage in or be amused by it. But as it turns out, it's really hard to get a precise bead on what is objectionable about it, and it's even harder to see why people should never engage in or be amused by it, especially given the possibility of certain attitudes and contexts among makers of jokes and wisecracks. Racism and sexism are by no means funny; indeed, they are immoral, full stop. But some jokes and wisecracks that play with racial and sexual stereotypes can be funny, and sometimes people may have good reasons to play with them.

I'm well aware that this is very dicey territory. In order to investigate whether attempts at stereotyping humor can be either funny or morally permissible, and to show how much context and intentions matter, I have to mention actual knife-edge examples of it, in the form of both jokes and wisecracks. These may well be cherry-picked for callout, cancellation, or consequence. I'll push back on the morality of doing so in these middle chapters.

It can of course be hard to navigate this complicated moral terrain when wisecracking. Those who do so well are those we describe as having good senses of humor. But what is a sense of humor, let alone a good one? This is the topic of chapter 6. A sense of humor is an actual sense, a way of perceiving certain features of the world. A good sense of humor perceives comic features of the world well. But what does *that* mean? To best answer this question, I explore what's going on with some people who have impaired faculties of comic perception. Some autistic people, for example, may have difficulty finding the funny in a certain kind of absurdist humor or insult comedy. Some psychopaths and narcissists find humor only in aggressive ridicule and sarcasm. Some people with mania find too many things funny. Some people with clinical depression have a hard time finding anything funny. Why? It will again have something essential to do with empathy and its impairments, and our answer will again reveal the tight relation between a good sense of humor and a good sense of morality.

Still, there are some people without any psychological disorders or deficits in empathy who nevertheless have poor senses of humor. They either find too much humor in things they should not be amused by, or they find too little humor in things they should be amused by. Should they be corrected, and if so, how? In the final chapter, I offer some practical advice. What I recommend to improve one's sense of humor is to develop a finely honed sense of the absurd, a way of sometimes seeing one's own life, and the lives of everyone around one, as without a point, as not mattering. This may seem a strange and dangerous recommendation: Aren't psychopaths, for example, the best (worst) illustrations of people who don't take the value of life seriously? I guess you'll just have to tune in to chapter 7 to see how I get out of that one. It won't surprise you to hear that empathy once again plays a crucial role, but in its Goldilocks form: You can't have too little or too much; it has to be *juuuust* right.

It should be obvious that humor plays a powerful and sometimes morally troublesome role in our everyday lives, but this role and its implications and connections have not been previously exposed and explored. In what follows, I aim to do so. Of course, that assumes I know something about it.

∴

Part One

HUMOR, MORALITY, AND THE RELATIONS BETWEEN THEM

∵

[CHAPTER ONE]

"You Had to Be There!"

The Nature of Humor

I was an assistant professor of philosophy for a few years at Bowling Green State University, in northwest Ohio. There I met some of the smartest and funniest people in my life. There I also met my colleagues. *Zing*!

Anyway, I went up for tenure in 2006. Doing so required generating letters of evaluation from famous philosophers in my field, compiling student evaluations and research publications, and documenting my service to the university. Once all of these things had been assembled, but before the department had voted on my case, I went out for dinner with several of my tenured colleagues. As we were waiting in the bar to be seated, the chair of the department, an enthusiastic and optimistic guy, was excitedly telling me how great my tenure file was: "The letters about you are over the top, and you've published so many excellent papers in great venues, and your teaching evaluations are great . . ." at which point he was interrupted by a wry colleague who darkly intoned, "Which makes it all the more difficult to have to tell you . . ."[1] This was one of the most hilarious wisecracks I'd ever heard. I would think that, of course, because I got tenure.[2]

You, however, may not think it very funny, or even funny at all. It's not a very relatable wisecrack for those outside of academia, after all, it trades in a bit of meanness, and while you might perhaps understand why those at the bar (who'd also been drinking) might laugh at it, it just doesn't tickle your funny bone. So what now? Are we both right? Both wrong? If only one of us is right, what could make that the case? How could we possibly settle this disagreement?

To understand how humor and morality interact and intersect with one another in our everyday lives, we first have to clear away two popular but mistaken views about their relation. The first is that humor is totally subjective, that if I think something is funny then it is funny to me, and if you don't think that thing is funny, then it's not funny to you, and there's nothing more to be said about it. We don't really disagree, on this view, we just have different humor tastes. Flatly stated like this, the view is false, but interestingly so, and we'll construct the right view from its ashes in this chapter.

The second popular mistake is to think that immorality can "infect" all forms of humor, and when it does, it has a trumping effect; that is, if attempts at "humor" contain any immorality, then they just can't be funny and it's immoral to be amused by them. We'll see why that view is mistaken in the next chapter.

Defining "Funny"

What is the nature of humor? It's my task in this chapter to tackle this hoary old question with the ramshackle vigor of a tenured philosopher. There are actually two questions embedded in it, one about the definition of humor, the other about its criterion. A definition is about meaning, of course, whereas a criterion is about what makes something that defined thing. So when it comes to the funny, we need to first understand what it means for something to be funny before tackling the question of what makes something funny.

One view people naturally gravitate toward is this:

The Funny, Failed Definition 1: What it means for something to be funny is for it to be the object of laughter.

But laughter just can't be the right response to focus on. We laugh for all sorts of reasons, only some of which have to do with what we really think is funny. Getting stoned can give people the giggles, as does getting physically tickled, and people laugh along with friends just because they are laughing. Fellow musicians may laugh in response to an unexpected musical improvisation, teammates may laugh at an extraordinary basketball dunk, or we may laugh while nervously watching a horror movie, even though none of these things are funny.[3] We may also judge things to be funny that we don't laugh at. Perhaps we've heard the joke too many times before, or perhaps we are tired or in a bad mood.[4] Perhaps we're at a funeral and squelch our laughter at the ridiculous hat someone is wearing. Or perhaps we are professional comedians who aren't easily tickled but can nevertheless discern what's funny.[5]

Laughter responds to way too many unfunny things, by our own lights, for it to determine what funniness is. Indeed, a lot of our laughter is just social grease, a polite way of responding in social surroundings that indicates that things are cool, that the vibe is chill. But again, we ourselves recognize that a lot of the things we're laughing at in those circumstances just aren't funny (think in particular about laughing along at your boss's terrible dad jokes or the news that your friends are having a baby). So let's try something else:

The Funny, Failed Definition 2: What it means for something to be funny is for it to be the object of amusement.

This is better, as amusement is surely connected tightly to the funny in a way that laughter isn't necessarily. But it's still not quite right, given that people can be amused or unamused by mistake. If someone is amused by the death of Nelson Mandela, or by the torture of a baby, they're just wrong. Those things aren't funny (good god, I hope you agree with this basic data point!). And amusement comes cheap for people who are stoned or drunk, those who may well look back on the things they were amused by in the morning as just not funny ("I can't believe we kept giggling over the shape of that trash can!"). Just because people are amused by something, even a lot of people, that doesn't mean it's funny.

In addition, some people are wrong if they aren't amused by certain things. Mahatma Gandhi was a charming wisecracker who once said, "If I had no sense of humour, I would have long ago committed suicide." Once, when he was heading off to attend the Round Table Conference in England, a reporter asked, "Mr. Gandhi, do you think you are properly dressed to meet the King?" His response: "Do not worry about my clothes. The King has enough clothes on for both of us."[6] If you aren't at least a wee bit amused by this wisecrack, you are making a mistake, I say.

Some may not yet be convinced. If so, then a better case comes from thinking about people who are in a bad mood or even depressed. They may still be able to judge that something is funny even if they can't be roused to amusement by it there and then. And once again, hearing the same wisecrack for the ninety-fifth time may not amuse you anymore, even though you still think that it's funny.

So for us to have a chance at adequately defining the funny, we can't target some merely descriptive property, something that in fact causes either laughter or amusement. What defines the funny has to contain a normative component. The object of our investigation must thus be on what's *amusing*.

The Funny, Properly Defined: What it means for something to be funny is that it is amusing, that is, it merits amusement.

If what's funny is defined as what's amusing, then it leaves open that some actually amused or unamused individuals can be wrong in the ways I've described, amused by some things they shouldn't be amused by, and un-amused by some things they should be amused by. To account for these mistakes, our focus has to be on this normative property, the amusing. But what exactly is the crucial normative feature here, *merit*?

Merit and Reasons

Amusement evaluates, it is a response to some event which appraises that event as funny. It can do so correctly or incorrectly. If something merits amusement, then if you are in fact amused by it, you have appraised it correctly. The hard question, though, is how this way of talking translates into what reasons we have to respond in various ways to the amusing.[7]

To see the relevant issues, start with an analogy. Suppose you've been helping to smuggle political refugees across a dangerous border, at great personal risk. What you've been doing is admirable, which means you merit admiration. Consequently, anyone who comes to admire you for your volunteer work is appraising you correctly. And anyone who comes to feel grief, say, in response to your admirable work is appraising you incorrectly, as what you're doing just isn't grievous.

But what does the fact of your admirability even mean? Your admirability provides a reason for anyone to admire you. But of course the fact that there exists "a reason" to admire you isn't enough. For it to play any practical role for us, this reason has to be accessible: we have to know that it exists and be able to grasp it for ourselves. Once I know about your good work, then I can recognize the reason to admire you. But that reason may have variable weight for me, ranging from tiny to tons, and it may well be outweighed by other reasons in my final determination of how to respond.[8] If, for example, I already admired you last week for a while but now I have to focus on my work, or if I'm in the midst of grieving for a dead friend, the reason I continue to have for admiring you is just outweighed by more important reasons right now, even though you're still of course admirable.

The same thing is true of the amusing. For something to be amusing is for it to merit amusement, which is to say that anyone exposed to or otherwise aware of it has a reason to be amused by it, even though that reason may be outweighed by any number of other reasons for a different response, such as that one is currently focused on other things, or one is grieving a lost friend, or that one has already heard the joke a zillion times. Call this reason for amusement a *comic* reason. The funny is whatever provides us with a comic reason for amusement.

With this definition of the funny in hand, we can turn our focus to the second general question guiding the investigation: What sorts of things give us a reason for amusement? This question is asking for a criterion of funniness, for what makes things funny. And here's where people will often say that it's basically all just subjective.

Subjectivity and Funny-Makers

The most radical subjective criterion of the funny is this:

Radical Individual Subjectivism: What makes something funny to someone is determined entirely and exclusively by whether that person is amused by it.

The view here is that the criterion of funniness simply comes from individual people's amused responses, and there are no standards for funniness independent of those subjective responses. If someone is amused by a joke, then it's funny to that person; if someone else isn't, then it's not funny to them.

But we know this view is false. If true, it would turn funny-making entirely into a matter of individual taste, akin to liking certain flavors of ice cream. This would mean there could be no actual disagreements over the funny, because there could actually be no reasons in favor of or against one response or another. If you like vanilla and I like chocolate (and neither of us likes the other), we don't actually disagree, as there are no reasons in favor of liking one flavor or another. We just have different tastes, and so it would be silly of me to say to you, "You're wrong to like vanilla; you ought to like chocolate instead." That is, there could be no genuine disagreement on simple matters of taste. But surely there is disagreement, sometimes really serious and even violent disagreement, over what's funny, as we know from our discussion of its definition. If you think a cartoon about Muhammad is funny, and I, a Muslim, think it's the least funny and most offensive thing in the world, we have a genuine disagreement: You are wrong, I think, and you have a powerful reason not be amused by the cartoon, which is the exact opposite of what you think about me. But of course, even in far less dramatic cases, there's clear disagreement about the funny: My wife thinks I'm just wrong to be amused by some absurd comedy sketches, and I think she's wrong not to be amused. These aren't mere matters of taste.

Because a normative standard has been built into the definition of the funny, what makes things funny can't stem from any individual person's actual subjective response to it. But perhaps we can hold onto our subjectivist intuitions about the funny by appealing to an *inter*-subjective standard. Of course, because some individual people make humor mistakes, we can't appeal to how all of us in fact respond to something as determining what makes it funny. But maybe we can appeal to how most of us in fact respond:

Intersubjectivity Criterion: What makes something funny is determined by what *most people are in fact amused by*.

So if a majority of people find something funny, then that's what makes it funny, on this view, and so all of us would have a reason to be amused by it, regardless of whether we actually were.

Unfortunately, this criterion is inadequate. This is because sometimes even a majority of amused people can be wrong. We've seen plenty of examples throughout the course of our horrible human history. The ancient Romans, during halftime of gladiator shows at the coliseum, roared with laughter at the sight of criminals bound to seesaws trying to escape ravenous lions (who always devoured them in the end).[9] Loads of people have been amused by those with various disabilities and "deformities."[10] Nazi guards were amused by their pitiable charges; enslavers were amused by the gun-enforced dancing jigs of those they enslaved; White attendees were amused by minstrel shows—these all seem to be examples in which a statistical majority of amused people was mistaken, in which case we certainly can't appeal to them to determine the funny-makers. So where else might we look? It may seem as if we need to look entirely outside of ourselves and our actual amused responses in order to find the right answer.

It's All Objective

It's at this point that nearly all theorists of humor suggest that we leave our subjective responses behind for an additional reason. We can't look at our own actual amusement to determine what's funny, they say, either individually or as a statistical majority, as that gets the cart before the horse. Surely when we're amused, we're responding to what we already think is funny, aren't we? But then that means our responses can't determine what's funny; rather, there are already things that just are funny, to which our amusement then responds, either correctly or incorrectly.

To find what the funny-makers are, therefore, we must go objective:

Objectivity Criterion, Empty Formula: What makes things funny is some objective property of the world, ___.

This is an empty formula because it doesn't yet specify what that property is. But we can fill it in in various ways by exploring several famous theories of funniness, as they all aim to be objective in this way. They each try to identify some property that exists independently of our amused responses that all and only funny things have in common, a property that makes those things funny thereby, and therefore gives us a reason to be amused by them.

The four major objective theories on offer are *relief/release*, *superiority*, *incongruity*, and *play*. In slightly more detail, they claim, respectively, that what makes things funny is (a) their causal power to relieve or release built-up tension; (b) their revelation of someone's superiority over someone or something; (c) their mismatch of some kind between expectations and reality; or (e) their playful, nonserious features. All of these theories fail, however.

We can drop the relief/release theory from our midst right away, for it was really offered exclusively as a theory about why people *laugh* (to release tension, a relief valve), and that's not the right focus for a theory of the funny, as we already know. Of course, even as a theory of laughter it's a bad one, as surely not all of our laughter involves a release of built-up tension (think of a polite chuckle at a stranger's bad joke, or a surprised burst of laughter when someone trips).[11] Were one to try to turn the relief/release theory into an account of what's funny, of what merits amusement, it would do even worse, as there are plenty of funny things that don't involve any release of tension (some clever wordplay, an absurd Gary Larson cartoon), and plenty of things that relieve tension without being funny (Xanax, a massage).

Each of the three remaining contenders does capture something more accurate about the funny, though. Start with superiority. It too was originally presented as a theory about the cause of laughter, evident in Hobbes's remark that laughter is the result of a "sudden glory" in perceiving one's standing relative to someone else, and so is morally abhorrent.[12] But it can be shaped into a more plausible-sounding theory of the funny:

SUPERIORITY THEORY: What makes things funny is entirely and exclusively a manifestation or illustration of someone's superiority over others.

Following closely on Hobbes, the first way to interpret this theory is that what's funny is that I, the viewer or hearer, am revealed to be superior to someone else, the butt of a joke. This version explains really well what funniness there is in pranks, as the pranksters see something funny in the fact that they have laid the butt of the joke low, in some sense, perhaps by getting her to panic or look foolish because of a false belief the prankster induced in her. Mocking, put-downs, and sarcasm also manifest superiority in this way, as does the amusement many feel in seeing someone take a spill (note the massive popularity of the TV show *America's Funniest Home Videos* back in the nineties and aughts, which eventually became almost exclusively a show running videos of people falling down, getting hit in the nuts by a ball, or getting hit in the balls by a nut).

One problem, though, is that the view as it stands has a hard time making sense of self-deprecating humor, where the joke-maker, in making fun of herself for some flaw, is also amused by it. But then it can't be necessary to humor that the amused person be the one who's superior to someone else.[13] Rather, it should be as I've put it in the formulation: things are made funny in virtue of their manifesting some superiority/inferiority relation, independently of who the amused party is.

However, not all cases of what's funny manifest any kind of superiority or inferiority. What does superiority possibly have to do with the funniness of a knock-knock joke or a pun-ridden wisecrack?[14] ("Who wants to hear my latest fishing story?" asks a friend. "OK, I'll take the bait," you say.) And superiority played little role in my tenured colleague's witty fake out. Furthermore, many demonstrations of superiority aren't funny in the least, as when I beat you down in a race, or when I beat you up in an alley. Superiority alone doesn't necessarily make things funny, and funniness doesn't always manifest or illustrate superiority.

What about incongruity? Same thing. The hardest bit off the bat is to get a clear and precise account of what incongruity is even supposed to be. I'll just cut to the chase and offer a rough formulation of what I think most theorists would accept:

INCONGRUITY THEORY: What makes things funny is entirely and exclusively incongruity, a mismatch of some sort between expectations and reality.[15]

Again, some pranks seem to display this property. The victim fully expects one thing to happen, whereas what happens instead makes her look foolish. And incongruity seems embedded in a lot of other humor as well. Many canned jokes aim to get you to think the answer will go one way when it goes another. "Taking the bait" in the fishing crack above involves exploiting the ambiguity of language, turning a standard cliché into something more surprisingly literal. My tenured colleague's wisecrack is certainly an example of incongruity, as one would expect that an enthusiastic citation of my accomplishments would lead to an overwhelming affirmation of my tenure status, not to its tragic denial.

But incongruity alone can't be what makes things funny. Consider a variation on the tenure wisecrack. Suppose that instead of listing all my strong accomplishments, the chair sincerely said, in a sad voice, "I'm sorry to say that you haven't really published that much, the letters we're getting about you are mediocre at best, and your service was limited to just one short committee stint," and then the other colleague interrupts to say, "Which makes it all the more delightful for us to be able to tell you . . ." This isn't funny, yet it is incongruous in a precisely analogous way to the original funny wisecrack. And think about all of the incongruous things we experience that just aren't funny: a Salvador Dalí painting, someone who forgets to switch to daylight savings time and misses a meeting, a candidate projected by pollsters to win an election who loses. Funniness can't consist exclusively in incongruity.

Some humor theorists have, in light of such objections, dropped the thought that incongruity is enough to guarantee humor. They insist, though, on maintaining that incongruity is necessary for it.[16] But even this more restricted view is false, as some funny things don't contain any straightforward incongruity. Suppose you see two seven-year-old boys laughing heartily at the farting sound a ketchup bottle makes when they keep squeezing it. Seeing their full-throated hilarity is, in and of itself, hilarious; you cannot help but be amused by their amusement.[17] But what they're doing isn't hilarious in virtue of its incongruity, because there's just nothing incongruous here: laughing at fart sounds is exactly what we expect seven-year-old boys to do! In addition, there seems no incongruity involved in a spot-on impersonation of Christopher Walken, or in Christopher Walken's own impassioned delivery of the line, "I gotta have more cowbell!" in that famous *Saturday Night Live* sketch. Incongruity on its own is neither enough for humor nor required by it.[18]

Some theorists require, instead of incongruity, the *resolution* of incongruity as the funny-maker. Incongruity in and of itself is irrational, after all, and it's just weird to enjoy what makes no rational sense.[19] But we can enjoy what returns us from seeming irrationality to sense-making once more. Incongruity resolution is certainly at the root of some humor. If I've been pulling your leg about my secret romantic tryst a few years back with Dua Lipa, you may be extremely puzzled for a long while by the utter incongruity of me—*me*—being with Lipa, but then when you suddenly realize that it's all a big joke, you may see funny in the resolution of that incongruity.

Nevertheless, this version is also a dead end. Not only is incongruity resolution insufficient for funniness, as it also occurs when a murder mystery is solved, but it too is unnecessary, as illustrated by the funniness of nonsense, non sequitur, or pure absurdist humor.[20]

The idea behind play theories captures something very familiar in everyday friendly banter. I was certainly playing with you in the Dua Lipa leg-pull. Or think about a friend who declares something rather surprising after reading the news—"Once again, Q got it right"—followed by your hesitating question, "Wait, are you serious?" She then smiles or winks. That's a crucial signal: She's just playing with you, pulling your leg, having some fun, and so what she said is perhaps rendered funny in virtue of its having been playful. We might thus try a theory like this:

PLAY THEORY: What makes things funny is entirely and exclusively playfulness, that is, nonserious, nonthreatening, spontaneous, disengaged activity simply aimed at enjoyment.[21]

Again, this view seems to apply well to some of our examples. When I tell Mark I'm going to write a book on humor and he responds, "That assumes you know something about it," he is quite obviously just playing with me. Language may be used in bona fide and non–bona fide ways.[22] In some contexts, saying something like what he said would be hurtful, an insult. But in signaling to me that he's just playing, Mark makes clear that we are in a world in which language is being used in a fun, nonserious way. As John Morreall notes, we are suspending "ordinary rules of communication and [giving] each other comic license to say anything, as long as the group enjoys it."[23] This also seems to be going on in my colleague's wisecrack: When he hints that, despite all my accomplishments, I'll still be denied tenure, he's just playing around.

But play isn't always funny. Suppose that in response to my claim that I'm writing a book on humor, Mark were to say instead, playfully twirling around, "A book? Yee-haw!" This isn't funny. It's play, perhaps, but it's clumsy play, like throwing a Frisbee directly into the ground. Bullies sometimes think they're just playing around too, but in surrounding and mercilessly mocking a kid on the playground—perhaps, purely hypothetically, by pointing and chanting "Shoemaker, Poo-maker, Shoemaker, Poo-maker"—well, they're not being funny at all (let me just take a moment to gather myself). Plus, playing an actual game—Life, chess, whist—isn't funny.

There are also funny things that aren't playful, including some mockery and satire. At the end of the 2020 US presidential campaign, Barack Obama gave speeches on behalf of Joe Biden that were full of Trump-mockery. In wondering about what happened to Trump to make him so narcissistic, Obama asked, sarcastically, "Did no one come to his birthday party when he was a kid?" Funny, but not playing around at all. Or suppose you're listening to a windbag linguist at a talk, making airy pronouncements with unwarranted authority. Suppose he arrogantly asserts that, while there are many examples in languages around the world of a double-negative meaning something positive ("I'm not not interested . . ."), there were no examples anywhere of a double-positive meaning something negative. You respond drily from the back of the room: "Yeah, yeah."[24] This is what the British call "taking the piss," that is, taking the wind out of the sails of the pompous, and it's often deadly serious. Funniness can't consist exclusively in playfulness.

None of these properties on its own can be what makes all and only funny things funny. Perhaps, though, together they are? Let's try that, then:

THE QUADRUPLE THEORY: What makes things funny is entirely and exclusively at least one or some combination of the following four properties: superiority/inferiority, incongruity, incongruity resolution, and/or playfulness.

Does every case of humor require at least one of these properties? I don't think so. I was recently doing some winter hiking, and while the trail was decently marked, I had greater confidence in keeping on the trail by following in the boot prints of two people who had obviously preceded me through the deep snow that day. About halfway through, however, one of the prints disappeared, while the other, larger set of prints kept going. I thought to myself, "Perhaps this the point at which Jesus started carrying the other hiker." I thought this was decently funny, riffing as it did on the famous "Footprints in the Sand" religious poem that was all the rage a few decades ago. But it wasn't funny in virtue of any of the listed properties: It didn't appeal to an incongruity or its resolution, it wasn't particularly playful, and it had nothing to do with superiority or inferiority. Instead, its funniness (at the time, which is perhaps different from why it may be funny to you) had to do with its drawing a connection to and caricaturing a familiar (and rather silly) popular allegory.

But even if there's an expansive way to identify one of the quadruple properties in that wisecrack, having all four properties isn't enough to guarantee funniness. Suppose it looks like I have a dancer's body from years of gymnastics: I'm lithe, compact, and my buttocks ripple. You say to me, "Oh, you must be such a good dancer!" and I respond, truthfully and with a wry shrug, "Nope, can't dance a lick!" This isn't funny, despite being self-deprecating, unexpected (incongruous), incongruity resolving, and playful.

Further, once we make explicit that our interest is in wisecracks (not just jokes), whose funniness often seems to come from their interpersonal features, it becomes clear that we must include reference to many other properties. Consider Mark's wisecrack yet again: "That assumes you know something about it [humor]." Contrast this with the stranger who makes the exact same remark with the same timing and nuance. It's not funny in the stranger's mouth. The only difference comes from our different relationships: Mark is my friend, and the stranger isn't. Or suppose another friend makes the same quip Mark does but this other person resents me for a past slight and so utters the same line with venom. This too won't be funny, and the only difference this time is in their different motives: Mark doesn't mean what he says to be mean, whereas the frenemy does.

Once we start down this road, we should recognize several other properties that often contribute to the funniness of wisecracks, including cleverness, quickness, timing, exploiting ambiguity, and, for lack of a better term, connection drawing, which includes making resonant references to pop culture, say, or revealing how something we've long seen from one perspective can be seen, amusingly, from another, as in the Jesus hiker crack. And there are surely others (indeed, they will include some of the immoral properties like deception, stinging, and stereotyping that will be considered and added to the list later).

So let's allow, as seems possible, that every funny thing does contain at least one of the properties of superiority, incongruity, incongruity resolution, and/or playfulness. While they sometimes contribute to funniness, they can't be the only things that do so. What also contributes will be found on a long list of properties, what I'll call:

THE KITCHEN SINK THEORY: What makes things funny is entirely and exclusively at least one or some combination of the following properties: superiority/inferiority, incongruity (mismatch, contradiction, or absurdity), incongruity resolution, playfulness, cleverness, quickness, timing, exploitation of a certain kind of relationship, ambiguity, intentions, motives, connection drawing . . . (and others).

The list as it stands is incomplete. I can't think of any more, but there probably are several more. Suppose that we could identify what the remaining properties are, if any. At that point, the kitchen sink "theory" would surely be correct, as it would contain all the funny-making properties. However, it would now just be a long list of wildly disparate properties, which seems to undermine its pretentions to be a true *theory*. It simply asserts that funniness consists in some property or a combination of properties on the list. But it says nothing about which combinations are funny-makers and which ones aren't, what the algorithm for the combinations might be (how much incongruity-plus-cleverness-plus-playfulness, and in what amounts, makes the combination funny?), and which properties can be funny-makers, if any, all on their own and in what contexts. Sometimes superiority or incongruity can make things funny, but sometimes they make things just mean or confusing. Sometimes a clever play on words can be funny, but sometimes it's just poetry. Sometimes a seeming insult made with good intentions can be funny, but sometimes it just expresses kindness. So what can be said to fill in these crucial details? The kitchen sink theory doesn't tell us.

More importantly, even when certain properties, in certain amounts, and in certain combinations clearly contribute to making things funny, and we can identify them as such, we don't yet know *why* they do so.[25] Why, for example, do superiority, incongruity, or playfulness make a thing funny, when they do? Why instead don't equality, congruity, or seriousness? For that matter, why aren't roundness, grammaticality, and onomatopoeia funny-makers? (Well, maybe the last one is.)

We wanted a theory of the funny, not just a list of properties that may or may not play a contributing role in the funny, in certain unspecified amounts and combinations, and as of yet we don't have anything like one. Going objectivist about the funny turned out to be the wrong move, given tons of counterexamples and the lack of explanatory power found in our ultimate kitchen sink list. But it also looked like going subjectivist and appealing to our amused responses was also the wrong move. Yet those would seem to be our only two options. So now what? Fortunately, there remains one version of subjectivism we overlooked.

What Makes This Song Great?

There's a fun YouTube series called "What Makes This Song Great?" hosted by Rick Beato. In the first part of the show, Beato pulls apart a popular rock song from the past fifty years, playing its various elements in isolation and telling us how they contribute to the overall sound. So we get to hear first how the drum fills increase the song's intensity, how the backup vocals provide some overlooked mood or syncopation, what effects pedal the guitarist was using, what mode of music scale the lead singer's melody was in, and so on. Beato then reconstitutes the song, putting all those elements back together, enabling us to hear the song in a new and more enlightened way. We get to appreciate how all the individual elements, in the right amounts, combined to generate the unique and special sauce that made that song so very memorable and popular.

But in doing this, has he really answered the title question? Well, yes and no. Yes, it's those particular properties, in those precise amounts and combinations, that make the song great—indeed, what other great-making features could there be but the elements the song actually contains? But we still don't know the answer to a more fundamental question, namely, why do these specific properties, in their specific amounts and combinations, make the song great? Why does the variation in Dorian mode of the verse's melody in Radiohead's "Paranoid Android" contribute to its greatness? Why does John Bonham's pounding, relentless, echoey drumbeat help make Led Zeppelin's "When the Levee Breaks" so head-shakingly awesome?

Music theory attempts to answer this question by identifying more general properties of which these specific properties are instances, including kinds of note intervals, chord progressions, harmonic convergences, scales, dissonances, intensity levels, rhythms, and others. These are the properties that make music great. But whatever increasingly more general properties we may identify, we will still be faced with the most fundamental question: *Why do those properties make music (or a specific song) great*? Why are they the great-making properties of music, as opposed to others (for instance, the sounds of chainsaws and retching)?

This deepest question cannot be answered without making essential reference to our human musical sensibilities. What makes a song great, ultimately, is just that it has some combination of sounds, convergences, progressions, intervals, degree of intensity, and beats that humans have been built to respond to with the pleasant buzz and hum of musical enjoyment. They are the properties that typically hit people in the musical sweet spot, properties that tend to trigger the aesthetic joy nearly all of us are deeply familiar with.

So the question "What makes this song great?" has two different types of answer. One type of answer is that what makes it great is that it incorporates a whole bunch of different objective musical properties that, in certain amounts and when combined in certain ways in certain contexts, generate a particular soundscape. But the deeper type of answer is that what makes the song great is that its particular soundscape *is the type of soundscape that tends to be enjoyable to humans.*

Some answer like this has to be right. But doesn't it have us just appealing to the same old actual subjective responses that got us into trouble originally, and that don't admit of any real disagreement or incorrectness? No. That's because, instead of appealing to our actual responses to determine the nature of good music, it appeals instead to our *musical sensibilities*, our human dispositions to musical joy, and these may or may not always issue in the right responses. They can misfire. And in the possibility of misfire, of mistake, there is also the possibility of doing it right, and so the possibility of reasons to do it right, and so, finally, the possibility of true disagreement, where one side is right and the other wrong.

There are lots of complications here, and the view hasn't at all been spelled out in clear detail. But this general form of an answer is what also applies to humor, and I'll develop the view and address all the complications while talking about that.

What Makes This Wisecrack Great?

What makes something funny? At one level, as with music, we can articulate general objective properties that we often find associated with or embedded in funny things, the properties I've listed in the kitchen sink theory (and whatever other properties I might have overlooked). But what explains why these properties are all associated with or embedded in the funny? Why these properties and not others? Here's the best explanation, I think, what I call:

THE HUMAN THEORY OF HUMOR: What makes the properties on the kitchen sink list the funny-makers is that they are just the sorts of properties that a functional, developed, refined, and unobstructed human sense of humor would respond to with amusement.[26]

I call this the *human theory*, as it proposes that funniness has its ultimate and exclusive source in human nature, in our sense of humor.[27]

Several questions immediately arise. First, is this really a subjectivist theory? Well, yes and no. It touts the kitchen sink theory as capturing (eventually) all the funny-making properties, and these are all objective properties, properties that exist in the world independently of any particular person's subjective responses. But it appeals ultimately to those subjective human response mechanisms to explain why those properties, and not others, are on the kitchen sink list to begin with: They are just the properties that our (suitably scrubbed) senses of humor are disposed to respond to with amusement.[28]

Second, though, if the view appeals to subjective responses at its core, how can it account for the normativity of humor, for why and how our actual responses might be mistaken or correct, and what comic reasons there are? On the human theory, normativity comes from the responses that a person with a certain sort of human sensibility would have, were they to experience events in the right context. So the reasons for amusement, as we'll see, are really about the reasons we have to get ourselves into that context (I will say much more about this point below).

Third, isn't this theory just empty, a kind of cheat, where we are "explaining" the mystery of humor's nature by appealing to the mystery of *human* nature?[29] Answer: The human theory is actually quite illuminating, shedding great light on both humor and our shared humanity. But to see just what it illuminates and how, we first have to see the two main arguments in its favor.

The first argument is simple, appealing to the theory's explanatory power, and it just falls out of what I said about the ultimate explanatory gaps in all of the objective theories, either individually or collectively. The *amusing* is a single, unified property, an evaluative property of various items in the world, which is just to say that it's a general property appraised as funny by a single, unified response, namely, amusement. But we are amused, it turns out, by a ton of wildly different sorts of things. The more funny-making properties there are (as listed in the kitchen sink theory) that contribute to or constitute that general property (the amusing), the more we are going to struggle to identify the source of their unity. Our puzzle isn't about why there are so many properties that contribute to general funniness; it is rather about why these many properties appear together on the list of funny-makers. *What do they have in common?* Indeed, several appear to have nothing in common: incongruity is quite different from superiority, as are timing, playful authorial intent, or the exploitation of ambiguity. The human theory offers the best (and certainly simplest) explanation for their unity: They are all properties that, in various amounts and combinations, a properly developed, refined, and unobstructed human sense of humor would respond to with amusement.

The second argument in its favor is that the human theory best explains and predicts the kinds of reasons we take seriously when engaged in humor explanations and disagreements with each other. Setting out this argument will enable me to fill in and explain all of the human theory's crucial details.

Suppose you overhear the wisecrack that opens this chapter: You're next to us at the bar, you hear the chair detail all my accomplishments, and then you overhear my other colleague intoning, "Which makes it all the more difficult for us to tell you . . ." You see me amused, but you don't think it's funny. Maybe you're just confused by it, or perhaps you're hurt on my behalf, as it seemed kind of a mean thing for him to say. Perhaps you think I'm just hiding my hurt and need defending. So you ask the wisecracker: "How is that funny?"

The theory is not saying that what makes something funny is just that any human, or most humans, will actually be amused by it. Some humans, like babies or those with profound intellectual impairments, have a severely diminished or nonexistent capacity for genuine amusement (though not necessarily for laughter), for recognizing and responding to funny-making properties. Others, like young children, have the capacity in place but haven't much developed it yet, so they can only recognize a small number of funny-making properties, as illustrated by four- and five-year-olds who make up excruciatingly bad knock-knock jokes,[30] or who try other sorts of random word salads that attempt to simulate the rhythm of jokes they've heard. They are effectively learning a new language—a language that rewards the teller with attention and affection—and as with the babbling nonsense words babies utter in trying to mimic language, so too young kids utter nonsensical "jokes" for a while before they start to "get" the jokes themselves and subsequently learn how to make them.[31] And then it's another little while before they start to engage in wisecracking banter with others, which involves a different—more creative, interpersonal, and empathic—set of humor skills.

So in order to be plausible, the human theory has to require that the senses of humor that determine what counts as an amusing property are at the very least functional and developed. A functional and developed sense of humor is a product of education and maturity, but it's nevertheless a human sensibility, a manifestation of our human nature. OK, but then if it's a sensibility we share in common as humans, shouldn't we all agree on what's funny? Obviously, we don't. We have humor disagreements all the time. So what gives?

When we disagree about humor, what precisely are we disagreeing about? What reasons do we appeal to? And how are such disagreements resolved? The answers are complicated but quite illuminating.

First, it's important to stress that these are genuinely normative disagreements. That is, they are disagreements about what people ought or ought not to be amused by. "Oh, c'mon, they were just clowning around!" attempts to put normative pressure on the unamused to be amused. "Oh my god, she's really hurt!" attempts to put normative pressure on the amused not to be amused. There are mistakes being made in both cases, mistakes that ought not be made.

But what is the source of a humor mistake? If I'm right that it's a functional and developed human humor sensibility that determines what's funny, and if we are among those humans with a functional and developed humor sensibility, then the human theory predicts that we ourselves ought to be able to see what's funny by our own lights.[32] And this fact in turn suggests that our best strategy to end disagreements over humor will be to offer the types of considerations aimed at getting our disputants to "see" for themselves what's funny or not. In other words, we would be expected to reason with each other as if humor disagreement could most effectively be resolved by (a) increasing each other's skills at seeing relevant funny properties, and (b) by clearing obstructions from each other's perceptual pathways, so that we are better able see the humor in front of us (or the lack thereof) for ourselves. And these are exactly the strategies we do see when we look closely at our interpersonal reasoning about what's funny or not.

To explain the first strategy, a functional and developed humor sensibility can always use greater refinement. People who like wine have functional and developed palates, but they are quite often unrefined. To become a good tastemaker at evaluative pronouncements on wine—this wine is actually better than that—you need to refine your palate. If you can't really tell the difference between grapefruit juice and red wine, you've got some discriminating to do. This usually requires lots of tastings (woo hoo!), so that eventually you can come to mark the more subtle differences that there are between wine and nonwine, as well as those between different types of wines. The refined palate is the one that can identify and discriminate between various tasty-making properties: "This one is oakier than that, this one is more berry-forward than that." So too with refinement in humor sensibilities: the refined humor palate is one capable of making more fine-grained identifications and distinctions between various funny-making properties. For example, refined humor sensibilities can better mark the difference between faux insults and real insults, and they can better determine when people are pulling their legs or being sincere. They can more readily see the amusing in the dry wit or clever wordplay. They are better able to catch subtle references or to suss out authorial intent. Most generally, the refined sensibility can, by its own lights, better track comic properties than the unrefined sensibility.

So how do we refine our senses of humor? In order to refine a sensibility, any sensibility, you have to use it, over time and in various ways, and this includes testing it and expanding its range and limits in new and unusual circumstances. Refining one's sense of taste for food requires trying out lots of different and unusual foods. Some you will not like at first, but you may learn to like them by trying them a few more times, and their "strange" tastes will often become more familiar and enjoyable (often in unexpected ways).[33] And even if you don't learn to like them, your sense of taste will have at least become more refined just in terms of your now being able to discriminate more finely between various tastes.[34] Our sense of humor is a sense in more than a metaphorical way.[35] And as with our senses of sight, hearing, and taste, there are more and less refined sensibilities, and the more refined ones are those that have experienced a bunch of different visible, audible, and tasteable things, and so have become more able to make relevant discriminations pertaining to the purpose of the sense organ. So too for humor: You'll have a woefully unrefined sense of humor if you never engage in wisecracking banter or don't observe or experience much of the world around you, including dipping your funny toes into the dark humor pool.

The first familiar strategy for resolving humor disputes, therefore, often involves assessing, criticizing, or correcting the stage of refinement of your disputant's sensibilities, as in "You know their teasing is just a way of expressing affection, right?"; or "She's just pretending to insult him, but they're longtime best friends, and she means none of it"; or "Their dark humor is really just a way of making fun of people who would be horrified by their playing around with gruesome topics, so don't take their dead baby wisecracks so literally." These are attempts to get people to step outside their current humor comfort zones, to open themselves up to the new, to expand and refine their sensibilities. And sometimes, once they do so, they can see how, by their own lights, what they're witnessing is amusing.

Let's suppose, though, that our disputants have equally refined humor sensibilities, that is, they're both equally good at making fine-grained identifications and discriminations of comic properties. They both have functional, developed, and keen comic vision. Now what? The greatest visual system in the world is no good if its perception is obscured in some way. So in trying to eliminate comic disagreements, our second strategy is to make sure that the other person's comic vision hasn't been blocked by some feature in their environment or in themselves. And there are several such "obscuring factors":[36]

- *Moods*: Different moods obscure comic visions differently. When you're in a pissy mood, you see far fewer things as funny that, were you your nonpissy self, you'd be amused by (recall the quarreling couples who just aren't amused by the other's attempt at levity). But the same is true for those in overly joyful or ecstatic moods, for whom everything—too much—is amusing. Again, once the ecstasy wanes and they return to their normal selves, they'll see that some of the things they were amused by while in that state just weren't funny.
- *Altered States of Mind*: The drunk and stoned, much to the irritation of the sober, may find many things amusing that they themselves won't find amusing in the morning. So too many of those on LSD or heroin fail to find things amusing that they ordinarily would.
- *Swamping Emotional States*: When you're enraged, it's psychologically

difficult, if not impossible, to be amused by anything. So too when you're grief-stricken, remorseful, or disgusted. These emotional states control your attention and guide your actions in a way that typically prevents amusement from gaining a psychological grip. Were you not in those states, though, you would ordinarily recognize various comic properties and find them amusing.

- *Ideological Biases*: Our biases are many, and they may be moral, religious, cultural, or political (I will refer to all of these generally as *ideological*). They are value-laden filters on our views of the world that we are committed to mostly on faith, trusting or hoping that they have solid justifying grounds, but sometimes unsure in our more private, reflective moments whether they actually do. These include religious and moral commitments, of course, but they also include various cultural, political, or economic commitments, all of whose ultimate rational or evidential grounds we tend to be hard-pressed to articulate or defend. They are often beliefs and values inherited from our parents or upbringing, but we may also simply find ourselves attached to them through some inscrutable psychological processes.[37]

I find the last set of obscuring factors the most interesting, as they are often the hardest for us to notice and so tend to be the most persistent of obscurants. We are more fearful when our ideological biases are threatened than we are when our more clearly and solidly grounded beliefs are threatened, and so we tend to be more defensive and inclined to lash out, or lash out more vociferously, against perceived attacks on them. When we know full well the clear-cut rational or evidential grounds of our other beliefs, attacks on them pose no such threat. You can make fun of me all you like for believing that the earth revolves around the sun, that regularly eating fast food is unhealthy, or that one ought to get vaccinated against a deadly virus, but it won't bother me one whit, because I have really good reasons for my beliefs, and I'm intimately acquainted with what those reasons are. But when you criticize or make fun of me for believing that karma will get bad people in the end, that Virgos are humble and industrious, that God exists and always answers prayers, that there's a reason for everything, that it's morally OK to eat animals, that a one-celled zygote is a person, that ivermectin wards off COVID, that mask mandates work to reduce the spread of viruses, that anyone can succeed in America if they just work hard, and, yes, even that all human beings are equally valuable and worthy of respect— well, then, sir, *that's not funny!*[38] If you get angry when your beliefs are mocked, that's typically a sign of defensiveness, a sign that you may have some kind of ideological bias at work, and such bias is precisely the sort of thing that can prevent you from seeing any funny in the mock. For you to see that funny, you've got to identify and eliminate—or at least detach yourself momentarily from—your ideological biases (which ain't easy; I offer suggestions on how to do so in chapter 7).

Thus far I've listed two general types of strategies we appeal to in order to resolve humor disagreements: refine one's humor sensibilities and/or eliminate any factors obscuring our comic vision. Neither strategy yet refers to any of the kitchen sink properties. Rather, they aim simply to make sure that you're in the right position to view those properties well and clearly. It's inevitable, then, that the third strategy of resolving disagreement draws attention explicitly to those properties. To the person at the bar who overheard and was puzzled by my colleague's wisecrack, I might argue that it was funny because it pulled a totally unexpected switcheroo on me: Where I was expecting more compliments and assurances, I got the rug pulled out from under me. The wisecrack manifested subversion of expectations, cleverness, killer timing, and theatrically veiled intentions (he acted as if he really meant it, that he was so sad to have to tell me I wasn't getting tenure). And so as long as the puzzled stranger at the bar has a refined sense of humor, is in a normal mood, and is sober, unbiased, and in no contrary emotional state, then when I draw her attention to those properties, and her view of them is unobstructed, she should see the same reasons for being amused that I saw.

Perhaps, though, despite all of these factors being in place, she remains unamused. What's gone wrong? Maybe nothing. That's because the role that the kitchen sink properties play in our humor disagreements isn't quite the same as the role that certain properties play in other sorts of evaluative disagreements. This is a very important point that has gone unappreciated in discussions of humor. If you are wondering what makes a wisecrack funny, then when I draw your attention to the relevant comic properties in our midst, I am actually not making an *argument,* at least in any standard sense. Indeed, if I were making an argument—"You should be amused by that wisecrack, because it incorporated subversion of expectations, cleverness, killer timing, and theatrically veiled intentions"—then that argument would be laughable (but not amusing), given the many examples of events containing some of those exact same properties that give you no reason for being amused: a Dali painting, proposing to your fiancée via skywriting, having your employee discover her promotion by slipping it into her fortune cookie. You cannot enable someone to reason their way into amusement simply by getting them to recognize the comic properties in their midst, and that's because those properties alone underspecify which sort of evaluative response is being sought.

What the hell are we doing, then, when we point these properties out to each other? The answer is found in the human theory of humor. It says that the kitchen sink properties are the ones that, in interaction with human humor sensibilities, are funny-making. So merely pointing out to you the kitchen sink properties located in some wisecrack will be insufficient to get you all the way to amusement, as your recognition of those properties doesn't necessarily yet involve your interacting with them with your humor sensibilities turned on.

Let me back up a second. Normally, when I'm giving you practical advice, I'm pointing out various properties to you, and in so doing I'm communicating them to you as facts, which are then meant to translate into reasons for you. Suppose we go to a restaurant together, a restaurant I've been to several times. It's your first time, though, so you wisely ask me what I've had before. I respond, "Well, the last two times I've had it, the salmon was dry, overcooked. The chicken is always moist, though, and well seasoned, and the cauliflower au gratin it comes with has a lightness that offsets some of the chicken's fattiness." I've provided you with some valuable facts, facts that then ought to translate into reasons in your own mind as you deliberate what to order, reasons counseling away from ordering the salmon and toward ordering the chicken. Your ordering the chicken would in fact be justified by these reasons (as long as other contrary reasons aren't in play, like that you are a vegetarian).

Things are interestingly different, though, when it comes to the funny. When I'm amused by a wisecrack, and I draw your attention to its various comic properties—its funny-makers—I'm not trying to communicate them to you as facts that then translate into reasons that justify your being amused. Rather, I'm trying to communicate my own amused state when I experienced those properties with my own humor sensibilities switched on. I am trying to communicate to you at the level of our senses, in order

> to induce a sameness of vision, of experienced content. If this is accomplished, it may or may not be followed by agreement, or what is called "communion"—a community of feeling which expresses itself in identical value judgments.[39]

These are the wise words of Arnold Isenberg, talking about what is communicated to the reader by aesthetic criticism, but it applies in spades to humor. In answering your question "Why is that funny?" I'm actually grasping for ways to communicate to you the feeling I got in hearing it, to explain to you what it was that generated my tickled, amused enjoyment. But I can't touch your forehead and zap that experience directly into you; all I've got are my words, and these are pretty inadequate words at that, so inadequate that some of the time I simply wind up saying, in exasperation, "You just had to be there!" But before I reach that frustrated point, what I'm doing is inviting you to try to see what I saw and how I saw it in that moment (which may be tough, thus the frustration). This is an invitation for you to try to experience the wisecrack as I did, by deploying your own human humor sensibilities so as to interact with those properties.

When my colleague made his wisecrack, I was feeling a little high from the chair's compliments, patting myself on the back a bit at how it probably meant I'd get tenure, thinking about what it would be like to be an associate professor, when I could say what I *really* thought about these people . . . , and then came the unexpected jerk back into reality: "Which makes it all the more difficult to have to tell you . . ." If only you could have been there, standing in my shoes, feeling as I did, you'd have felt that same blast of amused enjoyment at that balloon-popping wisecrack that I did.

What I'm claiming is that "reason-giving" in humor disagreements is ultimately not just about communicating facts that translate into reasons that then serve to justify your disputant's amusement. Instead, so-called reason-giving in the humor domain often aims to communicate understanding, by inviting empathy and communion.

Now suppose you take me up on this invitation, but you still aren't amused. Has something gone wrong? Not necessarily. Amusement at wisecracks is so of the moment, ephemeral, and highly dependent on subtle relationships and contextual features that we often simply lack the ability to fully appreciate what it was really like to have been there, a member of that specific amusement party. It may also be that we come from such different backgrounds, and we were raised in such different cultures or environments, that it's extremely difficult for one of us to occupy the other's perspective sufficiently to see the funny as they do. But then this is just another obscuring factor, an empathic blockage, one that prevents access to crucial information. We have to do our best to clear it away too, but that can be extremely hard.

Even so, when you try on someone else's sensibilities in the way I've described, you can at least come closer to seeing what they see as funny. And for those willing to take that empathic leap, it may tend to undercut a moralistic tendency that some people have, namely, to preach against what is to them unintelligible amusement, what they call "foreign," "alien," or even "inhuman." Alternatively, you might not feel amused by someone's wisecrack, even after trying on their perspective and seeing what they saw through your own refined and unobstructed comic sensibilities, because that person was in fact wrong to have been amused.[40] And this may be true because they failed to pay sufficient attention to the immoral properties that were involved in their wisecrack, such as meanness, deception, racism, sexism, or downright cruelty. Indeed, these possibilities are what the middle three chapters of this book are about.

Nevertheless, I think there is a common humanity in humor and humor disagreements, although it likely won't ever issue in universal amusement at all the very same comic properties. Our humor sensibilities are often shaped in dramatically different ways, raised as we have been in very different families, cultures, and communities. People around the world—people with fully developed and highly refined comic sensibilities—are still going to be amused by very different things, even when viewing them in a mostly unobscured fashion with refined comic sensibilities.[41] This is due not only to our different backgrounds and cultures, but also to our different ideological biases. The common humanity in our humor sensibility is not going to be made evident, therefore, in any actual shared amusement at all the same things, but instead will be made evident in our shared human capacity to empathize with one another, and so to come closer to a shared understanding of why others are amused by things that we ourselves may nevertheless not be amused by.

Conclusion

"How is that funny?" We started off with a natural thought, that what makes things funny is thoroughly subjective, a question to be answered simply by looking at what individuals or a majority of people actually laugh at or are amused by. This view cannot adequately account for the normativity embedded in our humor exchanges, though. We thus abandoned subjectivism by trying out a series of objectivist views of the funny, but all of them had serious counterexamples. So we tried collecting all of the potentially funny-making properties together into the kitchen sink theory. This was just a list, though, and an incomplete one at that. And even if we'd found every single property that went on it, the kitchen sink theory would tell us nothing about why those properties are on the list or what they all have in common.

Those explanations come instead ultimately from our senses of humor, so we had to return to a kind of subjective view once more, albeit of a much more sophisticated kind: What unites all the funny-makers on the list is that they're all properties that, in various weights, combinations, and contexts, tickle the human sense of humor, that is, they tend to amuse us. Or at least they tend to amuse us when our senses of humor are functional, developed, refined, and unobscured, when we're exposed to and engage our humor sensibilities with them, and when we've examined them from the perspectives of those who already perceive them in the funny ways. Whew! It's humans in those conditions who determine what funniness is, and so when you're engaged with and open to those funny-makers, you indeed have a reason to be amused. The human theory is a universal human theory of humor, albeit with lots of conditions that pay due respect to its incredibly context- and relationship-sensitive nature.

The main arguments for this view come from both its explanatory power (in providing unity to the kitchen sink list), as well as its capturing all the nuances of how we reason with each other in cases of challenge or disagreement. It offers the only way to account for all of the kinds of considerations people take seriously when thinking, talking, agreeing, and disagreeing about what's funny or not funny, and what we should or shouldn't be amused by. This conclusion is buttressed by thinking about the many different types of things we find funny, everything from slapstick to mockery to put-ons to absurdity to subtle satire. What could possibly unify all of these things under "the amusing" umbrella other than our sense of humor, a strange and wonderful sort of sensibility, when you think about it, one that just happens to be tickled by a wide range of strange things?

Now that's not to say that our sense of humor is just some random, bizarre, pointless, or grab-bag sensibility. The fact that we can't identify some property in the world that all examples of humor have in common doesn't mean that there's not something shared and unified about the sensibility that experiences them. As it turns out, there is one, but that shared feature is not found in the content of humorous things; rather, it's found in the function of our sense of humor. A sense of humor facilitates some of the most profound human connections we have. It is a deeply interpersonal sensibility, one that contributes enormous value to our lives. Of course, it is precisely because of this interpersonal role that morality is relevant to humor, in what turns out to be a variety of fascinating ways. Thus this book.

The human theory of humor gives rise to a very serious worry, though, for it may seem to imply that anything goes, that if humans with developed, refined, and unobstructed senses of humor were to somehow find torture, racism, or rape funny, then those things would in fact *be* funny. This isn't a far-out possibility, as we know from our horrific human history. But could people who are amused by those things ever be right?

This is the question motivating the next chapter.

CHAPTER TWO

"That's Just Not Funny!"

How Morality Does (and Doesn't) Bear on Humor

I was at a dinner party many years ago when the hosts' toddler got onto her spring-driven rocking horse by the dinner table. As she was enjoying riding the horse up and down, I snuck my hand over to the metal frame at the back and slowly glided the horse forward several feet, so it seemed suddenly to the little girl that her horse had come to life! Her eyes grew round in wonder, and she started jumping up and down deliriously to make the horse go faster. She'd been pranked, and it was hilarious to all in attendance.

Here's a prank with a different tenor. Stephen King's *Carrie* is a painfully naive and shy girl. When showering after gym class one day in high school, she gets her first period. She's been raised by a single mother, a religious zealot, who has taught her nothing about sexuality or her body, so when she sees the blood running down her legs, Carrie is horrified. The other girls see her reaction and make merciless fun of her for it. A few of them then devise a prank. They make sure Carrie gets invited to the prom by her crush, then they rig the votes to make sure Carrie gets voted prom queen. As she's standing onstage receiving the applause of her classmates, they dump a bucket of actual pig's blood on her. When they do this in Brian de Palma's filmed version of the book, there is a stunned hush from the students as they take in what's happened. But then one of the "mean girls" who was in on the stunt whacks the student next to her in delight, points to Carrie, and starts laughing. And when she breaks the silence, the rest of the students follow up with their own laughter. And it's all suddenly hilarious to everyone . . . until Carrie destroys them and the town with her telekinetic powers.[1]

So here's a question: How should we respond to such things? Could there be any funny in the Carrie prank, given its overwhelming cruelty? And wasn't the rocking horse prank just a little cruel too, as it deceived the poor kid into thinking she was riding a real live magical horse? And if it was a little cruel, what does it say about those of us at the dinner party that we were all so amused by it?

I think many people come to this table with a view already firmly in place about the proper relation between morality and humor, a view that, if true, would undermine the motivation for the rest of this book. It's a view most familiar in response to some jokes. When a joke is perceived to have any immoral features at all, many morally upright people respond by saying, "That's not funny!" Immorality in jokes or wisecracks, they think, eliminates all humor. My aim in this chapter is to show, first, why people might reasonably think this, and second, why it's nevertheless incorrect. Seeing why it's incorrect will enable us to find our way to the correct view about how morality bears on humor (and vice versa).

Reasons and Values

Funny things have comic value, and values generate reasons for us. So comic value is what generates comic reasons to be amused. But comic reasons are only one of many different types of reasons that can vie for our attention and favor, reasons that have their sources in many different values. Other types of reasons come from prudential, competitive, aesthetic, culinary, epistemic, and, yes, moral values. The reasons these different values generate for us—for both our actions and our attitudes—promote only the specific values that generate them. For example, culinary values generate reasons to do the sorts of things that will make the food you're preparing tasty. I may thus have a culinary reason to add a teaspoon—or a tablespoon—of cayenne pepper to my gumbo. Competitive values generate reasons to try your hardest to win in games and sports (in accordance with the rules). So when I've made it to first base in the championship baseball game, I may have a competitive reason to steal second base, insofar as that action will put us in the best position to win. And so it goes in other value domains. When I'm standing before my half-finished canvas, I may have an aesthetic reason to pick up a thick brush and open the can of red paint, insofar as painting a dramatic red blotch on it will, I think, best promote the aesthetic value of beauty in my art-making. When I'm considering heading into my favorite crowded bar during a pandemic, I have a prudential reason to stay home, as staying home best promotes the value of doing what's best for me in the long run. And so forth.

Obviously, reasons from different value domains may sometimes counsel contrary responses. The competitive reason I have to steal second base counsels an action in conflict with my prudential reason not to strain my vulnerable hamstring. My aesthetic reason to paint that red blotch on the canvas counsels something contrary to what my moral reason may counsel, namely, that because I'd promised my partner that I would begin using more sophisticated and delicate colors and strokes in my work, I shouldn't paint big red blotches on the canvas anymore. These different reasons pull me in different directions, so because I can't do two different things at once, I have to reflect on them in order to discern which reasons count more for me in my particular circumstances. Maybe winning the championship baseball game counts more than my physical health (I have all winter to heal), so I ought to go for the steal. Maybe the painting will just look too beautiful with the red blotch on it, so I break my promise and paint it anyway. These cases are sometimes resolved when we realize what matters more to us; at other times, we may just remain torn.[2]

This book is, in great part, about the way in which comic values generate comic reasons that may interact with, buttress, conflict with, or actually incorporate moral reasons—reasons generated by moral values—and vice versa. In particular, I'm interested in our reasons for responding to immorality-infused wisecracks in various ways. Comic values give us reasons for amusement. Moral values, when violated, give us reasons for what I will call "blaming anger." But amusement and anger are obviously quite different emotions, typically involving contrary evaluations, psychological states, and motivations. How, then, might they interact? To answer this question, we need to understand the nature of emotions more generally.

I Second That Amusement

Emotions in general are urgently attention-grabbing, action-readying, affectively-laden evaluative responses to the world around us. Fear evaluates things as threatening or dangerous (as fearsome), admiration evaluates something as having gone well above and beyond some standard (as admirable), and shame evaluates something about you or yours as worth hiding (as shameful). These evaluative responses include action tendencies: fear includes a motivational impulse to avoid the threat (either by fleeing, fighting, or freezing), admiration (of people) includes an impulse to emulate them, and shame includes the impulse to hide (or to cover your metaphorical or literal nakedness). Of course, we don't always act on these motivations—they're just tendencies—but the inclination, the impulse, is there.[3]

I think amusement has to be included on any plausible list of pan-cultural emotions, an urgently attention-grabbing, impulse-causing, affectively-laden evaluation of things as funny. There are a few people who deny this claim, though. One reason is that they don't see amusement as being "a direct adaptation to dangers and opportunities," so they think it lacks an essential evolutionary feature of other (pan-cultural) emotions.[4] Second, they deny that amusement has any action tendency. Says John Morreall, "Not only does amusement not motivate specific actions, but the more amused we are, the less capable we are of any action at all."[5] Robert C. Roberts agrees: "We explain people's action by referring to their anger, fear, and jealousy, but not by referring to their being amused."[6] Both claims are false, though.[7]

Start with the latter worry. Doesn't amusement have a clear motivational impetus, namely, laughter? One might think that laughter isn't an action, as it's involuntary, so amusement doesn't ready us to do anything, but that would mischaracterize the notion of an action readiness, which is simply an impulse to behavior of some sort, whether or not it is voluntary or intended in the robust "action" sense of some philosophers. Even so, I'm not sure laughter is the right characterization of amusement's action tendency, especially insofar as we laugh in response to all sorts of things that aren't amusing, as I detailed in the previous chapter. Laughter is often merely a kind of social grease. We may laugh nervously at an awkward social exchange, laugh at a friend's announcement that they're having a baby, or laugh anxiously at a suspenseful moment in a movie. Yes, laughter is often our best signal that someone is amused. But that signal can mislead, due to all of laughter's other possible causes, and anyway, because of amusement's feeling of pleasurable enjoyment there's a better characterization of the relevant action readiness ready to hand, one provided by Nico Frijda, namely, the *savoring* of that enjoyment.[8] Amusement is a lean-in emotion: it's delicious, it feels good, and when we experience that particular form of enjoyment, we want to roll it around in our mouths, as it were, soaking in all its particular flavors. A good wisecrack is like a delightful amuse-bouche, and it's no wonder "amuse" is found in both. We can savor funny wisecracks through laughter, of course, but we can also do so without it, as when we respond with a wry smile or crinkled eyes in appreciation of a friend's clever crack. At any rate, I don't think there's much reason to take seriously the worry that amusement contains no action readiness.

Turn, then, to the evolutionary story behind amusement. It's complicated, of course, and it's not a rabbit hole I'm going to go down into very far, as the correct story isn't essential to my account. All that I need is for my own discussion of amusement not to be incompatible with whatever that story turns out to be. But it's worth taking a moment to explore the leading possibility.

Most of the scientific research in this zone has been done on laughter, but some scientists have drawn from that research to build a theory about the adaptation of amusement.[9] The basic idea is that laughter shares much in common with the panting and false alarm calls of chimpanzees (and even rats).[10] It's a sign of play, in other words, and so it has developmental value in signaling nonaggression when the players are nevertheless engaged in what might otherwise seem to be aggressive behavior. So young chimps (and proto-humans) could jostle, tickle, and wrestle while growing up, activities that improve balance, strength, and fighting skills, but that don't (significantly) threaten injury. When you put on a play face (a smile or laugh), it signals that you're just playin'.[11]

Laughter isn't an emotion. But in writing about mirth or amusement (I take these to be synonymous) as the emotion that laughter often expresses, some evolutionary biologists offer quite a plausible story about it as an adaptation. Amusement is a pleasurable reward—it's a dopamine delivery service—for "data-integrity checking."[12] We have various belief commitments, sometimes overcommitments, deeply assumed expectations of how things will go based on scripts that play a powerful role in our lives.[13] Humor forces us to reevaluate these expectations by introducing a competing script, one that typically surprises us in a pleasant way. Jokes (again, the focus of virtually all of this research) present us with a cognitive or emotional conflict that we have to work our way through, and working through that conflict is pleasurable. Funny jokes reveal a "faulty mental space" in ourselves—"the identification of failure is central to humor."[14] When the disparity between our commitments and reality is revealed, it's surprising, delightful, and funny (so goes the story), so much so that we seek it out, creating bugs in our mental spaces by going to comedy clubs, reading joke books, and watching funny movies.[15]

On this story, the function of our humor sensibility—our disposition to amusement—is to make us better thinkers by enabling the discovery of faults in our cognitive structure in a safe space, a joke space. Humor helps us become more intelligent and creative. Indeed, goes one speculation, our sense of humor and our powerful (and serious) aversion to noncontradiction have a common source, namely, the "evolution of an effective control system for our time-pressured heuristic search engines: our brains."[16]

This model is fascinating and plausible. But its exclusive focus on individual fitness with respect to a specific sort of puzzle solving in jokes is too narrow. The model of course doesn't take sufficiently seriously interpersonal wisecracking, which is far more prevalent in our lives than hearing or telling jokes, and the distinctive sort of funniness involved in wisecracks implicates properties and capacities that go well beyond the mere discovery of faults in our cognitive structure. Indeed, some researchers wrote way back in ye olden tymes of 1992:

> We are lacking a substantial body of research that focuses on the use of humor in conversational settings. Such research is necessary for the development of a single, unified functional model of humor.[17]

Unfortunately, this research is still lacking. But for our purposes, perhaps this doesn't matter so much. We were, recall, just looking for a plausible adaptational story of amusement, and we may have found one. Nevertheless, it likely isn't the whole story, given that it doesn't clearly account for the social aspect of wisecracking (often absent in joke telling), which we are all familiar with: that magical moment when someone makes a great crack and we all crack up together in response, sometimes doubled over with laughter or with tears rolling down our cheeks. There is indeed something quite special involved in shared amusement like this at interpersonal wisecracks.

Of course, we can allow that the amusement here is still all about making surprising cognitive discoveries that tend to make us more intelligent and creative, and intelligence and creativity do make us more attractive to potential mates, friends, and partners (business and otherwise).[18] So one obvious downstream fitness-generating consequence of being disposed to amusement is that it increases one's social likability. And it does so in a few ways. Amusement feels good. Those who have a heightened facility for amusing people are themselves extremely likable, as is anyone who makes others feel good. People want to be around them. They make gatherings fun and easy. In addition, those who are amused are fun to be around. Causing them to be amused is enjoyable as well. When they enjoy your wisecrack, they are enjoying you, and that feels good in its own way. They make gatherings fun and easy too. Those who, like the queen, just aren't amused, well, they are party poopers, too tough to please, a hard slog to be around.[19]

But here's the thing. The best wisecrackers know when to start and when to quit, when to start and stop teasing or making fun, where to draw certain lines. Truly good wisecracking is tough, because it requires delicate timing and precision, and the wisecrackers really have to know their audiences well to pull it off properly, so that some people aren't (too) confused, (too) offended, or (too) hurt, for example.[20] So the social likability produced by being amused or amusing has to be tempered by a moral sensibility. An adaptationist story about our sense of humor will be incomplete without accounting for its crucial connections in our wisecracking lives to our sense of morality. We'll explore what those are.

Amusement is clearly an emotion, one that contributes positively to our lives in several ways. But when people push too hard for it or take it in dicey directions, it can generate a very different emotional response, namely, anger.

Anger

No one denies that anger is an emotion, nor do they deny that it was adaptive insofar as it served a powerful evolutionary function. The problem is that people disagree about what that function was and is.

There are two competing stories about anger. The first is that it was selected insofar as it served to enforce norms of cooperation and cohesion. Anger was aimed at group members who violated those norms, and it served both to get them back in line (or at least aimed to do so) and to warn others not to violate those norms.[21] It had punitive and deterrent effects, so in order for someone's anger to be appropriate it had to be deployed by and at agents with certain cognitive capacities. The angry enforcer had to be able to know what the norms were, know what violations consisted in, and be able to track violators, whereas violators, in order for anger at them to make any sense (given its punitive and deterrent aims), had to be able to govern their behavior by the relevant norms and in light of wanting to avoid being anger's target, and the angry people needed to know this about them.[22]

The alternative story about anger is motivated by the fact that some angry humans simply lack the cognitive capacities required by anger in the first story. In particular, human babies seem to get angry, but they can't possibly be tracking subtleties like what the norms are, what a norm violator is, and whether violators are able to govern their behavior by norms or a desire to avoid being a target of anger. When a baby cries angrily after her mother leaves the room, she just wants Mommy. Furthermore, people who do have these capacities nevertheless experience anger at many things besides norm violators. When the rain ruins your picnic, when you trip over a bump in the sidewalk, when your route to work is diverted by a road collapse that will make you seriously late, when your computer suddenly shuts down in the middle of writing an important document, you may well get angry. But none of these are for norm violations at all; indeed, they aren't directed at people at all. Why, goes the thought, if an anger mechanism evolved to enforce norm violators would it misfire on such a massive scale? The answer, from the tellers of the second story, is that that's not what the mechanism evolved for; rather, it evolved as an expression of goal frustration, where we are prevented or blocked from doing or getting something.[23] The baby's goals—of nutrition and nurture—are being frustrated when Mommy leaves the room. And the adult's goals—of having a lovely picnic, walking unimpeded down the street, getting to work on time, and finishing the document—have all been frustrated by the world.

One problem with this second story is that it's quite unclear what the evolutionary value of anger could possibly be when it aims at nonagential things. As my wife will say to me when I get angry at the weather for ruining my outdoor party, "What's the point of that?!" And we all realize just how silly it is to get mad at our computers or the sidewalk(!) for tripping us. The value of anger in the first story was clear and compelling: norm enforcement better enables both individual and group survival, norm enforcers are valuable to a tribe, and they are more likely to reap mating and other prudential benefits. It's unclear, though, how anger of the second sort could have those benefits if it's not retributive or deterrent, or if it's not even aimed at agents.

A second problem with the second story is that it's not clear how some of the things we consider to be norm violations are properly construed as frustrating our goals of doing or getting things. Some respect-based violations, in particular, may not prevent us from doing or getting anything at all. If you condescend to me, if you secretly peep on me while I'm in the shower, or if you make fun of me behind my back—these are all things that will tend to make me angry (were I to find out about them), even if they don't prevent or block me from doing or getting a thing.[24]

We could dissolve the tension between these two stories by finding a way in which they might both be true. The way I suggest is by allowing that there are actually two distinct types of anger. Indeed, I think this fact is revealed by their two very different motivational profiles.[25] How we tend to be motivated in response to norm violation is often quite different from how we tend to be motivated in response to goal frustration.

A lot of the time, when we get angry at others, they have both violated norms *and* frustrated goals, so the distinction may be hard to see. But suppose that you just don't like me, so you've hammered nails into my car tires. When I see my flat tires in the morning, with your note on the windshield claiming responsibility alongside a laughing emoji, I'll be angry. But I'll be motivated in two different directions. First, I'll be motivated to find a way around the goal frustration you caused by figuring out an alternative way to get to work (or perhaps I'll just call AAA). But I'll also be thinking about getting back at you or confronting you later, once that goal frustration has been removed. These are distinct motivational tendencies of my anger(s).

But we can separate them out. Perhaps as I'm driving to work there's a rockslide blocking the road. I may well again get angry, but now my anger will motivate me only to find a way around the blockage to get to work on time. I will most certainly not be motivated to get back at the rockslide! Alternatively, if I find out that you, who stayed in my Airbnb guest room last week, peeped on me while I was in the shower, I'll be angry too. You haven't blocked any of my goals, in this case, but if I ever track you down again, I'll be motivated to give you a piece of my mind.

These may be two types of anger, or they may better be construed as two different emotions with very similar psychological feels (anger and frustration?). That doesn't matter. What does matter is that we recognize their difference in our responses to wisecracks. We need labels to do so easily, though. Call the angry emotional response to moral violations *blaming anger* (or, as I'll occasionally say, "angry blame" or "moral upset"). This is a type of anger directed squarely at agents, a response to an agent's *having wronged* someone. It's a response with which we're intimately familiar, the kind of response that naturally bubbles up when someone, without excuse or justification, deliberately steps on your foot, punches you in the face, breaks a promise to meet you somewhere, breaks into your house, condescends to you, peeps on you, makes fun of you behind your back, stabs you, or cleans out your bank account. And indeed, these wrongs merit angry blame, in the same way that funny things merit amusement.[26] When someone deliberately stabs you, my friend, I'll be morally angry at the stabber, and I'll be astonished if you aren't morally angry as well, precisely because my anger recommends your anger.

Blaming anger often aims at retribution against the wrongdoer, though not always.[27] More generally, it aims to confront the wrongdoer, to communicate to that person that he or she wronged you, and it demands some form of acknowledgment in response (typically remorse or guilt, as well as subsequent repair or recompense).[28] None of these aims or demands makes a lick of sense, however, if we are targeting such anger at anything other than moral agents who have wronged us. You cannot seek retribution, or aim to communicate a demand for acknowledgment, or request recompense or repair, from the weather, the sidewalk, your computer, a system of government, or any states of affairs per se. You can only do so, sensibly, to other individual people.

That doesn't mean you can't sensibly get angry at those nonagential things, though. It's just that your anger will be a form of goal-frustration anger—what I'll mostly call "frustration"—as these things can certainly block you (or others) from doing or getting things you desire. But you can't properly blame those nonagents.

What grounds blaming anger at others, making it importantly different from mere frustration at them, are their intentions and motives, that is, what they are aiming to do and their reasons for doing it. Two people can perform identical actions—they can both step on my foot, say—but they may do so with very different intentions and motives: one does so aiming to hurt me because he hates me, the other does so aiming to kill a poisonous spider that's about to bite me. Both foot stompings may hurt equally, so they will both frustrate my goal of walking around pain free. Both may thus ground my angry frustration. But only the person with the nasty intentions and motives (the first one) will be the proper target of my blaming anger in addition, even though he performed exactly the same motions with his foot as the second person.[29]

Blaming anger, as we'll see, is what matters most for our investigation into immorality-infused wisecracks.

Prudence and Comedy

Funny wisecracks give us a reason to respond with the emotion of amusement, an enjoyable affective appraisal of the wisecrack as amusing, typically motivating us to savor its enjoyment by laughing or contributing a wisecrack of our own. Moral wronging, on the other hand, gives us reason for angry blame, an evaluation of the wrongdoer as having poor intentions or motives, and moves us to confront the wrongdoer to demand some kind of acknowledgment and remorse. These are quite opposed emotions: they move us in very different directions, they feel quite different from the inside, they evaluate things differently, and they seem to be psychologically incompatible, that is, it's really hard if not impossible to feel both simultaneously.

These facts give rise to two important questions. First, could it be possible for the very same thing to give us reasons nevertheless to have both of these very different responses? That is, could some things give us reasons to evaluate them as both funny and immoral? Or can it be only one or the other? Second, if we do have reasons to respond with both emotions, how the hell could we possibly do so?

As I mentioned earlier, I think that many people likely come to the table with the view that immorality kills humor, that any so-called humor that hurts others, disparages their identities, mocks them, makes them feel lower, reinforces in-group/out-group boundaries, and so on, can't give us any reasons to be amused, because such things just aren't funny.

This view is false, although in some really interesting and complicated ways, ways that will also inform us about how to answer the two questions just asked.

Jokes and Joke Tellings

There is a bit of philosophy that's been done on the relation between humor and morality, but it should be no surprise by now that it's all been about jokes. While these aren't my primary focus, the discussion that's taken place can at least get us started on how and how not to think about the right relationship between morality and wisecracks, so that's where I'll begin.

There have been some deeply confusing and troublesome labels for various views on this topic, so I'm going to ignore them all and just try to explain the views more intuitively.[30] In applying them to jokes, we need to address two questions:

1. Can a joke contain moral or immoral properties in and of itself?
2. If a joke does contain such properties, how should we respond to it?

Philosophers have been quite confusing in their answers to the first question. Many seem to favor the following view: Jokes in and of themselves have no appraisal value at all, that is, on their own they can be neither good nor bad, moral-wise *or* humor-wise. That's because jokes are meant to be told, they say, so we have to make a distinction between what they call joke types and joke tokens in order to make clear the relationship between jokes and morality.[31] Joke types are said to be recipes, words on a page (or in the cloud, or in our memory), merely a list of instructions for an actual performance. The performance of a joke type—the actual telling of a joke—is its joke token. As Carroll puts it, "When I ask you whether you've heard the one about the pig with two wooden legs, I'm inquiring whether you'd like me to token this type."[32] Because joke types can be tokened (told) with a wide variety of different aims, intentions, and degrees of success, and their humor depends (so these philosophers say) on those agential features, jokes in and of themselves have no appraisal value, including being funny, unfunny, moral, or immoral. It's only the telling of a joke (the joke token) that can have appraisal value.

There are many problems with this view, however. I start with what I think is a close analogy. Poems are surely meant to be read or heard. But we don't talk about poem types and poem tokens and say that only the latter have any appraisal value. Instead, there just are good poems and bad poems, and they are not being appraised as such in accordance with the intentions of those who print them out or who recite them to us. And when I ask you if you've heard the one about comparing thee to a summer's day, I'm not asking whether you want me to token that poem type; I'm asking whether you know and appreciate that beautiful poem, period.

So too, it seems to me, with jokes.[33] Jokes, sure, are typically meant to be told, just as poems (or any works of art) are meant to be shared. But that doesn't mean a joke is an abstract recipe, a joke type, that can only be appraised in its tokened form.

Come to think of it, this is true of actual recipes as well. My very favorite cocktail is a whiskey-based New Orleans standard, called a Sazerac. I once read a Sazerac recipe in the paper, provided by a famous local bartender. It called for twelve shots of Angostura bitters. Anyone who knows Sazeracs knows this is outrageous. You don't need to make one and taste it to know that it's outrageous. You should dash in no more and no less than *three* shots of *Peychaud's* bitters in making a Sazerac.[34] It was a bad recipe, therefore, full stop. I don't need to taste a version of it, or to hear someone else read it aloud to me, to know that.[35]

It should be quite obvious that we can and do appraise the value of jokes in and of themselves (sans telling). Just google "Jokes about Kazakhstan," where you can find this gem:

> The Scotland football team went to visit an orphanage in Kazakhstan this morning. "It's good to put a smile on the faces of people with no hope, constantly struggling and facing the impossible," said Anatoly, aged 6.[36]

This joke is funny, and we can easily appraise it as such independently of any performances of it.[37]

Now to this seemingly obvious counterargument, Noel Carroll retorts:

> In the greatest number of cases, as represented in joke books and, nowadays, on websites, the witticisms displayed—the joke types—are recipes or scripts or, at best, loosely advisory instructions to be performed. That is why they are typically so dead on the page (or the screen). It is what the performer does with them that causes or fails to cause comic amusement. (Indeed, if you laugh at one of these joke types from the page, it is undoubtedly because you are playing a performance of it in your mind's ear either in your own "voice" or that of a comic you admire.) Whether a humour type is effectively mobilized depends on its token execution, which relies on such performance factors as the comic's intonation and gestures (including winking) as well as such contextual information as

knowing who the comic is and what she stands for (thus allowing for un-marked irony). Thus, not only is it the humour token that is moral or im-moral; it is the token that is comically amusing or not.[38]

This view is also mistaken. Start with the point that if you're amused by a joke (token) on a joke list, it's "undoubtedly" because you've per-formed it in your head. Just in reporting what goes on in my own head, this is false. Perhaps my head is different from Carroll's (he does have way more hair). But in simply reading that Kazakhstan joke above, I find it funny. I don't "perform" it to myself; I actually perform jokes poorly. Analogously, when reading a moving poem, I may cry, which I may also do when reading a Sazerac recipe calling for twelve shots of Angostura bitters. But these aren't performances in my head. They are instead identifications of properties. Jokes, poems, and drink recipes all have properties, and it's those properties that we can evaluate against a standard, as, respectively, (un)funny, (un)moving, and (un)delicious.

Indeed, this fact becomes even more evident once we see that there are just different appraisable properties attached to so-called types and so-called tokens of these things. I could, for instance, make that horrible Sazerac recipe to perfection. If I did so, I'd have a horrible Sazerac on my hands, but if I followed its instructions to the letter, then my *making* of the recipe would be excellent. So there are just two completely different objects of evaluation: the recipe and its execution. And they may both be evaluated as good or bad, just in accordance with different standards: the cocktail recipe, in accordance with cocktail standards, and the cocktail making, in accordance with cocktail-making standards.

We should talk, then, in terms of jokes and their tellings and recognize that they are both perfectly appraisable things, albeit appraisable relative to different standards. We can appraise jokes themselves as funny or unfunny (perhaps leaning heavily on properties like subversion of expectations, say), and we can appraise joke tellings as funny or unfunny (perhaps leaning more heavily on properties like timing and voice-work). A funny joke may be unfunnily told, just as an unfunny joke may be funnily told.

Jokes, in and of themselves, can certainly have funny-making properties. But can they have moral-, or more to the point, immoral-making proper-ties, and so be appraisable relative to moral standards? The answer depends on what moral- and immoral-making properties are, precisely, and this is an incredibly controversial issue. The domain of morality is, as it turns out, very hard to define and differentiate from domains of the nonmoral. Sure, everyone agrees that kindness/meanness, fairness/unfairness, and justice/injustice are moral/immoral properties. But what about respect/

disrespect? What about sexual purity/promiscuousness? What about loyalty/disloyalty? What about cleanliness/disgustingness? What about deference to/rebellion against authority? What about righteousness/sacrilege? What about stinginess/generosity? What about developing/wasting your own talents? What about bravery/cowardice in the face of danger? What about great prudence/imprudence? These are all properties that some people around the world view as moral, while also all being properties that some other people view as distinctly *non*moral. If we can't determine what things count as moral properties, though, we can't settle the question of whether jokes have them.

Because I want to capture as many people as possible in my net, I'm going to be very permissive on this issue, allowing that all of the just-mentioned properties may count as moral/immoral. This means that jokes might have immoral properties within them, broadly construed. After all, a joke about Allah may well be deemed sacrilegious, and so immoral, by some Muslims. Someone might well think that a joke containing the word "fuck" is impure, and thus immoral. Someone might think jokes about feces or dead babies in blenders are disgusting, and thus immoral. Such properties will surely prevent these people from finding such jokes funny.

But while we do now have an answer to our first question—yes, jokes can have immoral properties—this doesn't actually tell us a whole lot. That's because only a certain subset of immoral properties really matters, and jokes can't have those.

Jokes and Responses

Comic properties give us a reason to respond with amusement. One might think, then, that all immoral properties give us a reason for angry blame. If so, then jokes that contain both comic and immoral properties might give us reasons for both amusement and angry blame. But jokes in fact cannot contain both. Recall from the earlier section that only moral wrongings give us reason to respond with blaming anger. Blaming anger is confrontational, and it demands pretty sophisticated responses from its target, namely, things like acknowledgment, remorse, apology, and recompense. It is appropriate, therefore, only for moral agents, people with certain high-level deliberative and volitional capacities.

What this means, obviously, is that even though some jokes might have some (im)moral properties, broadly construed as above, jokes themselves never merit blaming anger, as jokes aren't moral agents. Indeed, there is nothing to blame in jokes. Jokes cannot, in and of themselves, wrong anyone, because jokes don't—can't—have intentions or motives.[39] When it comes to jokes, then, we should be focused exclusively on the only relevant properties that they have, namely, their comic properties: Are they funny or not, that is, do they merit amusement?

If, on the other hand, we're evaluating joke *tellings*, then yes, angry blame may well be appropriate, precisely because tellers are (typically) moral agents, and they may tell jokes with various aims and motives.[40] But notice that now what we're evaluating is a performance, and not a joke as such. And the performances of jokes, just like the making of recipes or the reading of poems, may be good or bad, albeit relative to different evaluative standards. Sometimes a performance of a joke is good because it's funny, sure. But sometimes it's good because it's enjoyable on other aesthetic grounds. Ironic hipster comedians like to tell really lame jokes, aiming to generate groans, not amusement, but enjoyable groans nonetheless, given all the hipster irony floating around. And sometimes a comedy performance is funny without any jokes, as when a talk show host simply reads the newspaper out loud, quoting actual politicians, and then stares incredulously at the audience or raises an eyebrow.

So here's the takeaway: Jokes may be funny or unfunny depending on the presence of certain comic properties (e.g., incongruity), and performances may be funny or unfunny depending on the presence of their comic properties (e.g., incongruity, sure, but also timing, voicings, authorial intent, etc.). Because only performances involve performers, who are (typically) moral agents, only performances of jokes (and not jokes themselves) can give us any reasons for angry blame, because such an emotional response is appropriate only in response to the actions and attitudes of actual moral agents who wrong people with bad intentions or motives.

But wait a second! Didn't I allow that jokes could have properties that some people do deem immoral, namely, things like vulgarity, impurity, disgustingness, or sacrilege? And don't those properties make people angry (especially the last one)? If so, then it seems that I'm committed to saying either that they aren't really feeling anger or that their anger is inappropriate. And both implications seem problematic, either condescending or dismissive.

Well, actually, I'm not quite committed to either implication. I agree that such folks may well feel an appropriate kind of anger at such jokes, but it's the goal-frustration kind, which is the appropriate response to, well, goal frustration, regardless of whether any moral agent brought it about. Remember, goal-frustration anger can be appropriate in response to the weather or cracks in the sidewalk. But that feeling can't be angry blame. Suppose that the vulgar joke or the joke about Allah were produced by a chatbot. Would angry blame be appropriate? To whom? A generative language AI model? Programmers, who have no direct control over what this bot might generate? I can only make sense of the angry responses some may feel in the face of vulgar words or sacrilegious images in and of themselves as responses to the frustration of their desires to rid the world of vulgar words or sacrilegious images. But it couldn't be appropriate to feel angry blame at the jokes themselves, as they were generated by a learning program, have no intentions or motives, and can't feel remorse.

This isn't a condescending or dismissive view, then, despite its implication that some actual manifestations of blaming anger at sacrilegious jokes are just mistaken. People may in fact feel such blaming anger, but they shouldn't, as it's the wrong kind of anger for the setback at issue. Remember, blaming anger motivates confrontation and angry demands for remorse or acknowledgment, but there's just no one to confront or demand such things from in this case.[41] (Again, this would also be true for those who angrily blame their computers for "losing" their documents or the sidewalk for "tripping" them.)

Moralisms

We've now got a more precise distinction between jokes and wisecracks. Jokes in and of themselves are essentially amoral, so they can't be the proper objects of angry moral blame. Joke tellings and wisecracks, however, can be, as they may contain the poor intentions or motives that make such blame appropriate. Now people don't really tell jokes to each other all that often. Furthermore, joke tellings are typically funny or not to the extent that they serve the joke, that is, to the extent that they draw attention to the comic properties that make the joke itself funny. But these are also not the interpersonal moral properties that ground angry blame. It's only when jokes are told to specific people with malicious intentions or motives that they are ripe for angry moral blame. But then it's not the joke or joke telling as such that has any immoral properties; rather, it's that moral agent's use of the joke as a battering ram, say, that is immoral.

What I'm interested in from here on out, then, are actual wisecracks, bits of spontaneous interpersonal humor, as these may indeed contain immoral properties. Because wisecracks essentially involve interactions between moral agents, they may well ring morality's alarm bells on occasion, especially when they issue from poor intentions or motives. Wisecrackers can wrong people, for example, when their wisecracks include disrespect, deception, meanness, or stereotyping. When this occurs, then, what happens to our comic reasons to be amused? Are they affected in any way?

For years, on the Nickelodeon Channel's Kid's Choice Awards, celebrities would unexpectedly get "slimed," getting a green gooey substance dropped on them while they were giving a speech or performing a song. The celebrities usually didn't know that this was going to happen to them (although they must have known that it was a possibility, as it had certainly happened to others). Figure 1 shows a post-slime moment with Demi Lovato. Kids (and lots of adults) found this to be hilarious, and I concur: A totally unexpected sliming can be funny. One of the funny-making properties here is the incongruity of a beautiful and celebrated celebrity in a glorious gown covered in ugly green goo. Another funny-maker is the surprise factor. But, in figure 2, let's remind ourselves of the prank on Carrie with which we began. Note the very close similarity in prank results between the two in terms of beauty and goo-gown. Both also involve incongruity and surprise. But there's of course a major difference between them, reflected in their vastly different facial expressions: The first prank was performed in a kind of fun and friendly welcome-to-the-club spirit, whereas the latter was performed expressly for the sake of humiliation and in an exclusion-from-the-club spirit. These are crucial differences in the intentions and motives of the wisecrackers: The first prank was meant to be inclusive and fun, the second was meant to be excluding and cruel. These differences, to my mind, are precisely what affects the funniness of each as well: The first is, in its

FIGURE 1. Demi Lovato getting slimed on Nickelodeon.

FIGURE 2. Carrie covered in blood.

way, funny, whereas the second one just isn't (or at least it's far less funny than the first).

I suspect all of our responses to the two cases will be similar enough to establish an agreed-upon baseline starting point: Blameworthy immorality in humor—that is, humor that includes nasty intentions or motives—can definitely dampen its funniness. We might thus appeal to this data point to establish the view that I suggested at the beginning many people probably come to the table with, what I'll call

Hardcore Moralism: Any blameworthy immorality in a wisecrack always extinguishes its funniness.

This view is way too strong, however. We can see why by imagining cases in the middle of the pranking spectrum, where someone was slimed primarily with a fun and inclusive motivation behind it but also with a little meanness there too, maybe due to the slimer's envy of the slimed, causing the slimer to feel a bit of schadenfreude in seeing the embarrassed slimee, even if the slimee isn't totally humiliated. We may think in this case that, while a wee bit of a nasty motive makes the prank perhaps less funny than it would have been without that motive, it doesn't eliminate the funniness altogether. So a more plausible version of the view might be this:

Middlecore Moralism: Any blameworthy immorality in a wisecrack always makes it *less* funny.[42]

This view would be compatible with a wisecrack losing all of its funniness too if, say, it incorporated Carrie-style cruelty.

Here's a tough question for the middlecore view: What reason is there to think that morality affects funniness in only one direction, namely, in the negative one? Rather, if blameworthy immorality decreases a wisecrack's funniness, then praiseworthy moral upstandingness should, it seems, enhance it. Moral and immoral properties should affect humor symmetrically, one would think, unless we have some principled reason to think otherwise. But the incorporation of praiseworthy moral properties doesn't on its face seem to make wisecracks any funnier. The middlecore view suggests an unmotivated asymmetry between blameworthiness and praiseworthiness, at least as they pertain to humor.[43]

Carroll, who launched a criticism of this sort against what he labeled "moralism" about jokes, says that moralists never account for this point, but that's not quite true. Berys Gaut tried to defend a symmetry in his version of the view (again, about jokes):

> A joke is funny partly because it is targeted accurately, being precisely appropriate to its object. Since the ethical is a kind of appropriateness, this will enhance the quality of the humor of the joke. The fact that its humor is ethically merited can lend a joke a depth and appropriateness which it would otherwise lack, it can rule out coarseness or crudity, it can make the joke revelatory, emancipating its hearers from the narrow bonds of prejudice, getting them to see a situation in a better moral light and respond accordingly, and this being so, we should hold that the quality and power of a joke's humor can depend partly on the virtuous attitudes it displays.[44]

Of course, since the view under consideration is that immorality always reduces funniness, the symmetrical view would have to be that praiseworthy morality always enhances the funniness of a joke. But that is surely false. Adding a denunciation of climate change to a joke about cow farts won't make it any funnier (just odder). More importantly, the qualities of ethical appropriateness that Gaut cites seem to me often either to extinguish the funny or to severely dampen it, rather than enhance it. Emancipating people from prejudice is of course a good thing; trying to do it via wisecrack will often bring groans and even complaints ("Must you infuse even your humor with your righteous cause?"). The knowing nod or murmured approval of "virtuous" humor—this isn't the hallmark of hilarity; it's often instead the hallmark of sanctimony.

So there would seem to be an asymmetry, at least on its face, between how moral properties, bad and good, typically affect funniness. As a result, middlecore moralism, that blameworthy immorality always reduces funniness, is mistaken, given that symmetrically praiseworthy moral rightness in humor doesn't always increase its funniness.

There are two ways to respond here. First, we might try to hold onto some version of moralism about wisecracks by switching the focus of what's allegedly affected by blameworthy immorality in a wisecrack from the funniness of the wisecrack itself to the character of the people who are amused by it. Perhaps it's not that immorality eliminates or dampens a wisecrack's humor; rather, being amused by immorality reveals one's poor character. There is a view like this in the literature on jokes, and it's probably most familiar when it comes to racist and sexist jokes, where people allow that, while such jokes might be funny, nevertheless if you are actually amused by them, then you must share in their racist or sexist assumptions; that is, you must be a racist or sexist to be amused by racist or sexist jokes.[45]

Many people have already successfully argued that this *attitude-endorsement theory* is false, at least for jokes, so all I have to do is report a few of those reasons and apply them to wisecracks.[46] For one thing, some stereotype-based jokes (and wisecracks) can be funny even if one knows nothing about the group members being targeted, so the question of one's endorsement of some attitudes (positive or negative) against them is moot. Consider again the "Moronistan" space agency joke I told in chapter 1. It was originally spread widely, as I recall from my childhood, as a joke about the Polish government. John Morreall reports that he heard this joke for the first time, though, not as a Polish joke, but as a joke about "Frisians," and he was amused by it without knowing who the Frisians even were (they are an ethnic group in the northern Netherlands).[47] But one simply can't share the alleged ethnically stereotyping assumptions of some group if one has no idea who that group is.

Second, the attitude-endorsement view fails to take sufficiently into account the context in which wisecracks are made, as well as who is wisecracking with whom.[48] From one antiracist to another, a so-called racist wisecrack told in a racist's caricatured voice may be funny in virtue of its revealing the idiotic attitudes of the racist (see chapter 5). We have the ability to recognize these features in one another, and so we can find "racist" or "sexist" wisecracks funny without sharing in any of the dicey assumptions those wisecracks may contain.

Blameworthy immorality in wisecracks doesn't always reduce their funniness, nor does it necessarily worsen the character of those who are amused by them. Both hardcore and middlecore moralism are too strong. But we also know from the sliming versus Carrie cases that immorality can reduce funniness. So we should try to pay our respects to our starting data point by adopting the most chill version of moralism:

Softcore Moralism: Blameworthy immorality in wisecracks *sometimes* reduces or eliminates their funniness.

This view is, I think, correct. But it is compatible with a very intriguing possibility in a different direction:

Softcore Immoralism: Blameworthy immorality in wisecracks sometimes *causes* or *increases* their funniness.[49]

I think this view is correct as well. There are a few considerations in its favor. Start with the very first example of a prank I gave in this chapter, one in which I secretly moved the rocking horse the little girl was riding on so as to make her believe it had come to life. I deliberately deceived her. Compare it to a version in which there's no deception, in which I tell her, "OK, little girl, I'm going to move your rocking horse forward now, so it's not really alive." She may still be delighted, but it doesn't strike me as funny anymore, or at least it's far less funny than the version that included the deception. If you grant for now that deliberate deception is wrongful (a topic that takes up a lot of the next chapter), then that's a case in which immorality can make something funny, or at least funnier.

A second consideration is more abstract: Given that one of the kitchen sink funny-making properties is incongruity and another is surprise, and given that some moral transgressions are surprising incongruities (of perhaps a relatively benign sort), then some morally transgressive wisecracks could be funny (or be made funnier thereby).[50]

I've seen only Carroll argue explicitly against a view like this (for jokes, natch).[51] But he does so by attacking a straw man, starting with a joke about alien cannibals that he says is supposed to illustrate and support the view:

On a planet far away from Earth, inhabited by humans, there are butcher stores that specialize in human meat. When astronauts from Earth arrive, they discover display cases featuring trays of various sorts of human brains. Mathematicians' brains cost one ounce of gold per pound, the brains of physicists also go for an ounce of gold per pound. But philosophers' brains—they cost ten pounds of gold a pound. When asked for the reason behind the difference in price, the alien butcher explains: "Do you know how many philosophers you have to kill in order to collect a pound of brains?"[52]

For a softcore immoralist, this joke might be thought to provide some support for the view, as its cannibalism component is precisely what makes it funny (uh, and need I note that cannibalism is immoral?).

What Carroll argues against the view is that, first, to establish the softcore immoralist's case, you'd have to compare this joke-with-cannibalism (its immoral component) to the very same joke-without-the-cannibalism, and this is extraordinarily difficult, if not impossible, to do.[53] Furthermore, he asks, is there really any immorality in the joke? It doesn't, after all, mandate that we who hear it become cannibals; indeed, it doesn't favor or endorse cannibalism in any way. It merely describes aliens (humans?) who are cannibals, and so the joke could merely be an entertaining imaginative exercise (which isn't immoral). Indeed, he writes, "If an instance of humour is evil, then it is because it beckons audiences to believe in the acceptability of the immorality that it broadcasts."[54] Because this joke is compatible with merely imagining this world, without buying into its immorality, it fails to establish the softcore immoralist's desired conclusion that immorality can make a joke funny.

But he was the one telling us this (pretty unfunny) joke in the first place. And he's arguing against its value by pinning on the softcore immoralist a view that no reasonable advocate would hold, namely, that any funny-making immorality in a joke provides reasons in favor of *embracing* that immorality. That's just not the role played by funny-making immorality, though. Instead, the softcore immoralist can easily hold that the contemplation or imagination of any immorality included in the joke can and perhaps ought to enhance one's amused enjoyment at it. This more plausible version of the view allows that there could be an immoral component in a telling of the alien-cannibal joke (namely, the cannibalism), and that it could be a funny-making immorality after all. So Carroll's attack on the proposed view fails. And I don't know of another argument against softcore immoralism to refute.

The Correct View

One of my wickedly funny former colleagues was Ray Frey (known professionally as R. G. Frey). He was quite famous, having written important and influential papers and books defending utilitarianism and against animal rights. His students loved him, in part because of his dry and deeply cutting wit. One story I've heard repeatedly about him is that, in his graduate seminars, when someone would offer an objection to a view he was espousing, he would say, "Interesting. Just for ease of discussion, let's call your view 'The Crazy View,' and mine 'The Correct View.'" I follow Frey's hilarious lead here in simply stating my view of the general relation between the funny and the moral when it comes to wisecracks:

The Correct View: Sometimes the (im)moral properties in wisecracks can affect our reasons for amusement at them positively or negatively.

Now to this point, I've argued in the following directions:

- Against hardcore moralism, the view that blameworthy immorality in wisecracks always eliminates their funniness.
- Against middlecore moralism, the view that blameworthy immorality in wisecracks always reduces their funniness.
- In favor of softcore moralism, the view that blameworthy immorality in wisecracks sometimes reduces or eliminates their funniness.
- In favor of softcore immoralism, the view that blameworthy immorality in wisecracks sometimes causes or increases their funniness.

The Correct View simply combines all of these conclusions into a single statement, fit for a bumper sticker. As I say, I've given some arguments in its favor throughout this chapter, but as I have to explore specific examples of immorality to fully vindicate it, the next three chapters will constitute the real arguments in its favor, so I'll stop here.

Conclusion

From these first two chapters, we now have in place a general recipe for how to approach and appraise wisecracks. First, we need to determine whether the wisecrack has some funny-making properties in it (drawn from the kitchen sink theory). These are properties that clear-eyed, developed, and refined human humor sensibilities are disposed to be amused by (per the human theory of humor). If the wisecrack has such properties, then we have a reason to be amused by it. I haven't provided any more details of a first-order theory of funniness, one that would issue in determinate verdicts of funniness or not for any proposed wisecrack, as that's not the point of this book and anyway I'm incapable of doing so. What I'll do instead from here on out, when I need illustrations, is simply try to pick examples that most readers will agree are funny (although there will definitely be some disagreements when it comes to the political and stereotyping stuff, I can guarantee it—that will be part of the point). At any rate, second, if the funny wisecrack also incorporates some properties of moral wronging— meanness, disrespect, humiliation, deception, cruelty, negative stereotyping, and so on—then we may also have a reason to be morally upset by it, a reason to angrily blame the wisecracker. If we do, then third, we need to determine which of these two reasons weighs more heavily, so as to determine how to respond overall.

As I have noted, lots of people think that if there's any immorality in a wisecrack, then it's just not funny. These folks are likely to respond with straight-up blaming anger at such wisecracks. I've argued that their general view is mistaken, but philosophical arguments alone don't often have emotional sway. From here on out, therefore, I'll be offering a kind of anger management training course. It's not of the sort we're most familiar with, though, where people are counseled into seeing some moral violations as worthy of less anger than they ordinarily feel. Rather, I'll be counseling people in part 2 to see some moral violations as worthy of more *amusement* than they are ordinarily disposed to feel. In particular, people should be less angered and more amused than they may otherwise be by funny wisecracks involving, respectively, deception, mockery, and stereotyping. I'll then offer, in part 3, more general methods to alter and expand overly serious people's humor sensibilities so that they can more ably enjoy—and have good reason to enjoy—some of the great amusements of life. Who says philosophy isn't practical?

∴

Part Two

MORALLY TROUBLESOME WISECRACKS

A Guided Tour

∵

[CHAPTER THREE]

"Back When I Was in 'Nam . . ."

Deceptive Wisecracks

A police officer in Kansas resigned on Monday after admitting he had fabri-
cated a story that a McDonald's employee wrote a vulgar insult on his coffee
cup. The Herington Police Department officer, whose name was not made
public, claimed that a McDonald's employee had written "pig," preceded by an
expletive, on a receipt attached to his cup. The department's police chief, Brian
Hornaday, relayed the story on Saturday in a Facebook post that attracted
nationwide media attention but has since been deleted. The tall tale unrav-
eled when McDonald's provided video footage that proved its employees had
not written anything on the cup, Mr. Hornaday said at a news conference on
Monday. The 23-year-old officer then admitted he had lied about the supposed
incident "as a joke," Mr. Hornaday said.

Daniel Victor, *New York Times*, December 31, 2019

I once went on a ten-day trip to Israel with a whole bunch of Christian college students. It was arranged by my dad, a theology professor who took a
group of his students every year to the Holy Land, and this year he included
me. They were all lively, friendly, and convivial, but they did one thing that
drove me crazy: As soon as a slightly exaggerated or leg-pulling wisecrack
left their mouths, they would immediately rush to insist, "Just kidding!"
They were desperate to ensure that no one thought they really meant what
they'd just said. But this disclaimer also implied that they had been deliberately deceiving people, if only for a short while. And that sounds like they'd
been lying. And lying is a sin.

What was so grating about the disclaimer was that it was obvious that
they had been kidding, and so the rush to make it explicit ruined whatever
humor there might otherwise have been. The fun is in the foolin'.

Nevertheless, there is something to their worry. Lots of wisecracks seem
to incorporate deception, and they wouldn't be funny if they didn't. Probably the most familiar type involves getting someone who cares about you
to believe that you've failed at something when you've actually succeeded.
Kids did this all the time after their auditions on *American Idol*. Family

members would await anxiously outside the door to see what the fate of their loved one would be, and then that person would walk out with a dejected look, sometimes shaking their head sadly, before deliriously revealing their "ticket to Hollywood" to the now ecstatic family. One can imagine them all reliving the moment together again when it was broadcast, laughing uproariously at how they'd been fooled: "You really had us going!"

The old MTV show *Punk'd* pulled pranks on celebrities. The most famous involved getting Justin Timberlake to believe that he owed $900,000 in back taxes and that federal agents had arrived to seize his house, his valuables, and even his dogs. Timberlake was reduced to tears before the prank was revealed, at which point he . . . laughed (and faux-wrestled host and producer Ashton Kutcher, albeit with a barely concealed agglomeration of relief and anger).

We can easily imagine Timberlake punching or suing Kutcher instead. Obviously, then, someone who's been pranked may or may not be amused by it (just ask Carrie). But how the butt of the prank reacts can sometimes be irrelevant to the funniness of the prank itself, which instead is located primarily in the disparity between how the butt perceives things and the truth of the matter.[1] This means that only those able to see both perspectives at once are in the privileged position to see the funny in the prank (those "in on the joke"), which is mostly a matter of incongruity and superiority: how the duped and foolish-looking butt sees it isn't how things are.

Leg-pulling wisecracks (also called "put-ons") involve a leg-puller aiming explicitly to get someone (the leg-pulled) to believe something false, if only for a little while.

During a conversation with my son-in-law Nic about the best stand-up comedians in recent years, he told me with a straight face that his Mount Rushmore of comics was Dane Cook, Larry the Cable Guy, and Jeff Foxworthy. I started spewing my drink at this list of, uh, lesser comedians until he looked at me and said, "You don't really believe that, do you?" Crucial to the joke was my hesitation, my actually falling for it for a second. Once the deception was revealed, I could not have been more relieved. And, of course, I was then amused. (His favorite comic was really the late great Greg Giraldo.)

One of the scariest fictional leg-pulls is in the movie *Goodfellas*. After one of Joe Pesci's stories, Ray Liotta says, "You're funny." Pesci leads him to believe he's getting more and more angry at Liotta for insulting him ("I'm funny how, like a clown?"), and everything gets really uncomfortable and tense, until Liotta finally picks up on the signal that Pesci is putting him on, resulting in one of the heartiest, scariest, and most relieved laughs ever filmed.

As with a prank, the humor in leg-pulling is often located somewhere in the disparity between the target's false beliefs and the truth. While it may not matter to the funniness of a prank that the target never finds out she was being deceived, the humor in leg-pulling often requires some reveal, a signal that the leg-puller isn't serious.[2] (The relieved amusement in the Liotta scene comes bursting out of everyone at the table only after the reveal.) Often the ridiculousness of the deceptive claim is its own signal (as was supposed to be the case with my son-in-law's leg-pull). But sometimes we need to use that most ham-handed of reveals: "Just kidding!" Of course, the more you know people, the less you need to resort to something that explicit: a subtle smirk or twinkle in the eye can do the trick. Indeed, saying "Just kidding," as the Christian students did, very often just kills the joke. One mark of best friends is that neither ever has to say or do anything to reveal that they are kidding. Some of the funniest leg-pulling exchanges between best friends can be conducted with entirely straight faces.

Nevertheless, something more than a signal that you've been deceiving someone has to be in place to explain what's going on here. The officer who claimed that a McDonald's employee wrote "*&#$* pig" on his cup tried to weasel out of the uproar by saying that he'd lied as "a joke." But either he was also lying about his lying, or he was telling the truth and his joke just wasn't funny. In either case, funniness doesn't come from signaled deception alone. So what else might be needed?

In the previous chapter, I proposed that sometimes immorality in a wisecrack can make it funny. Over this and the following two chapters, I'll be testing this proposal with three specific immoral properties, wondering whether they might be added to the kitchen sink list of funny-makers, and, if so, how we should respond when they are located in actual wisecracks. This chapter will be on deceit, the next chapter will be on a certain type of stinging mockery, and the chapter after that will be on stereotyping (primarily racial and sexual). I won't have to convince you that deliberately stinging someone or racism/sexism are immoral properties, or that they are sometimes embedded in wisecracks. The question in those chapters will instead thus be about how those immoral properties affect the funniness, if at all, of the humor, as well as what we should do about it.

In this chapter, though, something different needs doing. Many readers may balk at the idea that there's any immorality in the pranks and put-ons described thus far, either because what's going on isn't "real" deception or because what deception there is isn't immoral. But this view is mistaken: Pranks and put-ons do require real deception, and that deception is of an immoral sort. Consequently, if some wisecracks require immoral deception in order to be funny, aren't those wisecracks immoral too?

Lying and Deception

Philosophizing about lying and deception has been big business over the past forty years or so. People have written plenty of articles, books, and anthologies, detailing everything from the definition of lying, to the fine distinctions between lying, deception, misleading, bluffing, and bullshitting, to the developmental and social psychology of lying, to the moral wrongs of lying, to the different conversational and political domains in which lies often play a key role.[3] I'm less interested in all these distinctions than I am in figuring out what goes on in pranks and put-ons that might be construed as immoral, a proper target of angry blame.

You deceive someone when you get them to believe what's not true or you prevent them from believing what is true. You may accidentally deceive someone, as when you announce what you mistook to be the winning lottery numbers to a friend, or when you put out your garbage on the wrong day and your new neighbor copies you. These aren't morally troublesome, though, as they lack any bad intention. It's only when you *aim* to deceive that moral wrongness can creep in.

We can deliberately deceive others in a whole host of ways. The most familiar way is by lying, which is best characterized as an assertion one believes is false made to someone else with the aim of getting that person to believe that assertion.[4] Some pranks and put-ons involve lies, some merely deliberate deception, but both, it seems, generate moral trouble.[5]

Or do they?

This question is really two questions. First, do pranks and put-ons really involve deliberate deception and lies? And second, even if they do, does that sort of deliberate deception really raise any moral trouble?

In *Punk'd*, the explicit aim of the pranksters (mainly Ashton Kutcher) was to tell the butt of the joke something the prankster knew was false, with the explicit intention of getting the butt to believe that false thing. In Justin Timberlake's case, the aim was to get him to believe both that the people going through his stuff were feds and that they were going to confiscate everything (including his dogs!). The alleged humor of the prank consisted in Timberlake's actually falling for those untruths. The reveal at the end brought some extra amusement at Timberlake's reaction, but the prank itself was (supposed to be) amusing throughout, while we watched how foolish Timberlake looked as he cried and carried on in response to what the fake feds were doing.

This is the primary aim of many interpersonal pranks: to expose and laugh at someone's foolishness in believing something absurdly false. This aim thus clearly requires that these pranks be built on actual lies, so that the butt believes and perhaps acts (foolishly) on those lies. This is deliberate and knowing deception, there's no other way to describe it.

The "absurd" part matters. It's not a prank—or at least it's not a very good prank—if you successfully deceive someone into believing that the square root of 1,313.25 is 36.238691370574155, rather than 36.238791370574155 ("Tee hee hee, gotcha!"). Actually, I need to qualify that point: It could be a good prank if you get your brilliant math nerd friend to believe this. But then note what's going on: The butt of a successful prank has to be able to recognize what they're believing as absurd, as silly, as something they could or should have seen through, and only the math nerd could have done so in such a case.

Of course, pranks may violate this constraint. Someone might prank a person with a serious intellectual disability into believing something she couldn't have seen through, but then it's been made cruel in a distinctive sort of way, I think, and been rendered unfunny by that sort of cruelty. For a prank to have a chance at the funny (and I think many have no chance, as I'll argue at the end), it has to target only those with the capacity to see through it.[6]

One difference between pranks and leg-pulling, I have suggested, is that, whereas the humor in the former mostly comes from the butt being in the deceived state, the humor in the latter seems to come mostly from the deception being revealed to the butt. If I've been leading you down the garden path with a great leg-pull, but then I suddenly wink, and you come to realize that I'd just been putting you on the whole time, that's the moment when amusement properly kicks in for both of us.

This way of putting it suggests a more morally innocent cast to leg-pulling than to pranks, as the moment of amusement comes from the reveal, that is, the moment of shared truth. But in order for that revealing truthful moment to contribute to any amusement, it's crucial that what is revealed was, up until then, deliberately concealed. Leg-pulling requires intentional deceit, aiming to get someone to believe something that you, the leg-puller, know full well to be false. The *American Idol* auditioners were pulling their family's leg when they came out of the room, downcast and shaking their heads. They weren't technically lying, which requires an assertion of something you know to be false, but they were still deliberately aiming to deceive their families and there seems in the end to have been no difference of any import between what they did and lying—you could even imagine them actually lying, as they shook their heads, "Nope, I failed the audition," before the reveal.

Of course, many examples of leg-pulling are straight-up lies. When my son-in-law tells me his Mount Rushmore of comics includes Dane Cook and Larry the Cable Guy, he explicitly tells me something he knows to be false with the aim of getting me to believe that false thing. Even when he signals that he was just kidding, and we are both amused, the humor depends on my having fallen, if only momentarily, for what was most definitely a lie, one that I ought to have seen as absurd. I was a gullible fool to believe him, and that's what is funny.

So there's a significant chunk of wisecracking that seems to require deliberate and knowing deception in order to be funny. I don't see how to deny this. Ordinarily, though, it's immoral to intentionally and knowingly deceive someone. So how can these wisecracks pass moral muster? There are three possible answers. The first is that the type of deception that takes place in pranks and put-ons just isn't of a morally troublesome kind. The second answer is hardcore in the other direction, saying that the deception in these wisecracks is indeed immoral deception, so deceptive wisecracks are in fact all immoral. The third answer—my answer—says that there is genuine deception in these wisecracks, of a piece with all other deliberate deception, and it is of a morally worrisome kind (as with all other deliberate deception), but wisecracks containing it can still be morally permissible (if not completely morally innocent) as long as they are made funny by the deliberate deception. Let's work our way through each possibility.

It's Not Immoral Deception

The first response claims that there's something about so-called deceptive humor that makes the "deception" involved just different from instances of morally worrisome deception. One could try to make this case in two ways. The first appeals to their different durations: leg-pulling humor lasts only a moment, one might say, but immoral deception doesn't. Unfortunately, this claim is both false and irrelevant. Some clearly immoral lies may be fleeting. Imagine a husband cheating on his wife with their neighbor being interrogated by his wife. He says, "I was nowhere near her house that night." She then presents him with their Ring camera footage showing him leaving the neighbor's house on the night in question. He immediately backtracks: "Oh, *that* night? Well, yeah, I was there that night, but only to drop off a wrongly delivered package." Alternatively, some leg-pulling can go on for years. Andy Kaufman, the leg-pulling king, used to open for himself as—and go on talk shows pretending to be—a crass, horrifyingly bad lounge singer named Tony Clifton. Some people at first thought Tony Clifton was real (he used to claim to hate Kaufman and didn't sound anything like Kaufman), others were sure it was Kaufman. But then, in a brilliant twist, Kaufman used to appear on stage during Clifton's show, having his partner in crime Bob Zmuda play Clifton. Kaufman died in 1984. But Tony Clifton has continued to appear in public since then, and as recently as 2012 was interviewed on Marc Maron's podcast. Kaufman *committed*, man.

Of course, Kaufman was performing, not wisecracking, per se. But my former colleague Ray Frey (labeler of "The Correct View" from the previous chapter) enjoyed putting people on for a very long time too. For example, he had a poster on his wall "signed" by the Blue Angels, the US Navy flight demonstration squad, thanking him for his "work with them" over the years. He never remarked upon it. But this guy put people on all the time, so no one knew if this was real or fake. He was clearly capable of putting up a fake sign and just letting the misleading impression sit like that, for generations and generations of students and colleagues (he was in that department for nearly thirty years). If that poster had really been signed by the Blue Angels, he had surely done something remarkable. But if it was a put-on, it was hilarious, remarkable for different reasons. And perhaps what's funniest of all is that we still don't know either way, and never will know, as he's now quite dead.

The "short" duration of leg-pulls or interpersonal pranks can't serve to differentiate them morally from nonhumorous deception or lies, as the former can go on for a long time, and nonhumorous deception or lies may last for only a moment. But even if there were a duration difference, it would be morally irrelevant. It's never the case that the short duration of some otherwise immoral activity somehow eliminates its immorality! Cheating, thieving, assaulting, murdering: these are all immoral regardless of how quickly you get each of them over with (imagine the sneaking cheater mentioned earlier finally explaining to his wife, "I only lasted two seconds, so it wasn't wrong!"). Of course, it's possible that the duration of some immoral activity affects *how* immoral it is. A long torture is morally worse than a short torture. But both are still immoral. Perhaps, then, briefly deceptive leg-pulls are less immoral than longer ones? Even if true, that concession gives away the game, as the attempt here was to show that deceptive leg-pulls aren't really immoral at all.

A second way to try to reach this conclusion would be to insist on some contextual differences between the two: the humor context, one could say, is a playful, nonserious context, and as such, any "deceptive" humor you engage in there doesn't raise any moral flags because it's not really lying or deception; it's only pretend or play. No one thinks that an actor uttering lines she personally doesn't believe is lying. Indeed, we might think that something like this must be true insofar as we wouldn't label serial leg-pullers with the vice of dishonesty, which we would for a serial liar.[7]

This is essentially the view of John Morreall, who distinguishes between contexts in which we use language in bona fide ways and those in which we don't. Typically, we use language for all sorts of ends. Most familiarly, we use it to convey information, but we also use it to advise, warn, suggest, and get each other to do things. When we are out late at the club and I lean in to tell you, "I have a headache," with those words I am, sure, transferring information to you about the pain in my head, but I'm more importantly suggesting that we go home, and in so doing I further aim to cause you to say, "OK, let's go."[8] But when we're wisecracking, goes the thought, we're not in this bona fide pragmatic speech zone. We're not aiming to communicate any actual information to each other, we're not doing anything *in* wisecracking (like advising or suggesting), and we're not aiming to cause others to do anything. So were my son-in-law to tell me his "favorite" comedians, I may respond, "Wait, are you serious?" precisely in order to determine whether we're in the bona fide or non–bona fide zone, because it's only in the former where communicating accurate information matters. If we're in the latter, then it's all just about amusement, and the ordinary rules and expectations of bona fide language are not in play.

In addition, says Morreall, in non–bona fide, wisecracking conversations, we have very wide latitude in the ways we can amuse others. We can do so through sarcastic remarks, funny faces, armpit farts, raised eyebrows, and much more. There is nowhere near such wide latitude in bona fide conversational contexts, though. As Morreall writes, "If my intention is to advise you that you'll need to put gas in the car, not just any words or actions will accomplish that."[9]

I have multiple disagreements with this view. Regarding the last point, we actually don't have a ton of latitude in expression if our aim is to amuse others, and we actually do have wide latitude if our aim is to communicate information in so-called bona fide contexts. Our latitude in wisecracking is restricted to what's actually going to be funny, if our aim is to amuse, and this can be much harder than it looks. If several people have been adding ever more clever quips at a dinner party, and I aim to keep the hilarity alive by contributing an armpit fart, or I yell "Zounds!" in an old-timey British voice, everyone's amusement will likely come to a screeching halt. And on the flipside, I actually have very wide latitude in how I'll communicate to you the need to get some gas: I can say, "We need to get some gas soon," or I can yell out, "Oh my god, we're almost out of gas!" or I can gently clear my throat when we near a gas station, or I can sing, "Gas, gas, we really need some gas, la-la!" Or, confounding everything, I can make a wisecrack about it: "If we don't stop for gas soon, my anxiety bladder will burst." So are we in a play context or a bona fide context? I don't see how we can plausibly mark a difference between contexts in the way Morreall suggests.

Indeed, we wisecrack all the time in ways that have the hallmarks of so-called bona fide communication, wherein we convey information, advise/suggest/warn, and aim with our words to cause others to do things. It's called mockery (which will be explored in far greater detail in the next chapter). When we're playing basketball and your shot sails wide of the backboard by ten feet, I may say, sarcastically, "Juuuust a bit outside," or perhaps "Ooooh, you wuz robbed," or "I knew you were taking steroids." These little zings convey that your shot was poor, advise you to consider doing better next time, and will likely cause you to focus more carefully on your shot-making in the future. Indeed, wisecracks are sometimes the kindest way to convey the information contained in hard truths, as the attached amusement may soften their blow. Saying, "My god, what a shitty shot that was!" is just plain mean.

Here's the deepest problem with Morreall's view, though: There's no clear way to characterize the alleged difference between the two contexts without begging the question, that is, without assuming the very thing he's trying to prove. Consider again the cop who said the McDonald's employees wrote "*&%$# pig" on his cup. Turns out no one wrote any such thing. His response: "I lied about it as a joke." So was he in the playful, joking, non–bona fide context or wasn't he? We want to say that he wasn't, that he meant what he said to be believed. But remember, that's precisely how deceptive wisecracks work too: a great leg-pull is meant to be believed; otherwise, it can't be funny! So what's the difference between the great leg-pull and the cop case? The cop's dissembling, I think we have to say, just wasn't funny. But we can't differentiate between play contexts and bona fide contexts by appealing to what's funny and what's not, as the very point of appealing to the different contexts in the first place was to inform us how to mark the difference between what's funny and what's not.

Leg-pulling and pranking seem to require genuine deception and true lies, so I don't see how one would get off the moral hook for deceptive humor by claiming that it's not "real" deception. The only difference I can see thus far between deceptive humor and deceptive nonhumor is simply that the former aims for funniness and the latter doesn't. But if the latter puts us on the moral hook for deliberately aiming at the deception, then so does the former.

Remember, though, that serial leg-pullers and pranksters aren't deemed dishonest, as serial liars are. The two remaining strategies respond differently to this data point: (a) Perhaps deceptive humorists are dishonest people after all, despite what we may think; or (b) leg-pullers and pranksters aren't dishonest, because the deception in their wisecracks is outweighed by something much more valuable. Let's take these one at a time.

Kant, Lies, and Deceit

The first strategy applies Immanuel Kant's ethical theory, whose motivating thought can be caricatured as your parents' hectoring question, "What if everyone did that?" Here's how it works. When you're considering whether or not you ought to do something, Kant asks you to think about your intentions and reasons: What would you be aiming to do and why? There's nothing unique about you relative to other rational agents; anyone capable of rationality ought to be able to act on the very same intentions and reasons that you do. So what Kant asks is for you to try to conceive of a world in which everyone in your place does what you are thinking about doing, with the very same intentions and reasons. He then asks a question: Can you conceive of this world without contradiction? If so, then what you're considering doing is permissible, but if not, it's not.

By illustration, consider Kant's own famous example. Suppose you are thinking about making a "lying promise" to me: You would be aiming to get money from someone, whenever you wanted it, by making a promise to pay that person back that you had no intention of ever keeping. Suppose we try then to "universalize" this lying promise, envisioning a world in which everyone in fact got money whenever they wanted it from another person by making a lying promise that they'd pay that person back. What Kant pointed to was not a world in which there would be all sorts of bad consequences of lying promises (e.g., broken business deals, resentment between friends, etc.); instead, what he pointed to is that such a world would embody a contradiction, and so would actually be impossible to conceive. Why? Stipulate that this is a world in which everybody gets money whenever they want by making lying promises. In this world, no one would ever believe anyone who said, "I promise I'll pay you back," because no one in those circumstances in that world would ever pay anyone back. As a result, no such practice where we count on people who say "take my word for it" could ever get off the ground or be maintained. But promises, by their very nature, are meant to be believed. So in imagining a universal law like this, we'd be imagining a world in which these things—promises—that are to be believed (conceptually) are simultaneously not to be believed (because in this world no one keeps them), and so we'd be envisioning a world in which people both would get money by making lying promises (by stipulation) and would not get money by making lying promises (because never believed). Contradiction, inconceivable.

The conclusion is thus that lying promises—and indeed lies of any kind—are always and absolutely immoral in virtue of being irrational: You commit the cardinal rational sin of contradiction by making an exception of yourself in this way, and in so doing, you fail to respect the rationality of the person to whom you've made the false promise. In other words, you owe it to others, as a matter of respect, to tell them the truth. Always.

Lying, Kant believed, is absolutely wrong in virtue of its aim, which is to manipulate people, without their consent, into believing something false—thereby bypassing their rationality, their autonomy, their *humanity*, in Kant's lingo. But if that's what makes lying wrong, it would have to make all deliberate deception wrong too. In deliberately deceiving you, I have aimed at getting you to believe something false, without your consent, even if I don't assert anything (and so don't, technically, lie). In trying to imagine a world in which everyone gets what they want via some deliberately deceptive behavior, no one's behavior in similar circumstances would ever be taken seriously as a source of reliable communication, so there'd be no practices of behavioral communication that could arise or be maintained. If I am thus thinking about getting what I want from someone via deliberate deception, my inability to conceive without contradiction a world in which that intention could be universalized (as a "law of nature") makes that considered action immoral. Or as Kant puts it: "A lie always harms another; if not some particular man, still it harms mankind generally."[10]

What the Kantian view thus implies for us, then, is that we have a "perfect" moral duty—an absolute and unexceptional moral obligation—to refrain from all interpersonal pranks and put-ons to the extent that they incorporate intentional lies or deception, however trivial or momentary they may be. Pranks and put-ons are just as immoral as all other intentional lies and deceptions, on this view, never to be engaged in.

The absurdity of this hardcore position is often taken to be revealed in an essay Kant wrote later in life, in which he considered the famous "murderer at the door" scenario: What happens if an ax murderer comes to your door, asking about the whereabouts of a person you are hiding? Can you lie? Kant sticks to his absolutist guns and says it would be immoral to lie to the ax murderer.[11] This is a bridge too far for many who otherwise find some plausibility in Kant's ethics.

Indeed, we can't possibly have a moral duty to refrain from all put-ons and pranks. Some lies and deceptions don't, it seems, manifest one whit of Kantian disrespect. If I lyingly say to you, "When I was in 'Nam, I called my machete 'Machete,'" I'm not disrespecting you. When my colleague lyingly intones that, despite all the seeming support for my tenure bid, he's sad to report that I won't make the cut, he's not disrespecting me. When the *American Idol* auditioners shake their heads dejectedly, they aren't disrespecting their families. I am just going to take this as an obvious data point, albeit one that reveals the bankruptcy of the extreme Kantian view.[12]

Nevertheless, the Kantian view does get something right (and that's why I discussed it). Kant is wrong that you have a perfect moral duty to refrain from lies and deceit, but he's right that you at least have a moral reason against engaging in them. So what might such a reason be?

Truth, Autonomy, and Knowing

Deceptive humor is neither absolutely and always immoral nor completely off the moral hook. That moral hook has to do with the role and value of truth in our lives.

Truth certainly has value. Most obviously, we are able to get around better in the world when what we believe is true. If I believe the poisonous snake is in the left bush and not the right, and my belief is true, I'm going to have a better chance surviving by running to the right. Truth is similarly valuable in communication: We typically rely on each other's word for making decisions and forming our attitudes. Honesty—reliable (and tactful?) truth telling—is a moral virtue, and it is attractive to others for these practical reasons.

Being in possession of the truth doesn't necessarily give us a reason to do anything, though. I certainly don't have any reason to tell others some of the truths I know ("2 + 1 = 3"; "my dreams are often fern-themed"), and sometimes telling the truths one knows can really hurt people ("I'm not sure I've seen a worse presentation"; "You could be the ugliest person I've ever met"), in which case we may have powerful moral reasons not to share it. I also don't necessarily have any real reason to try and form a belief about something just because it's true, such as the fact that the distance in a straight line between the outdoor drier duct at the back of my house and the base of the third sunflower in the yard is 872 inches, or the fact that the shade of Donald Trump's foundation is called Orange Glower.

Nevertheless, the fact that something is true probably does give us *a* reason to (try to) believe it, and surely sometimes gives us a reason to share it with others, especially when they have a need or desire to hear that information. But more importantly for our purposes, the fact that something is false almost always gives us a reason *not* to (try to) believe it or share it.

Being led to believe something false risks, at the very least, doing poorly at navigating the world. It risks undermining one's ability to exercise one's self-governing capacities by obscuring or concealing facts that are relevant to careful deliberation and decision-making. It risks preventing an accurate understanding of the world. In other words, it risks impairing the exercise of one's autonomy.[13] This is the truth in the neighborhood of Kant's ethics (one I actually have reason to share with you): Deception and lying of any kind risk damaging people's exercise of their autonomy. And risking that sort of damage does indeed seem to be a form of disrespect, as it aims to keep people from navigating their world as successfully as they'd like.

There are more subtle risks. Not only do we have moral status as autonomous, rational creatures; we also have moral status as knowers, as sources of knowledge.[14] Some have a higher status as knowers than others, sometimes through playing a role or having a social identity that society has deemed more valuable. When one is a doctor, or when one is a White male, one's credibility is typically viewed pretty highly. And some have lower status as knowers than others, sometimes in occupying a role unjustly deemed less valuable in society, such as being Black or a woman. A cop may view a Black man's witness statement as less credible than a White man's, or a woman's voiced idea at a corporate meeting may be ignored until a man voices the same idea. Obviously, then, our status as knowers can be ignored or damaged by injustice.

What also may damage it, though, is deception, of any kind. My credibility as a source of knowledge gets lowered when I'm regularly fooled into believing false things. People will take me less seriously the more I'm deceived. When I'm taken less seriously as a knower, I'm taken less seriously as a human being. Furthermore, I may internalize this view from others in a way that undermines confidence in my own beliefs and knowledge. And this risks, ironically, molding me squarely into the stereotypical type of person that society has (unjustly) constructed as being less credible, and so may serve to buttress that very stereotype.[15] Deceiving me may thus disrespect my status as a knower.

Deception and lying don't always cause such disrespect; they merely risk it. When the detective sniffs out the perp's false alibi, or when one partner immediately sees through the other's lame lies about not having cheated, no one's exercise of their autonomy or status as a knower has in fact been compromised by those deceptions. But the risk of it is enough to generate a genuine moral reason against engaging in the deceptions. That reason might not be very strong. But it is a reason. It has to go into the hopper, right alongside all of our other reasons, when we are thinking about what to do. Engaging in deceptive humor involves real deception, and as such, it's on the moral hook, giving us actual moral reasons against it, despite what many may think.

Conflicts of Reasons

A deceptive wisecrack can generate at least two conflicting reasons for how those who are taken in by it should respond. If the wisecrack is funny, it generates a reason to be amused by it. But it also generates a reason to be morally upset by it, as it risked damaging their exercise of autonomy and their moral status as a knower by deliberately blocking access to facts likely relevant to their decision-making.

But notice that these aren't all the reasons swirling around. To this point I've just discussed what reasons there are for responding to deceptive wise-cracks, with amusement and/or moral upset. But what reasons are there—if any—for making these wisecracks in the first place? Because making wise-cracks is a thoroughly interpersonal activity—a way of behaving that affects others—there are primarily just moral reasons at work here. But there are more and more varied moral reasons than we might have thought.

Do I have any reason to try to crack you up? Of course! When something I say amuses you, it makes you feel good: amusement generates that enjoy-able levity high. But it is quite likely to amuse me as well, so I'm in store for a pleasurable buzz. It may also strengthen our relationship, bringing us closer together. Recall also all the other prudential benefits of wisecracking I discussed in the introduction. So there are definitely some positive moral reasons—pleasure- and relationship-based—to engage in wisecracking with each other. If there aren't any conflicting reasons, we should go for it.

But adding deception or lying to a wisecrack creates precisely such conflicting reasons. I have a friend who works as a bartender in a popular bar in New Orleans. Often—too often—she is asked this question at some point during the evening: "Do y'all have a bathroom here?" She enjoys oc-casionally answering, with a straight face, "No, weirdly, we forgot to put one in." This is a put-on she finds endlessly amusing. Typically, following some confusion, a smile will spread across the patron's face as they realize just how silly this way of asking the question was (as opposed to "Where is your bathroom?").

There are reasons in favor of her making that wisecrack. It will definitely amuse her. It typically amuses the patron, once they realize their gullibil-ity, so that's also a reason for her to make it. It may also become a funny anecdote she can relay to other denizens of the bar (such as me), and it will amuse them (as it did). And while the bartender and patron don't have an existing relationship to buttress, it might nevertheless make the patron fond of her, especially if the patron appreciates people who dish out such humor. Perhaps the patron will return for more fun leg-pulling!

But insofar as the humor of this wisecrack requires straight-up lying, the reason against making it is that it risks damaging the exercise of an unconsenting person's autonomy, as well as his status as a knower. Perhaps the patron will be unable to deliberate clearly about peeing now, as he's been deprived of accurate information. Perhaps if his friends see him as being this gullible yet again, they will downgrade his credibility rating, relying on his testimony about other things less often ("He's so easily duped, you can't trust anything he tells you!"). And even if he immediately sees through this put-on, well, the bartender did risk all this, that is, she disrespected him, so he's definitely got a moral reason to be upset with her.

So should she pull his leg or not, and if she does, how should he feel about it?

It seems to me obviously morally OK for her to pull patrons' legs like this, and it seems obvious that they should not be angered in any way by it once they realize their gullibility. I have to take this moral verdict as just a fundamental data point. If you don't share it, if you think lying of any kind, even in a wisecrack, is always immoral and you should never do it, then you Kant read any further. Please stop. Seriously.

For those who share this verdict, though, there's still a puzzle to solve, namely, how is it that the moral reason against lying gets so easily beaten in this case? How could reasons in favor of causing a bit of amusement—a trivial and ephemeral moment of enjoyment—beat out a reason against disrespecting someone (by threatening the exercise of their autonomy or their status as a knower)?

The answer is that the amount of disrespect involved is utterly insignificant, that is, these risks are minuscule. Yes, it's possible that some patrons will hold onto their false beliefs that there's no bathroom until their bladder bursts, but this possibility is ridiculously remote (although actually kind of funny to imagine). And it's highly likely they'll figure it all out pretty quickly, perhaps by asking someone else or by seeing someone coming out of the bathroom, so the risk of damage is incredibly remote. Or if there is some damage, it will only be to their ego.

So when you consider together all of the moral (pleasure-causing and relationship-enhancing) reasons the bartender has in favor of making the wisecrack alongside the lone and pitiful moral reason against doing so (the very tiny risk to patrons' autonomy or status as knowers), the former reasons easily beat the latter. Comedy wins!

Here's a comparison: I risk damaging people's exercise of their autonomy every time I drive, as I might hit and kill someone by accident. That possibility is so remote, though, and my other (moral and prudential) reasons in favor of driving are so compelling, that the autonomy risk is easily outweighed.

We need to tread carefully, though. Just because a deceitful wisecrack will amuse a bunch of people, that fact alone won't always enable it to clear the moral bar. Consider a prank in which everybody but the butt finds it amusing; indeed, suppose the butt is quite morally upset by it. People sometimes get very angry after being pranked. Carrie sure did, and with good reason. If the butt of a prank will get really angry, shouldn't that fact matter for determining whether we ought to prank someone, or even pull their leg?

Yes, of course, although there's nothing distinctive about wisecracking on that score. Whenever I bypass your consent, jokingly or not, I give you a reason to be angry at me. This will be true if I give your phone number to a telemarketer, order for you before you arrive at the restaurant, or "borrow" your bike without asking. Consent of some kind is typically a necessary gateway to permissible interpersonal conduct.

Typically. But not always. You don't need my consent to be justified in knocking me down as I'm about to walk onto a collapsing bridge (perhaps I don't see the warning sign and I'm walking blithely with my noise-canceling headphones on so I can't hear you warn me).[16] You don't need my consent to be justified in telling me a painful truth ("This wasn't very much fun, and I'm afraid I just don't find you very attractive," says one person to the other at the end of a blind date). But you also don't necessarily need my consent to be justified in protecting me from some painful truth, as in the old movie cliché of a talent agent buying up all the newspapers that have printed a horribly negative review of their client's performance.[17]

In general, then, it may be OK for you to bypass my consent when it's for my own good. This is just plain old paternalism, of course, and its legitimacy is sometimes thought to be dicey. But I think most people are morally comfortable with some paternalism, especially in what's called its "softer" form, which, as in the bridge-crossing case, is really about preventing people from undergoing some harm that, if only they could see it, they too would admit is something they want protection from (by their own lights). I also think people are pretty comfortable with being "nudged" into buying more healthy cafeteria options, say, by their intentional placement at eye level, or by our default organ donation status being set up so that we have to opt out of donating upon death (as in the UK), rather than having to opt in (as in the US).

But what does any of this have to do with wisecracks? When you knock me down to prevent me from crossing the deadly bridge, you save my life, and in so doing, you've eliminated any reason I might have had for angry blame at you for knocking me down without my consent. So too, I claim, your being deceived in a humorous way can sometimes be good for you, and that goodness can easily outweigh any reason you might have had for angry blame at being duped without your consent.[18]

Here's one value of some put-ons and pranks: Being made to look foolish for gullibly believing an absurd lie can actually improve your belief-forming skills, making you less gullible and more critical in the future. It's a valuable corrective to sloppy thinking. I should learn to give my son-in-law the benefit of the doubt that he's got good comedy tastes. The bar patron should learn to put questions about bathrooms more carefully. Of course, deceptive wisecracks may not always achieve such success, but that's how epistemic lessons are: Sometimes they take, sometimes they don't. That doesn't undermine their potential educational value, though.

What I'm saying is that deceptive humor can make us better as knowers, and so may indirectly serve to increase our epistemic status. The better we get at sniffing out put-ons, the higher our credibility rating may go. And increasing our status as a knower may actually increase the effective exercise of our autonomy. Of course, we've got to take seriously the lessons these wisecracks impart for all these lessons and benefits to kick in, but deceptive wisecracks may at least make that possibility available.

Second, these can be fun lessons, as long as you can lighten up and enjoy the humor part that comes along with it. There is clear value in being able to laugh at yourself, to not taking yourself and your gaffes so seriously. We're all gullible from time to time, and the fact that we fall for silly or absurd deceptions can be hilarious. That it's hilarious means that we ourselves have reason to be amused. When we ignore that reason in favor of being morally aggrieved, we are ignoring an essential interpersonal value, namely, playing along.

These two prudential values help explain, further, why serial leg-pullers don't count as dishonest. Were I to hang around the death bridge tackling people who blithely attempted to cross, you wouldn't think of me as an assaulter, as someone who exhibits the vice of deliberate harmfulness. That's because what I'm doing is valuable to people by their own lights. So too, when I engage in deceptive humor that has these positive benefits, I'm not being dishonest, given the value to people of what I'm doing by their own lights. The vice of dishonesty, it seems, applies only to those who deceive others primarily just to get goodies for themselves, without regard for any benefit in their targets.

And this leads to a final point: The wisecracker's attitudes and motives matter crucially here as well. They may be cracking wise just to amuse you. They may just be aiming to amuse themselves. They may just be doing so to amuse others around them. They may be doing so just to get someone to think more carefully before asking questions with obvious answers. They may be doing so to get others to take themselves less seriously. They may be doing so exclusively to thoroughly humiliate someone, to expose that person to the world as an idiot. Or they may be doing so with several of these motives. Different motives make appropriate very different responses in the butt of these cracks (*sorry/not sorry*). So even if the wisecracking method of exposing your gullibility to the world has some funny-making properties in it (like cleverness, killer timing, surprise, or incongruity), you may still have a serious moral reason to be angry at the wisecracker if it was done maliciously, or without sufficient forethought about how it might negatively affect you. But if they only meant well, or at least meant no harm, you may have no reason to be angry at all, just as you have no reason to be angry with the bridge tackler who was aiming to save your life. And if their motives were mixed, and you still do have a genuine reason for anger (perhaps they did aim to humiliate you a little), sometimes you should nevertheless just ignore it and admit, albeit sheepishly, "OK, you got me."

Taking a Joke

This last possibility I find fascinating. The phenomenon is familiar. It involves what we refer to as the ability to "take a joke" (even though it's really about wisecracks). While this ability is most often tapped into by mockery, the intentional exposure of gullible foolishness that some deceptive humor achieves may also tap into it. The ability to take a joke raises all sorts of tough issues, some having to do with gendered aspects of some types of wisecracking, others having to do with in-group/out-group power dynamics. I'm not going to get into those features just yet. All I'm interested in right now is the fact that some people—for good or ill—are better able to take a joke than others, where this means that they are better able to set aside what are nevertheless legitimate reasons for moral upset at being deceived and enjoy the humor involved. We of course all know the opposite type as well, the person who gets overly angry when put on, no matter how trivial it was, the pinched person who bitterly whines, "That wasn't funny!" Here I cast no judgment either way (exaggerated rhetoric aside). The only point I want to make is that there are additional reasons that have to be put into the hopper when you're deciding whether to put people on, reasons that have to do with whether they can take it.

When someone gets really angry at a wisecrack, regardless of whether they are doing so correctly (responding to malice in the wisecracker), it typically kills the festive amused spirit. As a result, this possibility has to matter when you're figuring out whether to wisecrack with someone. You shouldn't poke at a beehive, even if it's hilarious to see the bees fly around in crazed circles before they start stinging you. This isn't a moral reason, of course, but it is a prudential one worth heeding.

Another reason in the mix may indeed be moral, though. Should you say things that are mildly offensive around someone who is, in your judgment, overly sensitive about such things? Should you curse in front of your religious grandmother? It seems that we do have moral reasons sometimes not to affront some people's sensibilities, even if we think they are too sensitive or unreasonable. If you can refrain from upsetting someone, you sometimes should, regardless of whether your intentions in doing so would have been pure.

But even if this last moral reason is in the mix, surely it also sometimes loses handily to other reasons. If my grandmother also gets morally upset whenever anyone mentions body parts, I'm not going to be able to communicate well with her when, in carving the turkey, I need to know if she'd like a breast or a thigh, or, more seriously, when she has fallen and I ask whether she can put any weight on her leg. I have more compelling reasons to communicate clearly with her, even if it will affront her sensibilities. And so too there may be compelling reasons to make wisecracks even to the exceedingly delicate.

So how do you know whether a wisecrack will amuse or upset? Empathy. To empathize with someone is to see and appreciate that person's values and cares from their perspective, as they do, and so to be disposed to respond emotionally in sync with them when those things they value and care about are affected. The role of empathy will keep arising in this book, as I believe it's one of the most important elements for success in both our moral dealings and our wisecracking with each other. In the case of both, you must know your audience.

Why Pranks Suck

As a way of summarizing, illustrating, and supporting the machinery I've built in this chapter, I'm going to apply it to pranks in order to explain both why they are the lowest form of humor and why we should probably not play them on each other (much). Remember, the so-called funniness of many pranks doesn't depend on whether the butt is amused by it. But then because they don't need the butt's amusement in order to be funny, they contain a slightly different mélange of reasons than do put-ons.

Consider a few pranks you can find on YouTube (under the inaccurate description "Funniest Pranks Ever!"). In one, a guy's mother is transferring several bottles of water from the kitchen island into the fridge. Every time she turns around to grab another bottle, her son, who is hiding below the counter on the other side of the island, puts a new bottle of water on the island. His mother puts away one bottle, and then another, but she keeps seeing the same number of bottles back on the island, at which point she says softly to herself, "What is going on?"

In a second prank, a guy dresses up a realistic female mannequin, and when his wife comes through the door, he starts kissing and fondling the mannequin. His wife goes ballistic at what she thinks is a woman he's cheating on her with, even high-kicking the mannequin in the face. She is by no means amused by what he's done, and one suspects she never will be.

A third prank involves a father and son sitting on a couch together. The son is gently tossing his newborn baby in the air while his father contentedly watches. When his father looks away for a second, the son sets his infant down on the floor beside the couch, and then picks up a similar-looking doll, which he then tosses high and fails to catch, and it slams to the floor. His father is absolutely horrified.

Each of these cases involves deception, a clear attempt by the prankster to get a friend or loved one to believe something false. That means there's a moral reason on the table against doing it. But let's allow that it would be funny—perhaps it has the requisite sort of funny-making incongruity or surprise—so the prankster has a prudential reason to do it, namely, that it would amuse him (it's almost always a him, I note without comment). So far, the situation is analogous to leg-pulling. But pranks like these typically also aim at the embarrassment, shame, terror, or humiliation of the butt in a way that leg-pulling—where the ultimate point is to share in some amusement with the butt—do not. So insofar as none of these pranks is likely to generate amusement (the levity high) in the pranked person, there's no moral reason in favor of pranking if you're the lone prankster (and assuming there's no audience, as there wasn't initially in any of these examples; consider them in abstract from the eventual YouTube audience[19]). Indeed, there's an additional moral reason (beyond the deception) not to prank, namely, that it will embarrass, confuse, shame, terrorize, or humiliate the butt.

So let's tot up these reasons. On the side of pranking, we've got a prudential reason (it'll amuse me, thinks the prankster). On the side against pranking, we've got two moral reasons: it involves nonconsensual deceit, and it aims to cause embarrassment, shame, terror, etc. in the butt. What to do?

I think the first prank is morally fine, but the second two aren't. In the first prank, Mom is being caused to believe that she didn't put all the water bottles on the island away, so the aim is simply to see how long she'll keep at it before realizing that someone is messing with her. Now if Mom had dementia, there would be nothing funny about this prank, or so it seems to me, nor would it be funny if, instead of putting away water bottles, she was being made to lose count of how many bullets she was loading into a gun for a game of Russian roulette. So what's required for the prank to be funny is that (a) Mom at least has the capacity to figure out on her own what's going on, and (b) the stakes are low. What's funny is that she hasn't quite figured things out . . . yet. But she can. One can imagine her finally saying, "Wait a minute—son, are you doing that?" Temporary confusion or disorientation isn't bad in and of itself. Many of us deliberately seek it out, for example, when we get high, try to solve a puzzle, ride a roller coaster, or play in a locked room mystery. And confusion or disorientation can be good for us, as it may kick our brains into high gear and force us to be more careful in our thinking. So there's not too much morally to worry about in the first prank, either aimed for or achieved. Further, because it's so trivial, she likely can also share in the amusement afterward (it's more like a leg-pull in that regard), so that adds a moral reason in favor of pranking that the other two don't share.

Indeed, the other two pranksters aim squarely at psychologically trau-matizing the butt, and so there's much more to worry about morally. In the second prank a husband intends to make his wife believe he's cheating on her, and in the third a new father intends to get his own father to believe that he's just dropped the newborn on its head. Even if both beliefs are absurd (the husband would never cheat, the father would never risk his newborn's life like that), and even if there's a prudential reason for pulling these pranks (it'll amuse the prankster), that lone reason would be heavily outweighed by the moral reasons on the other side: the general reason against inten-tional deception, of course, but also the powerful reason against causing psychological trauma to others, however briefly. Psychological trauma, unlike confusion, is bad in itself. It may be possible to override the moral reason against causing it, but it will require a reason way weightier than the prankster's amusement provides to do so. And, of course, the butt of these pranks has every reason to be angry in response.

It should be obvious that this treatment applies in spades to the Carrie prank discussed in the previous chapter. Even if there was something funny in the prank (and I seriously doubt there was, but I'll grant the possibility), and even if the pranksters had a prudential reason to pull it (it would amuse them), and even if there was a moral reason in favor of it (it would amuse the entire student body), there were two powerful moral reasons against it that clearly outweighed the rest, namely, that it required repeatedly deceiving Carrie and it was immensely cruel in its aim to shame and publicly humiliate Carrie. The pranksters had deeply malicious motives. Carrie's anger, if not her telekinetic revenge, was abundantly appropriate in response, as it always is to cruelty.

Interpersonal pranks are the lowest form of humor not because they require deception (leg-pulling does that too), but because they often aim to cause intrinsically harmful psychological states. So even though they may be funny, and they may occasionally rise to "worth pranking" status, their humor has to overcome some pretty powerful moral reasons to get there. It may also be hard to figure out on the fly whether the pranked person will be angered or amused by it. One might think, then, that better-safe-than-sorry counsels just skipping them altogether.

Be Careful What You Leg-Pull For

There is one last moral wrinkle to consider in deceptive humor. Leg-pulling has gotten off the moral hook more than pranks to this point. But leg-pulling generates a psychological vulnerability for the leg-puller worth remarking upon, something that generates one last prudential reason to consider before engaging in it. When I pull your leg, I'm aiming to deceive you into believing something false that, when it's revealed, allows us to share in amusement at the fact that you fell for it. But some of the best leg-pulling is meant to be seen through, rather than having to be revealed. And sometimes, when it's not seen through, it can hurt the leg-puller's feelings, as what's really revealed is that the relationship wasn't what the leg-puller thought it was.

Return to the case of my son-in-law Nic telling me his favorite comedians were the less-than-inspiring group of Dane Cook, Larry the Cable Guy, and Jeff Foxworthy. I fell for it for a second. But I might well have fallen for it too hard and too long, and so treated it as believable that he really liked them. Indeed, I may not have seen through his leg-pull at all, and so replied, in true Midwestern fashion, "Oh, that's interesting," while thinking to myself, "My god, what terrible taste he has." And Nic might well have then remarked, "Wait, you didn't really believe that about me, did you?" Well, I did. And he may be hurt that I would ever think such a thing. What was supposed to be funny about the leg-pulling was that I would fall for it for just a bare second, and then I'd immediately recognize that he'd just been kidding. The fact that I didn't (in this hypothetical) means that I actually believed Nic had a terrible sense of humor. And the fact that I believed that this was possible of him, even though it was false, could hurt his feelings and hurt our relationship thereby.

No one's in the wrong here. "Be careful what you leg-pull for," though, should be the precautionary mantra of put-on humor. You might find out what a "friend" really thinks about you, or how far their benefit of the doubt extends. For instance, suppose you and I are friends, and as we drive by a Black man in handcuffs by a police car I aim to pull your leg by parodying what a bigot who saw it would say, muttering "Guilty!" as we pass him by. You may respond not with amusement but with horror that I would ever say or even think such a thing, as it seems to reveal to you that I'm actually a racist who believes all handcuffed Black men must be guilty of the crimes for which they've been arrested. You don't see through my put-on; rather, you think I'm for real. Now we may sort out this misunderstanding, and your initial impression may recede as a result. But what's been laid bare is that you could so easily think of me as a racist, and, well, that really hurts. And what's been laid bare to you is that I could so easily wisecrack about racial injustice. And these newly recognized features could well cause the beginning of the end of our friendship.

Deceptive humor is dangerous. It flirts with psychological trauma, disrespect, and hurt feelings. I can now more easily understand why the Christian students rushed to say "Just kidding!" all the time: It was to avoid risking any of that. Of course, in dispelling deception by saying "Just kidding!" one can easily wind up dispelling all the humor in a wisecrack. And that risks making *humor* worshippers angry. Again, I think the best lesson coming out of all of this is to know your audience. Barring that, you can always do what I did back when I was in 'Nam: *Run away!*

CHAPTER FOUR

"Lay Off!"

Mockery, Misfortune, and Meanness

At a rally in South Carolina in November 2015, then-presidential-candidate Donald Trump seemed to mock a disabled reporter, Serge Kovaleski, who has a condition causing contracture of the joints in his right arm and hand. It was a then-stunning, soon-to-be-familiar, type of thing for a presidential candidate to do. It started when, earlier that year, Trump claimed he'd heard about thousands of Arab Americans, from the top of buildings across the river in New Jersey, cheering when the Twin Towers came down on 9/11. This was deemed a lie by the press, as there seem to have been no such reports. But it turns out that Kovaleski, then a writer for the *Washington Post*, had indeed written an article shortly after 9/11 reporting that police had detained several people cheering and holding tailgate parties on rooftops in New Jersey after the towers came down. When the article was rediscovered in the wake of Trump's claims, Kovaleski (by then a *New York Times* reporter) said he didn't remember anyone saying that *thousands* of people had been cheering, or anything like that. Trump took this to be backtracking, of an order meriting mocking. So that's what he did. He begins by saying, "Oh, you gotta see this guy," and then, as he flops his dangling hands around in front of him, he puts on a panicked and dumb-sounding voice, saying, "Oooohh, I don't know what I said, oooohh, I don't remember!" The crowd howled with laughter.

The media published a picture of him doing this side-by-side with a picture of Kovaleski, with their arms in roughly similar positions. Outrage predictably ensued, with Trump haters up in arms that a presidential candidate would mock a disabled person, and Trump lovers claiming he'd simply been ridiculing a ridiculous backtracker and member of the fake news media, and anyway Kovaleski's arm is motionless and can't flop around in the way Trump was doing it, plus Trump didn't even know what the guy looked like, plus Trump always did that when mocking anyone's cowardice, plus Trump loves the disabled, and so on.

So let's just suppose Trump was making fun of Kovaleski's disability, as hard as it may be to imagine. Could such mockery ever be funny? And if so, could it ever be morally permissible to be amused by it, or to engage in such mockery oneself?

It's worth noting that many of the same people who were morally outraged by Trump's mockery of Kovaleski often themselves laughed and hooted at mockery of Trump. For example, they loved Alec Baldwin's famous impersonation of Trump on *Saturday Night Live*, which was clearly meant as a rather brutal takedown, with Baldwin exaggerating Trump's pouty lower lip, his wild hand gestures, and his way of speaking. But many psychologists have suggested that Trump himself might have a psychological disorder, malignant narcissism, which they consider to be a disability. If so, how would mocking him for things he might have done under the grip of *his* disability be any different, in moral terms, from his mockery of Kovaleski for Kovaleski's disability?

These are actually hard questions, harder than one might think. There are several steps to take in answering them. One is to figure out what exactly mockery is and whether it's ever funny. A second is to explore what reasons there might be, if any, to mock someone. A third is to determine whether mockery of some people, such as those with disabilities, is just off the moral table. A fourth is to see whether some popular objections to mockery, including the famous "punching down" metaphor, withstand critical scrutiny. There are going to be some genuinely surprising and controversial results here.

Mockery and the Funny

What is mockery?[1] It is to make fun of someone, to hold them up for ridicule, as the object of scorn, derision, and laughter (laughter at, not with), with the aim to disparage, embarrass, shame, or humiliate. The character of Nelson, on *The Simpsons*, captures the essence of mockery succinctly, with his finger-pointing "Ha-ha!"

Mockery, crucially, can be funny, although sometimes it's not. People who are quarreling may do vicious impersonations of each other, repeating what the other person has said in a mincing voice. This is mockery, but nothing about it is funny, nor is it meant to be; it's meant instead merely as ridicule, as insult. Intentionally insulting someone, when your aim is only to hurt them, is obviously immoral if there are no mitigating factors. For mockery to have any chance at being given a moral pass, then, its disparaging aims had better be leavened by humor.[2]

Suppose two friends are driving to a concert. One of them was responsible for just one thing: bringing the tickets.[3] Halfway there, he realizes he forgot them and says so. The other replies, "Oh my god, if you were twice as smart, you'd *still* be stupid!"[4] This has funny in it, as it flips an expected script about doubled intelligence (that if you were twice as smart, you'd be really smart). Now compare this to "Oh my god, you are so frickin' stupid!" Not funny, only stinging. There is something about the comic mockery in the first version that dampens or helps absorb the sting of the very same insulting thought that was expressed in the second version. Funny mockery can sometimes deliver what are in fact insults in a more cushioned way than unvarnished insults do, and that's because their sting is served up with the pleasant buzz of amusement. It's like cherry-flavored cough syrup (instead of castor oil).

It's worth taking a bit of time to get clear on mockery's norms, on what it takes for something to count as a fitting bit of mockery in the first place. When I say "fitting" mockery, I'm not talking about mockery that's morally or prudentially justified. Instead, mockery appraises people in a negative light (about which more later), and so to say that mockery is fitting is just to say that its appraisal of someone is correct, that what they did or how they are is somehow *mockable*. It could be fitting to mock someone, then, even if doing so would be immoral or imprudent (for example, if the object of your derision is John Cena, better to keep it to yourself, even if he did do a mockable ad with a purple cow).

So what makes mockery fitting, that is, what are the conditions for proper mockability? To mock someone is to make fun of them for something, but it can't be for just anything. Rather, they actually have to have the quality you're mocking them for. I can't fittingly mock you for being bald when you're hirsute. I can't fittingly mock you for a lisp when you don't have one. I can't fittingly mock your failing grade in art history unless you actually failed that easy-A class. Mockery has to capture some truth (or at least truthiness) about the mocked.

Second, mockery aims to shine a public light on this truth, perhaps just to the mocked person, perhaps just to a bystander, or perhaps to both. This means that, while you might rehearse some mocking comment about someone to yourself, it doesn't really count as mockery until you voice it.

Third, the features that mockery highlights have to be its target's perceived flaws, their failures to meet some standard. There are many standards people might fail to meet, including, to name just a few, standards of prudence, morality, athleticism, cooking, game playing, lawn manicuring, painting, singing, beauty, height, weight, and many more. Mockery may be fitting in any of these domains.

Fourth, the flaws mockery accurately exposes ought to be ridiculous in some way. If I have failed to win the one-hundred-meter dash at the Olympics only because I came in second by .0001 seconds, and in so doing I've posted the second fastest time ever recorded, my failure to win just isn't mockable. If, however, in running the one-hundred-meter dash at my church's charity competition, I stumble out of the starting blocks and land flat on my face, well, that's mockable. It's a spectacular failure, a ridiculous failure, a hilarious failure.

Fifth, fitting mockery aims at a sting, a *zing*, in its target. The target, ideally, should feel at least a wee prick of pain—in the form of embarrassment, foolishness, regret, humiliation, shame, or hurt—when mocked. Of course, this may not occur (thus the "ideally"). When I mock Biden or Putin to my friends, neither will ever hear or be hurt by my stinging remarks. But the idea is that they would be stung were they to hear it. And the same goes for people who are asleep, in a coma, or cognitively impaired, as they can be mocked too: Were they there, or all there (at full capacity), they'd feel the sting as well.[5]

You may disagree with this account of mockery. Can't we, after all, mock people for having risen above some normative standard, for being really nice or kind, say?[6] No. Mockery fits only failures, not successes. It involves making fun of someone and inviting others to laugh at them. You can't ridicule someone for an admirable trait. Imagine talking to your true moral hero, whoever she may be—Greta Thunberg, perhaps, or Mother Teresa, or Gloria Steinem, or Phyllis Schlafly—and then trying to "mock" her for doing precisely what you truly think is great about her ("Nice job, Gloria Steinem," you say sarcastically, "in making the world so much better for women."). Instead, it seems, you could only be making fun of yourself for falling below this person's moral ideals, or perhaps making fun of (satirizing) the kind of person who really would think those admirable traits of your hero weren't actually admirable. Alternatively, if what you say to a really nice person does count as mockery, it could only do so if what you're more subtly doing is making fun of them for what you take to be an actual flaw associated with their niceness, namely, that they are *too* nice, are a pushover, or signal their niceness in a smug way.

None of this is to say that you can't aptly mock admirable people; it's just to say that you can't aptly mock them for their admirable features. While I can't aptly mock Gloria Steinem for her positive contributions to the cause of women, I can fittingly mock her for criticizing female supporters of Bernie Sanders as just mindlessly following where the boys go.[7]

Another possible pushback to my account: Surely there's plenty of mockery that doesn't actually sting. As you'll hear again and again, I'm bald. People mock me for my baldness all the time, but it doesn't sting (I swear!). I also have several bald friends who report (at our monthly meetings) lots of wisecracks about their baldness but for which there are no stings attached either. Nevertheless, aren't these mocking attempts to draw public and ridiculing attention to our actual and ridiculous conditions?

It depends on the details of the wisecrack. Some don't aim to sting. I once asked my friends for advice about whether I should join a clinical trial studying a new drug for a condition I had. The primary side effect would have been "hair loss," and one of my "friends" said, "If that's the only side effect, then you literally have nothing to lose." This is a funny crack about my baldness, but it didn't aim to sting, and I don't consider it to be a mock. But it also depends on the sensitivities of the person being "mocked." It could be that my bald friends and I have all built up sting-resistant callouses on our tough bald heads, so mockery that does aim at a sting fails to deliver it. That doesn't make it not a mock. It just doesn't get to us. Although if you keep at it all night, it just might. More on this point later.

If I've gotten the conditions of fitting mockery right, then the moral worry about it should be clear: When you aim to draw attention to an embarrassing truth about someone, a truth they may well not want revealed or reveled in, and you hold it up for public ridicule with that stinging *ha-ha*, you are deliberately aiming to do something likely to cause that person some psychological distress (even if it doesn't always succeed). That, on its face, is immoral.

The immoral in mockery is highlighted when we consider its ugly role in human history. I have said that mockability is about the ridiculous. But what people have taken to be "ridiculous" has, over the centuries, most often boiled down to misfortune and disability. Plato says ridiculed people are those "who are weak and unable to retaliate when they are laughed at," as well as those who have undergone some "misfortune."[8] Cicero describes the object of ridicule as "a kind of . . . deformity."[9] Hobbes mentions "some deformed thing in another," "the imperfections of other men,"[10] or someone's "infirmity or absurdity."[11] Descartes says that those ridiculed include "people with very obvious defects such as those who are lame, blind of an eye, hunched-backed, or who have received some public insult."[12] But if these are the sorts of things that have been thought to be "ridiculous," ripe for mockery, then shouldn't we just deny right now that mockery could ever be either funny or morally OK?

The Funny in Mockery

In order for it to have any chance at morally mitigating its aimed-for sting, mockery has to have some funny in it. So where could it come from? Mock-

ery is perhaps the clearest example of superiority humor. And why is superiority a funny-maker? The answer given by the human theory of humor
(from chapter 1) is that it's just one of those properties that humans with
developed, refined, and unobstructed senses of humor would find amusing.
But then given all these cruel and horrific examples of superiority mockery
in history that many humans found amusing, shouldn't we seek reform?
Our sensibilities aren't set in stone, are they? People shouldn't be amused
by superiority humor, you might think, if it consists in mocking misfortune,
disability, deformity, weakness, and infirmity. Superiority humor needs to
go, and none of us should be amused by mockery!

I agree with some, but by no means all, of these complaints and recommendations. First, many of the examples of ridicule noted earlier were
examples of people laughing at other people. But laughter isn't our focus.
Instead, our focus is on the funny, on the truly amusing, and we might plausibly insist, therefore, that the examples weren't actually amusing. After all,
it's only the developed, refined, and unobstructed senses of humor that determine the properties that merit our amusement, and those who laughed
at "hunched-backeds" don't strike me as having senses of humor with very
much development, refinement, or clear vision. Indeed, throughout the
history of humanity, there might have been very few such senses of humor, just as there may have been few genuinely refined and unobstructed
senses of musical, artistic, or moral taste until quite recently (the current
consensus view that slavery is immoral is relatively new). So we shouldn't
be surprised if a lot of earlier humans found amusing certain attempts at
superiority humor that just weren't funny. But that doesn't yet mean that
there are no amusing examples today of superiority humor.

Second, the objection is too sweeping. Yes, some people have found
amusement in ridiculing people with deformities, and so forth. But that
doesn't mean that all superiority humor, or mockery, is of this form. Indeed, there are several examples of superiority humor that I think most everyone will agree can be funny.

For example, think about the funny in self-deprecation, a form of superiority humor in which I put myself down for your amusement. In early bits,
Louis C. K. used to wisecrack about being overweight: Why, he asked, do I
weigh myself when I do not use this information to guide my life in any way?
And self-deprecating mockery is a huge part of interpersonal humor. On an
LGBTQ dating site, one person advertises, "I'm balding but I still have my
teeth"; another writes, "I'm an elderly man with a promising future behind
me"; and an older woman writes, "A 49 model, well maintained, some rust,
the odd scratch in the paint but otherwise newly polished and shining, want
to crash with fast sports car driven by girl."[13] At a party I held a few years

ago, various guests were revealing their recent illnesses. One had been hospitalized for a thyroid scare, and another had surgery scheduled for skin cancer, so I turned to a third person and asked, jokingly, "So what's *your* problem?" His response was classic self-deprecation: "I'm physically fine. My problems are all psychological." Putting oneself down in these ways—self-mockery—can be funny and endearing, and lots of people enjoy it and engage in it.[14]

"OK, fine," you might say, "some superiority humor might be funny in its self-directed form. But surely all superiority humor directed at others is unfunny!" I doubt you believe this either, at least if you've got friends or a family, where mockery is rife. It's most often hilariously deployed when someone does or says something dumb.[15] My son-in-law Nic and I were once golfing on a course in southern Louisiana. On one of the fairways by a waterway, there was a gator-looking creature, motionless in the sun with its jaws open, about ten feet from where Nic's ball was. He pointed at it nervously, saying "Uh, David?" I replied, seriously and confidently, "Oh, that's just one of those fake gators they use to scare off predators on the course." I swear that's what I thought! It was motionless, after all. Plus I was focused on my own shot. So Nic strode up right near it and hit his ball, and we scooted off to the green. The next hole had us playing on the other side of the waterway. As we looked over to where the "fake" gator had been sunning, Nic wryly remarked: "Uh, David, that 'fake' gator seems to be gone." Sure enough it was, with the water rippling nearby. He has never let me live it down: "Nice how you nearly let me die," he'll say; or, "Now I see how you really feel about me"; or "Wouldn't the gators be the very predators the golfers need protection *from*?" And so on. Hilarious. Just hilarious. I can't . . . stop . . . laughing. Seriously, it was pretty funny because what I'd said was pretty stupid. And I said it with such confidence. It was crying out for ridicule.

In the linguistics literature, there are transcripts of exchanges between family members who mock each other all the time for slight mistakes. In one of them, Joe is putting dirty dishes into the dishwasher after dinner, but before she's seen him doing this, a visiting relative, Lynn, asks, "Do you need me to help you dry?" Joe responds, "If you want to get in the *dish*washer."[16] And later, talking about their sister, Joe accidentally slurs, "how much our shister wastes money," which Lynn mockingly highlights, "Your *shi*ster?"[17] Repetition in a funny voice is a very familiar form of mockery (and is perhaps the basic source of the funniness of impersonations more generally).

What's funny in these cases is a family member's silly failure, either of observation or of speech. And the same sort of thing takes place between friends all the time. One pitcher on a baseball team may mock his wild-throwing teammate by pretending to be him and throwing a ball into the stands. One friend says to another slovenly dressed friend in a bar, "I appreciate your respect for me in dressing up for the occasion." One bandmate says to another who has just flubbed a solo, "Who'd you actually sell your soul to down at the crossroads, Satan or Stan?" There are of course funnier versions of all these mocking wisecracks. But the point is that they can be and are funny, and they are all forms of superiority humor that aim at a bit of a sting. What's funny is someone's failure, where others are laughing at them from above.

Being the butt of mockery isn't always fun, of course. It can be embarrassing or worse to have your flaws exposed. But embarrassment isn't a bad thing in and of itself. Being embarrassed for his flubbed guitar solo will drive home the need for the mocked band member to practice more next time. Embarrassment can serve as a valuable corrective, readying us to toe that normative standard properly once more. Do you think I'll ever again confidently assert that a gator on a Louisiana golf course is fake?

Is one more extension of the funniness in superiority humor possible, to people one doesn't know or even to one's enemies? Easily. Indeed, it's very familiar from satire and political humor. *Saturday Night Live* skews to the left, politically, so many of their lefty comrades find it quite funny when the show makes fun of the hypocrisy of Trump, Mitch McConnell, Lindsay Graham, or other righty politicians. This is often superiority humor, though, where the audience finds amusement in recognizing their own superiority to the hypocrites being made fun of on-screen.

It's unclear if such audience members would find amusing structurally identical superiority humor running in the other political direction, but they should, as the exact same sorts of reasons are in place. For example, the *Babylon Bee* (a conservatively skewed *Onion*-esque publication) runs a number of hilarious stories skewing the pretentions and hypocrisies of people on the left, with headlines like "Liberal Activist Explains Notion of Tolerance to Man She Just Called a 'Worthless [Expletive]'"[18] and "Academy Strips 'Schindler's List' of Best Picture Award Due to Lack of Diversity."[19] These righty-favoring cracks have the same superiority structure as the lefty-favoring cracks, so if the lefty cracks are funny, so are the righty cracks. If people could clear away their obstructing ideological biases, the humor in both would be clear.

Some superiority humor, in the form of self- and other-mockery, can indeed be funny. We have a reason to be amused by it, and we have a reason to engage in it, as it can cause pleasurable amusement, in ourselves and others. But surely there are limits, aren't there?

Mockery and Meanness

Even if we allow that some mockery can be funny, most philosophers have despised it, for a number of moral and prudential reasons. Plato's objection was that the aggressive superiority inherent in mockery conceals a kind of envy or malice toward the victim that could morally harm those who laugh (by screwing up their souls), and which also might undermine the bonds of friendship crucial to a *polis*.[20] The Stoics always aimed to dampen or eliminate emotional responses that might prevent or disrupt being guided by reason, and this was true as well, for Plutarch, of "the seductive pull of shared laughter" at someone: it might make you too giddy to think straight.[21] Aristotle worried instead that the aggressive wit of mockery reveals a kind of "educated hubris," or "well-bred insolence" (depending on translation, but both sound bad), rendering one vulnerable to crashing back down to the earth sooner or later (today's mocker is tomorrow's mocked).[22] Hobbes called mocking humor "vainglory, and an argument of little worth, to think the infirmity of another, sufficient matter for his triumph."[23] Spinoza said that either the mocking victim's characteristics won't be as ridiculous as the mocker portrays them, in which case the portrayal is false (and the mocker is a liar), or those characteristics are ridiculous, in which case mocking them is just about the worst way to help the person improve.[24] And Hutcheson noted that ridicule may be an effort to make the mocked person contemptible in the eyes of others, which is apt to provoke severe moral anger and be dangerous for the mocker.[25]

All of these complaints may at times be true, but at most what we get from them is cautious counsel: Be careful what you mock for and how you mock. None of these complaints speak to whether mockery fits, though, to whether it can be an accurate appraisal of someone's ridiculous flaw. Nevertheless, the complaints together strongly suggest that, regardless of whether mockery of someone would be accurate, we should never do it. Drawing attention to someone's flaws and foibles for the sake of public amusement aims to hurt that person, to deliver a sting, so it's mean, and that's why no one should engage in it, one might think. Why cause pain to anyone in this fashion, even if it's funny?

I reject this objection. That mockery aims at a sting is, yes, a moral reason against engaging in it, but it's only one of many reasons in play with this type of humor, and on its own it may be quite weak.

Reasons to Sting

There may be all sorts of reasons, both moral and nonmoral, in favor of do- ing things that you know full well will cause someone embarrassment or hu- miliation. Start with (nonmoral) aesthetic reasons. Perhaps I'm making an unauthorized documentary about you, and I want it to manifest the aesthetic virtues of a great documentary, making it above all authentic and honest in the exploration of its subject matter. Manifesting these virtues may require that I expose something deeply shameful that you once did. That aesthetic virtues may require exposing people to public ridicule is perhaps best illus- trated in the harrowing documentary *The Act of Killing*, in which those who perpetrated the Cambodian genocide were convinced to act out, for the cam- eras, how they did so (and they are able to do so unmolested by a government that continues to protect them). There was clearly a kind of subtle but power- ful ridicule the filmmaker was engaging in, as the men all still thought them- selves justified and took their terrible playacting in these roles very seriously. They were monsters, of course, but they were also deliberately revealed to be ridiculous monsters. This exposure surely passed the moral test.

Switching to the athletic domain, if we are playing in the big champion- ship basketball game, I might have an athletic reason to embarrass you by dunking the basketball in your face, as it will manifest the athletic virtues of competitiveness and winning by sapping the energy and motivation of your team and electrifying my own team and the fans, giving us the mojo we need to bring the trophy home.

I may also have prudential reasons to draw attention to my own foibles in an embarrassing way. This is most obviously true in self-deprecating humor, which can defang or preempt mockery by outsiders, turning it into an ex- pression of autonomy and vitality, into strength. Exposing one's own flaws via self-deprecating humor has been found to increase, across the board, one's attractiveness to others.[26]

There are also moral reasons in favor of embarrassing yourself through self-deprecating humor. For one thing, it puts people at ease, especially members of put-upon out-groups.[27] And it can minimize power differen- tials between managers and employees.[28]

"OK, fine," you might now admit, "there may be nonmoral reasons in favor of other-mocking, and there may be prudential and moral reasons in favor of self-mockery, but these weren't the kinds of cases we were worried about. Instead, we were saying that there can never be moral reasons in favor of mocking *others*."

Sure there can.

The Moral Values of Mockery

Cicero identified one significant moral value of mocking others: It's a powerful method of social bonding. Often when we mock each other, we are identifying and reinforcing our shared norms and values, signaling to each other what behavior "we" won't stand for.[29] But mockery also bonds an in-group tightly when it's turned on outsiders, as it rallies the troops to do battle against those ridiculous "others." Indeed, Cicero thought mockery's most natural arena was the political, where it's still a potent weapon (regularly illustrated in the British Parliament). Mockery can occasionally bring down the mighty.

Of course, this feature of mockery contains real danger: In defining and closing ranks around our in-group, mockery also defines and shoots arrows at "them," the out-group. Mocking "them" is funny for "us," and "we" may not take seriously that "they" may be significantly hurt by our mockery (or worse: significant hurt may be "our" aim). And among the "them" have been those sufferers of misfortune and disability noted earlier. This is a real moral problem, and I'll come back to it.

Francis Hutcheson identified the second major value of other-mockery: it is corrective. When you mock people for their faults, he said, they "are apt to be made sensible of their folly, more than by a bare grave admonition. Men have been laughed out of faults that a sermon could not reform."[30] Mockery can, quite effectively sometimes, change people for the better. While he worried that some mockery "may be abused . . . before people of little judgment," he nevertheless urges that, "with men of any reflection, there is little fear that it will ever be very pernicious" and that it "may do good in a wise man's hands, though fools may cut their fingers with it, or be injurious to an unwary bystander."[31]

We can see both values manifested in the linguistic fieldwork. It's often hard to remember and catalog great examples of wisecracks because they are so of the moment. Thankfully, then, Elisa Everts (who was a grad student studying sociolinguistics in Chicago) recorded an hour with her funny Kansas family (her mother and three siblings) back in the early aughts, during a visit back home for their regular Memorial Day Weekend get-together. Everts reveals a very close family in action, a closeness illustrated and reinforced, she explicitly notes, by mocking and teasing. Some of this comes in the form of repetition and exaggeration. When Everts uses the term "stinkin'" three times in reporting various events in her life, her brother starts repeating it for emphasis, as if to say, "Do you realize you've been using this silly word throughout our conversation and this isn't how you normally talk?"[32] When her brother pronounces "wildest" with a serious southern twang as *waldest,* one of the sisters mockingly translates: "That's like wild, only it's *wald.*"[33] Elisa is recovering from laryngitis, and so is speaking in a high squeaky voice, an affect repeatedly impersonated and made fun of by the others. Each member of the family is both mocked by and mocks the others—no one's immune—and they target everything from speech patterns, to inability to spell, to why one of them would own a Honda instead of a Harley.[34]

These family members love pointing out those slips to each other, and they do so—intentionally or not—as a way to "identify and enforce group norms," in Everts's words.[35] They are, with their mocking, reminding each other that they are members of a group in which playful exchanges like this can take place, "where we do not have to stand on formality."[36] The trust and closeness achieved comes from the mocker reminding the mocked of the vast amount of history, affection, and norms they share, a reminder of the ties that bind them so tightly. But the mockery serves as a corrective as well, though not one that's preachy or coercive. They aren't smug lectures or smarmy Post-it Notes left on a fridge. Instead, they are delivered through play, so they can lean on amusement's buzz of pleasure to salve their sting.

All of these features can make mockery an enjoyable form of normative policing, a previously unrecognized kind of blame.[37] A well-timed sarcastic comment about my ill-fitting hat, a vocal impression of me that captures the affected way I've been pronouncing words since returning from a visit to England, a sly crack about getting a word in edgewise after I've been dominating the conversation—these all serve to enforce group norms that I've failed to live up to. In enforcing the norms, you're bonding our group members together (a group, we might say, which is constituted by those norms) and you've offered a funny corrective, one that will likely serve to get me back on the path from which I'd strayed.

Of course, many mocking families (and groups) have been and continue to serve as structures of oppression, molding little girls and boys into gender roles that perpetuate inequality, or indoctrinating kids into ideologies of White supremacy or homophobia. Many parents may make fun of their effete sons or tomboyish daughters to get them to toe the "right" gender lines. The problem in these cases, though, isn't the nature of mockery per se but the nasty norms that it's policing. So the bonding and corrective roles of mockery will have true value only when they are enforcing good or at least morally permissible sets of family and group norms. Of course, identifying what those are, exactly, is well beyond my needs or abilities here.

Nevertheless, the positive moral values of mockery can, I think, in combination with its funniness, outweigh the moral reasons there are against causing its stinging pain. And that establishes the first main point of this chapter: Mockery of others can pass the moral test.

Even if this is true, though, you might still think that some people have qualities that make mockery of them always either unfunny or immoral, which brings us right back to Trump and Kovaleski.

The Mocked

Note what Everts says about where her own family draws the line:

> The mocking really means you're all right. If you weren't all right, no-body would joke about it. It is only funny to joke about incompetence if the incompetence is superficial or temporary. If a person has a disability that renders them genuinely incompetent, talk about the incompetence is avoided altogether. This is evidenced when some of the jokes get too close to home and are negatively sanctioned.[38]

In the remainder of this chapter, I'm going to develop and critically examine this thought, which I'm sure many people share: Mocking people who have suffered misfortunes, especially people with disabilities, has to be immoral, one might well think, never to be done, regardless of any other positive values of mockery that may be in play.

We'll explore this thought by considering a contrasting thought that many people also have about mockery, just at the other extreme: Some-times facts about people seem to make mockery of them almost obligatory, even if other positive values aren't in play. Many on the political left surely thought or still think this about Trump, but there remain many people who to this day continue to see him as their champion, so he's too controversial a figure to point to in illustrating this point. Rather, I'm going to consider the case of Peter Cvjetanovic, who was photographed with a tiki torch and an angry face marching in Charlottesville during the White nationalist rally of 2017.[39] The photo was shared widely on Twitter, where nearly universal mocking ensued. Ultimately, thousands of people signed a petition to get him kicked out of his university once several folks posted his contact infor-mation. This is called "doxing," or sometimes "doxxing" (I'm not sure about "doxxxing"). While it's done most often these days to "encourage" people to toe a progressivist line, it actually got rolling back in the early nineties, when anti-abortion activists published names and addresses of abortion providers in what they called the Nuremberg Files, and whenever an abor-tion provider was wounded, his or her name was grayed out, whereas if one were killed, his or her name remained on the website with a red line through it.[40]

Perhaps the full-bore aim to punish Cvjetanovic went too far. But I'm guessing that most everyone would think that he at least was fair game for mockery, that it was perfectly morally permissible, and maybe even morally obligatory, for folks to mock him. But why would it be immoral, full stop, to mock disabled people and others who have suffered misfortune but be morally justified or even obligatory to mock people like Cvjetanovic?

There are two types of reasons people give to morally differentiate between these two cases. The first appeals to desert, and the second appeals to the direction in which the mocker is punching. Neither is adequate.

Desert

Many writers on blame insist that it requires a moral justification. Blame hurts, and you can't hurt people without good moral reason. The leading justification for the infliction of the punishment and pain of blame is desert, saying that blame would be unjust unless deserved. I earlier claimed that mockery is a kind of interpersonal blame for norm violations, so it might naturally be thought that mockery requires desert too, that it's morally permissible to mock someone only if they deserve it, and so to mock an innocent person would be unjust because undeserved. People like Cvjetanovic deserve it, you might think, but disabled people never do, so we can only permissibly mock the former. Among philosophers, Descartes actually makes this requirement explicit, putting the justification for scorn—"a sort of joy mingled with hatred"—to perceiving, unexpectedly, the "small evils" in others, that is, to perceiving that they are "deserving" of it.[41]

While there is, as usual, a lot of philosophical disagreement over what desert actually is, most do at least agree on its general structure: Someone deserves *something* in virtue of *something*.[42] The second something is called the "desert base." It's what makes appropriate the distribution of the first something, which is a benefit or a burden. The burden we are interested in justifying, of course, is the sting of mockery. The desert base of mockery would most plausibly be a mocked person's flaw.

"Flaw" is pretty vague, though, applying to a huge variety of things. My flaws, for example, range from major moral vices to minor skin blemishes. Deserving a burden for a flaw, then, is thought to require responsibility for the flaw: you can't deserve something if you aren't responsible for its desert base.[43] On this view, a pimply teenager doesn't deserve to bear any burdens for her acne, because her skin condition isn't her fault. But as a student, she does deserve an A for her essay, given her responsibility for its excellence. An athlete deserves the gold medal he earned by running the race so well, but as a criminal defendant, he may not deserve any punishment for a crime he committed while sleepwalking (and so was not responsible for).

To apply this view to mockery, we could say that if someone has a flaw for which he's responsible, then and only then may he deserve mockery for it. Cvjetanovic was obviously responsible for marching with a tiki torch in the Charlottesville protests, as well as for having the racist beliefs he had, so he deserves mockery for those flawed actions and beliefs. Alternatively, if someone is not responsible for her misfortune, she can't deserve mockery for it: the pimply teenager shouldn't be mocked for her acne, nor should children for their drunken father's shameful behavior. To the extent, then, that people aren't responsible for their disabilities, they can't deserve to be mocked for anything pertaining to them either. Mockery of the disabled would be immoral, in other words, because undeserved, and undeserved because nonresponsible.

This view fails, however. When I was a teenager, puberty frightened me. In particular, I didn't like the look of the hair growing in bushels on my legs. So I decided one day to shave it off. I started with an electric razor at my ankles. After shaving the hair on the front of my legs halfway up to the kneecap, I thought, "Wow, this is taking a long time, and I'm no longer sure I should be doing this." So I stopped right there and decided to let all the hair grow back in. It never did. To this day, I have a landing strip running down my shins. It looks ridiculous. It *is* ridiculous. It is eminently mockable, and it is, in fact, regularly—rightly—mocked by my family during shorts season. But I am not responsible now for the mockable state of my one-third-hairless forelegs. Either I'm a sufficiently different person from that stupid teenage boy so as not now to be responsible for his stupidity; or I am the same person as that kid, but insofar as he had no reason to think that what he was doing would result in my now-mockable plight, he couldn't have been (so I couldn't thus be) responsible for putting my legs into that state in the first place. Responsibility isn't necessary for mockability.

Indeed, the question of whether someone does or doesn't deserve mockery is typically quite irrelevant in interpersonal life. In family and friendship mockery, especially, responsibility and desert often play zero role in what we regularly think is perfectly fitting and funny mockery. Return to the Everts family. For them, mockery rarely tracks desert or responsibility at all: *waldest* just came out accidentally, and Elisa's much-mocked laryngitis wasn't her fault. Friends are regularly mocked for things that are simply no fault of theirs, including physical weaknesses, athletic failures, showing up late due to traffic, saying something stupid when drunk or coming out of anesthesia, and much more. In all these cases, desert is irrelevant.

Further, despite what the family members themselves say, they occasionally *do* target disability in their mocking wisecracks. At one point, Everts describes a comment about the blinds that is taken, to much amusement, to do double duty as a crack about their mother's own partial blindness.[44] All of these kinds of mockery are extremely familiar in my own life, within my own family, and I suspect it's true of you and yours as well. We tend to make fun of "our own" on a regular basis, for accidental gaffes, genetic conditions, and even physical flaws or impairments, all things for which desert and responsibility are irrelevant.

One final argument is worth advancing. The most compelling thought about desert comes from cases where innocent people are blamed or punished, treatment that must, it seems, be unjust because undeserved. If Paulo stole the cookies yet I blame Paula, the pain I've caused her in blaming her certainly seems unjust, and the reason why is just that she didn't do it, so she doesn't deserve my blame's pain.

This could be true of much of blame's pains.[45] But it is not true of mockery-blame. Remember, what matters for mockability—for fitting or apt mockery—is "truthiness." If I mock you for some attribute, you have to actually have that attribute in order for my mockery to be appropriate. You also have to have it for my mockery to sting. So here's my bold proposal: Mockery-blame can deliver its characteristic sting only to the extent that its target actually has the mockable flaw being singled out for ridicule. If an innocent person is punished, that treatment may be unjust because the pain of punishment can be delivered regardless of that person's innocence or desert. But in mockery-blame, I say, the mockery's sting can be delivered only if it zeroes in on and highlights some truth about the mocked person, that is, only if the mockery is truthy.

For example, suppose that you are sitting in the stands of a basketball game in which I'm playing, but you are rooting for the other team. I make a long three-pointer without so much as disturbing the net, but from your angle it looks like what you now shout out, in the familiar sing-song style: "*Air ball! Air ball!*" This won't bother me in the least; indeed, I'll find *you* a bit mockable yourself for making such a mistake. There is surely no injustice in your inaccurate mockery of me, as there's just no sting delivered. But then suppose that, a few plays later, the referee calls a foul on me that I simply didn't commit, and as it's my sixth, I'm thrown out of the game. Now there *is* a kind of unjust setback that's been delivered: I didn't deserve that, we might well say.

The difference comes from the source of pain or setbacks in various kinds of treatment. It's only undeservedly unjust for you to treat me in some evaluatively-called-for way where there's pain or setback that can be inflicted on me regardless of the accuracy of your evaluation. But mocking-blame's sting comes *only* when its evaluation is accurate. There is thus no undeserving injustice in inaccurate mockery, in mockery of the innocent. So too, I say, there's no requirement for desert in accurate mockery either; all that's needed (and which delivers the sting) is the accuracy of the appraisal. Whether the sting is deserved or not is irrelevant.

Desert won't help us articulate a principled moral difference between mocking those with misfortunes or disabilities and mocking Cvjetanovic. What might do the trick instead?

Punching, Up and Down

People on the political left often say that mockery is wrong when it punches down. The complaint has mostly been applied just to jokes or to particular comedians. But we ought to be able to apply it to mocking wisecracks pretty easily. The idea is roughly this: It is morally OK to punch up, that is, to mock, ridicule, or satirize those in power or with some kind of privilege or authority, but it's not OK to punch in the opposite direction, to mock the weak, the underprivileged, or those who have been marginalized or oppressed. This difference could then account for why Trump's mocking Kovaleski was wrong but why it's OK for people to mock Trump or Cvjetanovic.

Notice first that the objection is ambiguous between mocking those who are down, full stop, and mocking those who are down for the *features* that make them "down." People who offer this objection don't really differentiate between these possibilities, but they often do talk as if it could never be appropriate to mock people who are "down" for anything at all, even for things having nothing to do with their "downness." Surely this is false, though. It would mean, for instance, that no one could ever mock Dinesh D'Souza, a person of color, for supporting the birther movement against Obama or for calling Rosa Parks "overrated." It would imply that no straight people could mock Milo Yiannopoulos, who at the time identified as gay,[46] for establishing a "Privilege Grant" for White men only, or for calling alt-right ideologues "dangerously bright." It would mean no one, including other women, could ever make fun of Phyllis Schlafly (as did Gloria Steinem and others) for defending traditional gender roles while she herself was a lawyer, political leader, and editor. People with social identities of those thought "down" clearly can do mockable things.

The more plausible interpretation of the metaphor, then, is that it's morally impermissible to mock those who are "down" *for* the features pertaining to their "downness." You couldn't thus permissibly mock D'Souza, Yiannopoulos, or Schlafly, for, respectively, anything to do with their race, sexual orientation, or gender. What made Trump's flopping-armed mockery immoral, then, was that he was mocking a "down" Kovaleski precisely for what renders him "down," namely, his disability.

The primary problem with this metaphor, however, is that there's just no clear ideology-free way of determining who's "up" and who's "down." Those who are "up" are alleged to be those with social identities that come with power, authority, and privilege, people who have cultural weight on their side. But these are also very vague terms mostly deployed rhetorically, and they mean different things in the mouths of people with different ideological biases.

To explain, start with this uncontroversial point: These terms are all comparative. Being powerful, say, is like being tall. There is no such thing as being tall full stop; to be tall just means to be taller than members of a comparison class. But because one may find oneself in different comparison classes at the same time, whether one is "tall" is completely context dependent. I'm tall relative to my grandson, but I'm not at all tall relative to a group of NBA players.

So too there's no such thing as being powerful, or having authority or privilege, full stop; one is only more or less powerful and so forth relative to some comparison class. Putin is more powerful than his citizens in determining their rights and liberties, but not at all powerful relative to the citizens of Bali. I have more authority over my children than my neighbor does, and she has more authority over her children than I do.

Nearly everyone has some power or authority on some dimension or other with respect to some comparison group. The bartender has power over who gets to do what in the bar during her shift, but then her hours are set by the bar manager, and when she goes home, she may be powerless in the face of an abusive partner or evicting landlord. Even the homeless person under the bridge may have more power or authority than the other homeless people nearby in virtue of his dominance over a tiny piece of real estate.

The same thing is true of privilege. For example, it's often rightly noted that White men have many privileges in the US that other citizens don't have. When driving or shopping, they typically never have to worry whether they'll be tailed or stopped by cops for arbitrary reasons. They also see themselves widely represented in the media, they can be assured when they ask to see the manager that that person will often look like them, and they are the winners of the implicit bias sweepstakes. But poor or unedu-cated White men, in particular those from the Appalachian region, have long been the target of discrimination, are regularly ignored in public pol-icy, and have often been made fun of by comedians and others. The same is true of gay White men. So are these men privileged or not?

The obvious answer is that they are in some respects but are not in oth-ers. But this is true—to varying degrees—for nearly everyone. There are many different contributors to social identity—race, gender, ethnicity, class, social status, age, sexual orientation, etc.—and because there are so many different ways to possess different degrees of these features, there are both many axes of privilege and "many axes of oppression,"[47] and one per-son can of course appear on each list in some respects. That is, one person can score high on the privilege scale for their race or gender identities but score high (low?) on the oppression scale in virtue of their sexual orienta-tion or class identities.

Further, there are no context-free locations of marginalization: Those who are marginalized are so within certain domains, but they may not be in others. Evangelicals, especially White evangelicals, are thought by many to be perpetually "up." But it's well known that they are marginalized and heavily underrepresented in most branches of the academy, where profes-sors are overwhelmingly secular and tend to hire those like themselves. The same is true of those adhering to conservative political ideas, as most professors are also overwhelmingly of a left-wing bent who hire the like-minded.[48] So then is mockery of conservatives and evangelicals from those outside the academy punching up, while mockery from within the acad-emy punching down? Does a professor's mockery of an evangelical for her Christianity change direction once she leaves the university parking lot?

Indeed, might not those who many view as "down" actually be "up" in some domains, domains where they in fact exercise significant degrees of privilege, authority, and power? On this metaphor, how are we to view CEOs like Richard Branson, founder of the Virgin Group, who has dyslexia and learning disabilities,[49] or Paul Orfalea, founder of Kinko's, who has dyslexia and ADHD? What of J. K. Rowling, who suffered for years from chronic depression? When she makes her comments about trans women, is she punching from above or below?

One of the most despised and marginalized groups in many pockets of America (and Germany, and the Netherlands, etc.) are White suprema-cists and neo-Nazis. Their speech is restricted (in academia and most busi-nesses), their rallies are heavily protested these days, their members are excluded from a wide variety of jobs, and they are occasionally attacked in broad daylight by those who hate them for who they are, as happened to right-wing extremist Richard Spencer: Someone came from his right, as he was walking down the street, with a flying punch to the face. Indeed, this was *literal* punching, but what was its metaphorical direction? Up because he's a straight White male, down because he's a reviled and marginalized neo-Nazi? The actual punch looks horizontal.[50]

I'm not being a troll, I swear. Rather, my aim is to bring out the fact that metaphorical appeals to the direction of punching mockery are really focused on larger power structures and relations, whereas my discussion of wisecracks is focused on interpersonal interactions, in which there are just so many intersecting axes of both oppression and privilege that reference to the much more structural up/down approach is simply unhelpful.[51] Further, given how what counts as "up" or "down" mostly depends on the ideological biases of those who appeal to it, it can't provide an ideologically neutral and principled way of differentiating between cases like Kovaleski and Cvjetanovic. We can do better.

Piling On

I think we need to abandon the problematic directional punching metaphor in favor of a different one, namely, *piling on*. Doing so will yield many of the same conclusions held dear by the punching crowd, but without the problems I've just detailed.

Mocking you points out and exposes for ridicule a flaw in you, and its funniness sometimes depends on just how ridiculous that flaw was, that is, how far you fell below the standards for that kind of thing. Mockery generates amusement for the mocker and various audiences in virtue of their superiority to you in that respect. But if we both know that I'm superior to you in numerous areas—enjoying greater success, wealth, good looks, the respect of others, and, yes, power, privilege, and authority across many domains—then my mocking you for a flaw will often just be overkill. I've already won at life, so when I make fun of you, aiming to reveal yet another area in which I'm superior to you, I'm being unsporting, crass, and classless. It's like running up the score in a game, or showily lapping a slower racer (while jogging backward and shaking your heinie).

Those with social identities classifying them as members of historically marginalized groups have typically been rendered worse off than other people in many of these sorts of ways, due to their (often ongoing) oppression, so it's no surprise that people with certain social identities have been identified with the "down." But people can be worse off relative to others in many other sorts of ways, not just in terms of those particular social identities (and some with membership in historically marginalized groups can be really powerful and well-off—note Branson, for one). Indeed, one can be worse off than others in terms of features like income, dance skills, aesthetic talent, math ability, nose size, and family provenance, all things that mockery may target. If the worry people have when using the directional punching language is more carefully and clearly described as a worry about piling on, then moral complaints about mocking should apply more widely when the mocked fall into any of the categories of the unfortunate, untalented, incapacitated, unskilled, or of a lower socioeconomic status generally, and not just when they are members of groups that have been targets of oppression, or in virtue of their having a particular social identity.

Note the most familiar objection we tend to launch in ordinary cases of interpersonal mockery, and which is the title of this chapter: "Lay off!" In other words, *that's enough*! This is not an objection that the mockery isn't funny, nor is it an objection that the target doesn't deserve it or occupies a lower location in social space than the mocker. It's rather a moral objection against mockery whose stinging weight has just become too much for its target to have to bear. Piling-on mockery may not cease to be funny, just like a basketball team running up the score against a far weaker opponent won't cease to be winning. It's just that its weight becomes too much for anyone to reasonably have to handle, often in light of all the rest of life's burdens the person has already had to deal with. Calling for someone not to mock the "down" is better translated as a way of saying, "Ease up, they've been through enough already."

My "piling on" construal of the moral objection to mockery explains a lot (and, again, its verdicts will largely coincide with the purported verdicts of the structural up/down objectors). First, while the "up" have been rhetorically restricted in the US primarily to the White, Christian, and/ or male, the "piling on" objection allows that people can be relatively unburdened on a much wider variety of dimensions, including looks, wealth, talent, family provenance, social connections, and, yes, political power or privilege. The reason it may actually be morally OK to mock such folks is that they can take it. They've got a such a buffer of good fortune that they can absorb the sting that mocking delivers. So go ahead and mock the rich, mock those celebrities, and by all means mock the president.

We can also see how construing objectionable mockery as "piling on" might finally enable us to differentiate in a morally principled way between mocking those with disabilities and mocking people like Cvjetanovic. People with disabilities, we might think, are much more likely to be less well-off on many dimensions than those without disabilities, so because they've already been severely disadvantaged by having a disability, mocking them for features pertaining to that disability would be piling on, in a morally objectionable way, whereas Cvjetanovic seems like he's had it pretty good in life, so mockery of him for marching with the tiki torch isn't morally problematic at all, as he can surely take it.

I think the "piling on" objection constitutes an actual moral stopper to mockery, undercutting or outweighing any comic reasons in its favor. But as it turns out, it doesn't necessarily provide a principled moral distinction between mocking the disabled and Cvjetanovic, nor does it necessarily yield the verdict that those with disabilities can never permissibly be mocked for their disabilities. For one thing, being disabled certainly does not mean that one has necessarily been overburdened or rendered poorly off at all (or at least it depends heavily on what the precise disability is; more on this point later). To assume otherwise—that all disabled people are inherently overburdened and rendered poorly off by their disability—is condescending and objectionable stereotyping. It is condescending because it presumes disability is always a burden and makes people's lives worse off simply for having one. "Oh, you poor thing!" is the maddening thought here, relying on an assumption from a place of superiority that is egregiously false.[52] It is objectionable stereotyping because it wrongly attributes properties thought to apply to some group to all of its individual members as such.

Furthermore, once we construe the moral stopper as being triggered by piling on, then the number and volume of mocking voices has to matter a lot more than they've been taken to, and that undermines the attempted moral differentiation at issue. For instance, while it was surely permissible for me alone to mock Gal Gadot for organizing and singing in the smarmy and patronizing celebrity-packed video of "Imagine" during the COVID quarantine of March 2020, what happens when that zing becomes amplified, shared, and joined a million times over via social media?[53] Surely she could absorb the hit of my single pitiful mock—she's Wonder Woman!—but what about millions of mocks? Don't these individual punches collectively add up to a knockout? And what, indeed, about the relentless mocking of Cvjetanovic? At some point, wouldn't the mockery and punishment he received have to be way heavier to bear than, say, one private person's mockery of another private person's disability?

It's from this point that we see how the "piling on" objection actually applies much more widely than just to in-person mockery, for it can also provide a powerful objection to some social media callouts and attempts at cancellation: their sheer weight can bury people alive, in a way that's wildly disproportionate to any wrongs that may have been committed.[54] What's interesting here is that it's the collective heaviness of the pile-on, and not any one individual's contribution to it, that becomes too much to bear. Responsibility in callout culture thus bears a surprising inverse analogy to responsibility for addressing climate change: In both cases, nothing I do as an individual may make a bit of difference, whereas when we operate as a collective, significant effects occur.

To explain, the question of whether there are genuine moral reasons for any individual human to do anything as a way to mitigate climate change—recycle, fly less, drive electric cars, consume less red meat—is vexed.[55] *Humanity* might have a powerful reason, but I'm not humanity, so why do I have any reason, especially if my failure to do anything will have no noticeable effect on the problem? There's an inverse puzzle for would-be caller-outers: While the collective Twitterverse has a powerful moral reason not to pile on someone in a way disproportionate to their "crime," no individual's callout may make any difference at all (at least to the weight of the burden), so it's hard to see why any individual tweeter wouldn't have a reason to call out someone they deem to have done something immoral. After all, isn't this just our much more democratic (and progressive?) way of holding people accountable for their immorality? And isn't our susceptibility to being called out just what it means for us to be accountable to each other?

The collective action problem of climate change is enormously difficult to solve. One possibility, though, is to recognize that, while I may have a direct reason not to recycle or fly less, as doing so would cost me time and energy and have no effect whatsoever on the climate, I may nevertheless have a kind of *indirect* moral reason to do those things insofar as seeing me do them may influence others to do them as well, and the more people I can influence to do those things, the greater chance we will have at generating the collective weight needed to make an actual impact. My reason for recycling and such may then outweigh my reason against making such sacrifices, even if doing so will have zero direct effect on the climate.

The same might be true—inversely—when it comes to public callouts. We live in an age when we can call people out very publicly in an instant, and depending on our numbers of followers, we have the capacity to influence people in a way unheard of and unforeseen in earlier times. When people do what we deem immoral, we as individuals may each have a moral reason to call them out: they are accountable and so, we may think, they need to be held to account. But if we each act on such a reason, we are very likely together to create the kind of disproportionate burden that violates the no-piling-on constraint. So we may also each have an indirect reason not to call people out in public forums, at least to the extent that doing so is likely to influence others to pile on in a way that will, collectively, be quite immoral. Thus, just as our indirect reason to recycle and such (that it will influence others to do so) may outweigh the direct reason we have against it, so too our direct reason for holding some people to account through public callouts may well be morally outweighed by the risk of starting or contributing to a pile-on.

In any event, my main point has been to figure out the clearest and most charitable way of articulating the moral objection that many people have to mocking those with disabilities, an objection that might nevertheless allow mockery of someone like Cvjetanovic. The piling-on objection is indeed a compelling objection to some mockery (as well as to some public callouts), and it provides a far clearer and ideologically neutral moral reason against it than the punching up/down metaphor. But it still doesn't help us to differentiate between mockery of the disabled and people like Cvjetanovic, because it condescendingly and falsely presumes that disability, in and of itself, is burdensome, a weight no reasonable person should have to bear, and it also mistakenly assumes that people like Cvjetanovic can't be disproportionately burdened or buried by the collective weight of the many who pile on.

We thus haven't yet captured a clear and principled moral difference between mocking the disabled and mocking people like Cvjetanovic. So instead here's a radical thought: Maybe there's no moral difference between the two after all. This result could be cashed out in two ways: perhaps neither are permissibly mocked or both are. It's this second—most radical— possibility that is surprisingly worth our attention.

What Is Disability?

For a very long time, disabilities were characterized in terms of what's known as the *medical model*, which viewed them as human flaws, deformities, and infirmities that always make people's lives worse for having them and should thus be fixed or eliminated, if possible. On this model, for example, eyes that can't see don't function properly; blind people are thus physically flawed and live worse lives than they would if they were sighted. We should thus aim to help them by fixing their visual impairments, if at all possible, so that we can eliminate their disability and enable them to be "normal."

By contrast, the *social model* of disability asks, "What is normal?" Disabled people have actually been disabled by society, on this model, which has been built on the basis of a discriminatory norm of "normality" that robs those labeled "the disabled" of all sorts of opportunities. Social institutions, jobs, and buildings have been constructed, for example, in a way that heavily favors the sighted and those able to climb stairs, preventing equal access for those with various physical disabilities to a variety of opportunities. Disability is a socially constructed category, then, consisting of some impairment or deviation from a physical or psychological norm plus social prejudice against people with such impairments/deviations. To eliminate the disability, therefore, we shouldn't "fix" the disabled person and make her fit the normal norm; rather, we should change ourselves, our norms, and our society, so as to eliminate the discrimination by enabling those with disabilities as they are to participate fully in social life and pursue whatever opportunities are available within it on an equal footing with any other person.[56]

Viewing disability in this social constructionist way has wrought widespread positive changes over the past half century. It's the reason for closed captioning in TV broadcasts, wheelchair accessible buildings and bathrooms, audio signals on crosswalks, sign language interpreters for public speeches, and much more. It has dramatically altered the way in which children with dyslexia, autism, and various intellectual impairments are taught in schools (as they now receive individualized instruction based on their specific learning styles). And it has also spawned close-knit Deaf, autistic, and blind communities and cultures, which its members very much want to advance, defend, and preserve, and whose members are simply not any worse off for their disability as such.

There are some serious problems associated with the social model of disability, I hasten to add, including how we are to understand just what an impairment is, or how we might conceivably apply the model to those with profound intellectual impairments or chronic pain (how could an adjustment of our social structure eliminate these disabilities?). Nevertheless, the general approach is enormously plausible for some prominent disabilities, especially autism, blindness, dyslexia, deafness, and various physical deformities or disfigurements, all human differences in response to which there's been plenty of (historical and ongoing) discrimination and exclusion. The onus of eliminating these disabilities would indeed seem to be on the society that constructed them as such, sometimes literally, by making many buildings simply inaccessible to those with various physical impairments. Change the structure of those buildings, change the structure of society, be welcoming, not discriminating, to disability.

Many humans in our brutal history have been mocked for their disabilities (think about carnival freak shows alone). Let's take the social model seriously, then. It would seem to imply that people should never again be mocked for their disabilities. That's because mockery aims to reveal, poke fun at, and sting people for their embarrassing inferiorities. Society has been constructed in favor of abled people, and disabled people have thus been treated as inferior, as falling short, embarrassingly, of some "human" norm, entirely in virtue of being disabled. But their impairments are mere differences in the human condition, and not inferiority-makers. In order to eliminate discrimination against them, therefore, we need to change the structure of our society so that these differences are no longer treated as disabling, embarrassing, or as inferiority-makers. Insofar as mockery violates this dictate (it explicitly embraces superiority humor), then the social model would seem to rule mockery morally out of bounds for disabled people.

That's a powerful argument with deep roots in the social model of disability. But there's an even more powerful argument with even deeper roots in the social model that has the opposite conclusion.

Mockery, recall, can promote many positive values. It can serve to bond those who engage in it. It can be a kind of initiation rite, suggesting, "If you can take it, you're all right, you're one of us." It can be a genuine expression of affection among people who otherwise have trouble expressing affection. It can serve to articulate, enforce, and reinforce group norms. It can also deliver a backhanded compliment that recognizes and salutes the mocked person's *high* status (as when professional golfers mock each other: "How could you make such an amateur's mistake!" which indicates just how good they know they really are). These are all extremely valuable interpersonal goods. To withhold these goods from those with disabilities is to, well, continue to disable them. It's to discriminate against them in a crucial arena of interpersonal life solely in virtue of some arbitrary impairment or deviation from a physical or psychological "norm." It's exclusionary. It's to deprive them of opportunities for engagement and solidarity and bonding that remain open to others. And that's immoral.

If we embrace the spirit of inclusion that drives the social model of disability, I find this to be the more powerful argument. If our aim is to eliminate what discrimination we can from the social world by changing our social (and interpersonal) structures and institutions to eliminate disabling impairments, if our aim is inclusivity and mocking can be inclusive, then including disabled people into the mocking world may be morally permissible and, perhaps, a moral duty.

I'm not a moral monster. I'm quite aware that disabled people have been mercilessly and brutally mocked throughout human history, and there's no question that it was deeply immoral. I am also most certainly not advocating willy-nilly mockery of people with disabilities. Instead, I am saying that *sometimes* mocking people for their disabilities *may* be morally permissible within *some* interpersonal groups (and, in fact, it may *sometimes* be morally required). But there are several important caveats and conditions here:

- The normative recommendation from the social model is all about inclusion, so in order to ensure equal opportunity and access to mockery's values, any mockery of those with disabilities should of course be inclusive and mutual, a genuine part of, and a contribution to, interpersonal bonding within some established and familiar group (so these normative recommendations will apply almost exclusively to friends and family).

- The mockery cannot violate the no-piling-on restriction. If it does, it's morally impermissible. (This restriction also applies to mockery of people like Cvjetanovic.) Now I don't deny that there will often be serious knowledge gaps to overcome here, including how much of a burden is "unreasonable" for someone to have to bear, and how much of a burden any individual has actually undergone. This latter gap is especially pertinent to those with disabilities, who may well have undergone so many slights and microaggressions throughout the course of their lives that any mockery would indeed be too much, and knowing what that amount is or what's too much for them may simply be beyond anyone else's complete epistemic grasp. But again, this gap doesn't provide a distinctive or principled reason to exclude those with disabilities from mockery; it counsels instead that you restrict your mockery only to those whose vulnerabilities and limits you know pretty well, and this will, again, most often be friends and family, those with whom you've got some shared history.
- In order to generate reasons for engaging in mockery in the first place, it has to be funny! (The sting must be salve-able.)

None of these conditions were met in the horrifying historical cases. The historically mocked were systematically excluded from society and were among the least well-off, so virtually any stinging mockery of them would have been a morally objectionable pile-on. I also doubt that any such mockery was funny. People may think that pure ridicule ("What an ugly hunch, hunchback!") is funny, but it's not. Such mockery was and is thus quite obviously immoral, without redemption. But that's not to say that all mockery of disabled people was or is immoral or unjustified, especially if it may contribute to the elimination of the disability (a discriminated-against difference) in interpersonal life. Genuinely inclusive mockery can do just that.

"Only I Get to Say That!"

Being funny is necessary to salve mockery's sting, and so funniness is what puts mockery on the road to moral permissibility. But this raises an obvious final objection: "Mockery of disabled people," many likely think, "just can't be *funny*." Disability, in other words, simply has no funny-making proper-ties. There are several replies.

First, once again this response is just condescending to disabled people. It's as if those with disabilities are in fact impaired in a distinctive way that places them outside of the ordinary interpersonal domain. They are treated as "special" in a way that translates squarely into exclusion. Ironically, and sadly, many abled people view disabled people as so "special" that they call them "heroes" just for doing everyday things. Australian comedian Stella Young (born with osteogenesis imperfecta) calls this attitude "inspiration porn."[57] But disabled people aren't inherently admirable just in virtue of having and living with a disability.

Second, the claim that there's nothing funny about disabling impair-ments is false. The problem, as usual, is finding good examples of funny dis-ability humor, as authors in the scholarly literature have simply not wanted to talk about such humor at all, perhaps fearing that it would be further disabling (or perhaps fearing a backlash from readers). Nevertheless, there is clear evidence from within certain disabled communities that there is plenty of inter-member mockery afoot, so we can at least start there.

Some members of the Deaf community make fun of both each other and those with other physical or mental impairments. (It should go without saying that they mock members of the hearing community rather merci-lessly for their cluelessness when it comes to deafness—these are called "zap jokes.") That's because "a rejection of disabled status is properly considered to be part of Deaf community identification."[58] If you as a Deaf person reject the view that people like you are in fact disabled, then making fun of each other for your hearing impairments or affected ways of talking simply can't count as making fun of your "disabilities." Your impairments become just one among many human differences, deficiencies, and flaws, all equally ripe for mocking.

Those with various physical impairments engage in "crip humor," both as a way of bonding the in-group and as a way of enlightening outsiders to the fact, again, that their particular "flaw" is just one among many mock-able flaws that humans can have. So if mocking someone for his big feet or tiny hands can be funny and permissible, so too might mocking some-one for his lack of feet or claw-like hands (as in ectrodactyly). The elimina-tion of interpersonal discrimination for impairments and differences may well be partially brought about by the introduction of mockery into these communities.

One might say that these examples show that it's OK to mock others for their disabilities only if you yourself share them, so only "crips" get to en-gage in "crip humor." But if we take the social model seriously, the fact that two people have a disability in common is ultimately, goes the hope, to be seen as an arbitrary and morally irrelevant fact about them, just like the facts that two people have the same eye color or the same kind of mole on their cheeks. What matters instead, for equal access to the values at stake, is that the attitudes the parties have toward the relevant features and each other are of the right sort, and that the mockery's function is inclusive and contributes to interpersonal bonding.

But if these are the relevant requirements, then they could conceivably be met as well between people who don't share a disability in common. Someone without any (identified) disabilities could permissibly mock a close friend's disability, simply as some impairment or other, as long as it wasn't piling on and the mockery was inclusively mutual, funny, and part of the bonding constitutive of affiliative and affectionate interpersonal life. This was the sort of thing that actually occurred in the Everts family, as the nondisabled family members would riff on their mother's partial blindness with mocking comments about the "blinds." It's also the sort of thing Larry David occasionally does on *Curb Your Enthusiasm*, mocking his blind friend for not seeing what's in front of him, as well as a friend whose physical impairment causes him to walk extremely slowly. What's crucial here is that the vulnerability to mockery is mutual, that his disabled friends mock him right back for his own impairments (his social anxiety, his seemingly constitutional inability to adhere to various conventional norms). These are friends who mutually mock each other for their wide variety of human differences—not that there's anything wrong with that.

What's Required for Funny Mocking Impersonations

This conclusion is likely still too jagged a pill for many to swallow, given how cruel many real-life cases of disability mockery still are. Indeed, Trump's arm-flopping impersonation of Kovaleski remains an astonishing affront. And I recall as a teen watching in horror as a bully in my junior high school followed a Deaf girl through the halls while making the braying and nasally seal-ish sounds stereotypically associated with Deaf kids who dared vocalize. How could this sort of mocking impersonation ever be permissible, one might think, even in so-called mutual and inclusive environments?

The answer is that it's not permissible, but for a perhaps unexpected reason: it's not funny. And it's not funny because the impersonations involved exploit stereotypes about people with disabilities in a completely pedestrian, unintelligent, and unsurprising way. Humor that exploits stereotypes will of course be the focus of the next chapter, so I don't want to give too much away here, but I can say a few things now that ought to ameliorate the worry.

Suppose, to take a less controversial sort of case, you lived in Brooklyn for the past few years, and so in trying to impersonate you, I say a lot of "youse guys" and "fuhgeddaboutits!" I am, quite uncreatively, deploying a stereotype about Brooklynites from the movies, attributing a way of talking that some Brooklynites may have to a specific person—you. This is just lame and unfunny. In order for an impersonation of someone to be funny and to sting them (as a form of mockery), recall the very first condition of mockability: it has to capture something true about that specific person. If you're from Italy and I mimic you eating a "pizza pie-a!" the only apt response is a groan. If you're over six foot five, my impersonation of you that consists in pretending to hit my head every time we go through an underpass will rightly fall flat. And if you're a woman, my mimicking the way you talk with a high-pitched squeaky voice will be boring, not funny.

The funny in mocking impersonations comes primarily from their specificity, from the impersonator's finding something particular to the mimicked person that reveals a truth about them. Those who are brilliant at it—think Dana Carvey or James Austin Johnson from *Saturday Night Live*—will often watch tapes of those they impersonate over and over and over again, until they find the "hook," the little glimpse of universally recognizable truth in that specific person. When we are amused by a great impersonation, what it does is enable us to see the impersonated person in a new light, and we come to notice that feature about them more readily from that point forward. That's why impersonation can serve as a powerful form of mockery if what's being highlighted is in fact a ridiculous flaw that that particular person actually has.

Trump's mockery of Kovaleski did not, um, reach these humor heights. It was a classic case of an impersonation rendered unfunny by the exploitation of a tired old stereotype of a disabled person: "the spazz."[59] It wasn't specific to Kovaleski at all (who is actually unable to move his arm). And the bully following the Deaf girl was also exploiting the tired and unfunny stereotype about all Deaf people who vocalize, attributing those generic features to this one specific girl. This was surely also the case for much of the history of horrible mockery the philosophers despised: It was exploiting tired stereotypes without surprise, without cleverness. And mockery without funniness is, as I pointed out earlier, just plain cruelty, which is always immoral.

One way, then, for disability mockery to be funny is for it to be specific, targeted at a particular person's impairment (or impairment-related features) in a clever and surprising way, a way that reveals some truth about that particular person. This is, again, something best left to close friends and families, as they will tend to have the best epistemic access to those features. But it can surely be accomplished. Perhaps you and I are close friends. You can spot and mockingly impersonate my slight way of slurring my "sl" sounds. Perhaps I can spot and mockingly impersonate your raspy Bostonian way of pronouncing the "an" sounds in "Grand Canyon." Perhaps my way of speaking is traceable to my deafness. Or wait, perhaps yours is. Or both? I've forgotten. Does it any longer matter?

A Haunting Hypothetical

I've made the case I set out to make in this chapter, that mockery may be both funny and morally permissible across the board, in principle directed at anyone. But I'm haunted a bit by the scenario that opened this chapter, and I want to explain what's haunting me.

To avoid any armchair diagnoses of real people, let's just suppose that the president of one's country has narcissistic personality disorder (NPD). This is a personality disorder that psychologists and psychiatrists designate as a mental illness. It has its source in a lack of empathy, and its primary symptoms are a sense of grandiosity and entitlement, a desperate need for attention and admiration, a discounting of other people and their feelings, and a refusal to take blame or responsibility for anything. Its etiology is complex, likely a result of different extremes in parenting styles plus some neurobiological factors. In any event, it's not an illness that anyone is responsible for having. Many of those who have it tend to live unhappy lives, full of petty resentments and grievances, and they typically make the lives of those around them downright miserable. People don't want to be friends with them, and they have a hard time understanding why people act as they do around them. People who have mental illnesses that negatively affect their well-being are typically deemed to have a disability. Consequently, it might be that one's president, in this purely hypothetical scenario, has just such a disability.

Now suppose this president were to do a variety of eminently mockable things. For example, during his campaign to rouse Christian voters, when asked what his favorite Bible verse is, suppose he goes into admiration-seeking mode, despite his obvious ignorance: "Well, I think many. I mean, you know, when we get into the Bible, I think many, so many. And I tell people, look, 'An eye for an eye,' you can almost say that." Perhaps when there's a White nationalist rally met by protesters and violence, he says, currying favor from his base, "There were very fine people on both sides." Perhaps, when challenged, he calls himself "like, really smart," and a "very stable genius," or perhaps he tweets, "Sorry losers and haters, but my I.Q. is one of the highest—and you all know it! Please don't feel so stupid or insecure, it's not your fault." Perhaps, when getting briefed on a pandemic about to ravage the nation, he second-guesses the scientists and says, "People are really surprised I understand this stuff. Every one of these doctors said, 'How do you know so much about this?' Maybe I have a natural ability." Perhaps, as a way of expressing his stable genius in fighting that pandemic, he wonders aloud if people could eliminate it by injecting bleach into their lungs. And suppose that, whenever he's criticized, he goes on a Twitter rampage, trying to exact vengeance by mocking the source (often women, often for their appearance), with no consideration of the consequences for that person or the nation.

Now suppose that he is relentlessly mocked for these mockable things. Perhaps *Saturday Night Live* enlists a big star to do a mean but funny impersonation of him every week. Perhaps the "very stable genius" line is printed up and worn widely on T-shirts. Perhaps he is the regular punch line of late-night talk show hosts and comedians. Perhaps he is publicly mocked behind his back by his fellow NATO leaders. Suppose further that this mockery seems morally fine to half the voting citizenry. Nevertheless, it is mockery for his disability. What this hypothetical president does and says is exactly what we should expect someone with NPD to do or say in his position, things directly caused by his empathy-draining mental illness, which has him believing that the world is out to get him, that the feelings of other people simply don't matter, that he is truly great and entitled to all the applause and praise he can gather up, accolades he desperately craves.

Is it still morally OK to mock this hypothetical president? It seems to me that it is. But matters are starting to feel much more morally complicated. And here's where an even more disturbing thought enters. Suppose that this hypothetical president, in wreaking his revenge on those he perceives as persecuting him, mocks a reporter for his disability. He does this fueled entirely by his aggrieved narcissism, as he sees mockery as the fitting thing to do in response (given the need to publicly humiliate that "inferior" person). The mockery isn't funny, even though the crowd laughs at it, for reasons I've just given, and the mocker-in-chief isn't interested in inclusion or mutuality with the reporter; rather, he wants to ridicule the reporter only in order to incite and bond his audience together, by getting them to see themselves as united against that elitist reporter. Because the mockery is unfunny, it's immoral (and even if it were funny somehow, it would be immoral, given its piling-on aims).

But here's the thing: Very often in our interpersonal lives, we think we ought to let people off the blame hook for immoral actions they perform when caused to do so (primarily) by a serious mental illness. If someone with schizophrenia treats you cruelly because he thinks you're the devil, or if someone with clinical depression fails to keep her promise to show up at your party, you won't (and shouldn't) blame them, because their actions were caused by their illnesses, not by them.[60] So if someone's serious NPD were to cause him to immorally mock someone, it may come to seem that he too should be let off the blame hook, as what he did was caused by his mental illness, not caused by him. So even though this hypothetical president mocked a disabled reporter, he may not be the appropriate target of blame for it, even though what he did was immoral.

This seems quite a topsy-turvy conclusion. But I'm not sure how to avoid it, and it haunts me.

CHAPTER FIVE

"Somebody Ought to Throw Those Boys a Basketball!"

Stereotyping Humor

I was at a bar in Little Rock, Arkansas, watching the NBA finals on June 17, 1994, when the game was interrupted by a bizarre scene on an LA freeway: tons of police cars were slowly following a single white Ford Bronco. It was, of course, O. J. Simpson in that Bronco. As the slow-motion "chase" dragged on, another White guy I'd been chatting amiably with at the bar leaned over and, with a twinkle in his eye, said in a low voice, "Who'd'a thought O. J. would'a gone and turned n——r?"

This was a nasty wisecrack. When I heard it, I was stunned, tongue-tied. I had no sharp rejoinder; instead, I just felt sick. After a few awkward moments, I moved to another spot at the bar, and that was that.

Two years later, on his first major HBO special, *Bring the Pain*, Chris Rock made an interestingly similar wisecrack, in an (in)famous routine whose theme can be summed up by his repeated refrain, "I love Black people, but I hate n——as." "N——as," he says, are Black people who are violent and lazy, and who eschew adult responsibilities. They brag, "I take care of my kids," when, as Rock replies in an apoplectic voice, "You *supposed* to take care of your kids!" And he rejects the notion that this image is a media construction:

> When I go to the money machine tonight, all right, I ain't looking over my back for the media, I'm looking for n——as! Shit, Ted Koppel ain't never took shit from me. N——as have, so, you think I've got three guns in my house 'cause the media outside?

As I said, the White Arkansan in the bar—who I will from here on out refer to as Double-A, for "Arkansas Asshole"—was actually working in an adjacent comedic vicinity, marking a distinction as well between what he perceived "good" and "bad" Black people to be. To him, the previously inoffensive and "colorless" O. J. had, quite unexpectedly ("Who'da thought . . . ?"), revealed himself to be a stereotypically thuggish Black guy after all, which now made a certain slur for him appropriate. In comparison, Rock's remarks involved admitting—unexpectedly, subversively—that the stereotypical characteristics some White people attribute to all Black people are in fact—irritatingly, maddeningly—true of at least *some* Black people, and that those people do deserve to be called out with (a variation on) the nastiest slur of all (albeit only by other Black people[1]).

Both Double-A and Rock were exploiting or assuming shared knowledge of racial stereotypes and using racist slurs in their wisecracking. I found and still find Rock's routine brilliant and hilarious, and I'll say why momentarily. However, many other White people that I've known didn't and don't (or did but now don't). Rock's mostly Black audience fell out during the filmed routine; indeed, I'd never heard such explosive laughter at a stand-up show. But some Black people then and now have expressed mixed emotions, even downright hostility, about the wisdom of performing the routine.[2] In *Salon*, for instance, Mychal Denzel Smith witheringly wrote that Rock was doing "respectability politics," the sort of thing Bill Cosby also famously engaged in, yelling at Black men to "pull your pants up," blaming Black people for the problems in their community, rather than focusing on the one causal constant: racism.

> It's that racism that produced a situation whereby people were forced to go into survival mode, and more often than is comfortable to admit, survival techniques look like outlaw activities. . . . But instead of asking why the options for Black survival are so limited, the proselytizers of respectability politics would rather reify the theories of Black inferiority that excite the White racist imagination.[3]

Set aside for a second this complaint. Even if one shares it, I nevertheless think we can start with the likely universal view that even if Rock's remarks were problematic, they were at least way funnier than Double-A's, and perhaps Double-A's remarks weren't funny at all.[4] Why? What's the difference between them?

One could of course point to Rock's skills as a comedian, his epic abilities of timing, voice, pace, delivery, and cadence.[5] But take all that away and there's still a comedic difference between their respective stereotype exploitation, a difference located in the different worlds they occupy and the different stereotypes they exploited. One of many privileges of being a White person in America is that they (I) enjoy a positive benefit-of-the-doubt bias in stereotypes about them: they are generally viewed in a positive light, so that when some White people do bad things, they are viewed (by many people, not just by White people) as merely "bad apples." Bad apples can ruin the bunch, but they aren't viewed as manifesting any essential features of White people; they are instead acting out of (that is, against) character. These bad apples can thus be called out without their reflecting poorly on White people as a race. Being able to call out their own bad members without negative attributions to Whiteness generally is a privilege that pretty much only White people have (at least in America), as a result of a history of White supremacy and racism.

Black people, on the other hand, and as a result of that same history, have no such privilege. Instead, the default stereotype is that those within the group who have bad traits actually manifest the essence of Black people. So when there are Black people who don't exhibit those traits, they are stereotypically thought to be exceptions, "good apples," if you will, in an otherwise mostly bad bunch.

Double-A was operating under and exploiting the latter default stereotype, and so was attributing what he took to be essentially "Black" traits to someone formerly viewed as a good apple (among Whites). What Rock was doing, however, was subverting that stereotype and talking about Black people in the way that only White people normally get to deploy in talking about themselves: as essentially good but with the same sort of bad apples that White people also have in their group. That is, Rock was simply shrugging off the default attribution biases and asserting equality by also sharing publicly the kind of view some Black people have about some members of their group, the very same kind of view about "their own" that White people get to enjoy by (racist) default. This is a subversion of racism via the exploitation of racial stereotypes and deployment of racial slurs.

Both Double-A and Rock were engaged in funny-making attempts, as they were both exploiting a surprising shift in expectations. The question is whether there's also immorality involved in what they were doing and, if so (in one, both?), how we should respond in light of it.

In this chapter I'll be exploring these questions for stereotyping humor in both jokes and wisecracks. This is humor playing on, around, and with racial or gender stereotypes (with the occasional ethnic crack thrown in). Note my inclusion of jokes now. As usual, nearly all previous writing on this topic has been about jokes, not wisecracks per se.[6] Chapter 2 argued in favor of a kind of amoralism about jokes, the view that jokes as such (on the page, say) contain nothing sufficient to make angry blame appropriate. This view applies as well to racist and sexist jokes, although I recognize that such a stance is much more controversial. Nevertheless, I can sidestep all that controversy for two reasons. First, I'll just refer to the humor examples I discuss as "exploiting racial or gender stereotypes," whether or not they are most accurately described as racist or sexist jokes. Second, the only compelling objections to such jokes are to their being expressed, not to their mere existence on some page of a joke book or in the cloud. As a result, they are much more like wisecracks, where not only can properties like the joke teller's timing and delivery contribute to their funniness, but so can the teller's intentions, motivations, and attitudes. So the main focus here will be on stereotype-exploiting joke telling and wisecracking.

This more neutral talk of "stereotyping humor" is actually to be preferred over talk of "racist and sexist" humor, for several reasons. First, some stereotyping humor just isn't racist or sexist, even though it may mention race, sex, and gender or exploit racial and gender stereotypes. Rock's routine is one example, and we'll see others later. Further, the use of racist or sexist slurs by those who tell a joke or make a wisecrack may or may not render the humor itself racist or sexist. Even though Rock's remarks deployed a racial slur (or a very close variation), what he said wasn't racist; it rather aimed to subvert racist stereotypes. But this leads to the third point: What makes humor racist or sexist is just a ridiculously hard question, and that's because in order to answer it we first have to answer the question, "What are racism and sexism?" And there is, quite simply, no consensus on an answer. Regarding racism alone (but applicable to sexism as well), some think that it consists essentially in a hateful attitude; some claim it requires a false belief about the group members in question; others say that it's about an overall ideology of superiority or domination; some claim it must implicate social and institutional power dynamics; and still others think it's essentially about disrespect.[7]

While I myself am inclined toward the last definition, I don't need to settle this controversy here either. Whether some joke or wisecrack counts as racist or sexist isn't what matters to our investigation; rather, what matters is whether stereotype-exploiting humor more generally can be funny, can also contain some immorality, and, if so, can still permissibly be told and enjoyed.

Where's the Funny?

We need some jokes to work with. Here's the problem: There's been really only one joke discussed in previous academic work on the topic, and it's pretty painful. It was first presented by Ted Cohen in a philosophical book about jokes:

How did a passerby stop a group of Black men from committing a gang rape? He threw them a basketball.[8]

Cohen maintains that, while many people are bothered by this joke (as is he), if there is some moral objection to it and jokes like it, "the problem is confounded by the fact that they *are* funny."[9] Noel Carroll objects, arguing that a joke needs an audience to complete it, and some jokes like this generate serious imaginative resistance in morally upright audiences. Jokes are play, and when you put a play frame around a morally heinous activity, you are inviting people to imaginatively entertain something that morally good people can't do (or better: can't bring themselves to do). Even if there are what would ordinarily be funny-makers in the joke (for example, surprising incongruities), they can't be enjoyed as such by people of goodwill. As he puts it:

> Sometimes . . . owing to excessive moral outrageousness, the anaesthesia of the heart will be too difficult for an audience of moderate moral sensitivity to sustain. And they will not be amused. Thus, contra Cohen, some immoral joking will not be comically amusing because it is recognized or understood to be wickedly motivated by righteous listeners of normal ethical sensitivity.[10]

This point is a bit baffling, though. That people of good moral will aren't in fact amused by a joke implies nothing for whether they still have a reason to be amused (or not to be amused) by it. In other words, the fact that ethically sensitive people aren't amused by a joke doesn't mean it's not amusing. Some people just hear mention of someone's race in a joke and immediately hiss and refuse to be amused. They just don't want to "go there." But there can be jokes mentioning race where race is irrelevant to the humor or where the jokes straightforwardly aim to subvert racism, and they can also be quite amusing, which would make these "ethically sensitive" people who see no reason for amusement just plain wrong.

Second, even if there is a moral problem with this joke, it is extraordinarily difficult, as Cohen rightly notes, to put your finger on what that problem is, exactly. After all, the content of the joke is pure fiction: There was no group of Black men, there was no passerby. Is it that the joke contains the idea that Black men are criminals and mindless basketball players? But why should a mere idea be unsettling, especially if one knows it to be false? Perhaps it will lead others to believe the idea and treat Black men poorly as a result? But why should it? Why think a mere joke will have such pernicious consequences? And let's suppose that it would never lead anyone to believe anything like this about Black men or to treat anyone poorly. Wouldn't there still be something disturbing about the joke? Cohen then surveys possible moral theoretical replies, grounded on harm or poor character, and again comes up short. He leaves us with a banal recommendation: If you get upset by some types of jokes, avoid people who tell them. What's most important, he thinks, is that we not make the mistake of letting our moral disgust obscure the fact that such jokes can still be funny.[11]

Unfortunately, while Cohen is right that the joke has some funny-making properties from the kitchen sink list in it—it contains unexpected incongruity, the flip of a script—Carroll is also right that most people just don't or can't find it funny, given the reference to gang rape and the fact that it traffics in some really nasty stereotypes (that all young Black men are sexual predators and thugs). While I could make the points I want to make with this lame old joke, I think we just need to move on from it (for now) and focus instead on some different examples, ones that haven't made any appearance before in these sorts of discussions about humor.

The jokes I'm about to relate are provocative, and they may cause some people genuine moral discomfort. But of course that's part of the point, and I hope you'll trust and bear with me for a bit to see why.

What do ten thousand battered women have in common? They should've listened.

Why can't Stevie Wonder read? Because he's Black.[12]

What do you call a Mexican on a bike? Thief.

A priest and a rabbi are walking near an elementary school during recess. The priest elbows the rabbi and whispers, "You wanna screw some kids?" The rabbi responds, "Out of what?"[13]

All of these jokes exploit various stereotypes of disparaged, oppressed, put-upon, or marginalized groups: women, Black people, Mexicans, Catholic priests, and Jews. There are hundreds more we could trot out, but I won't bore you. Or at least I won't bore you in *that* way; I may, however, bore you in a different way, by analyzing the hell out of the first two of these jokes, an analysis that can be applied as well to the other two (and to some other stereotyping jokes more generally), and which will provide an answer to Cohen's puzzled question: How can a stereotyping joke of this ilk be both funny and the cause of serious moral discomfort?

Start with the joke about battered women. You may well be morally upset in response to reading it. I have found that many people are, women and men.[14] Alternatively, even if you're not morally upset by it, you might still feel a kind of visceral emotional response upon reading it, as it may sickeningly remind you of trauma you yourself have experienced or have been close to. This may well prevent you from finding any funny in the joke. I fully appreciate this feeling.[15] Of course, such a sickened feeling isn't restricted to jokes; it may also be triggered by any kind of reference to battering, including in novels, plays, poems, visual arts, documentaries, news stories, classroom lectures, and more. But there may be something particularly sickening here, insofar as joking about battering plays "lightly" with it, seeming to fail to take it sufficiently seriously, and that may strike many as morally egregious.

The fact that this perfectly understandable feeling may prevent the "anesthesia of the heart" necessary to finding any funny in the joke doesn't speak against its being funny, though; rather, it speaks only to how difficult it can be for some people to find it funny. And indeed, in my informal surveys of people about this joke, many people do find it funny, and not on gendered (or sexist) lines, as you might expect. Some men respond to this joke with disgust and anger, and some women find it hilarious. It's thus worth exploring both responses.

The disgusted or morally angered reaction is surely a response to the fact that the joke seems to trade in the deeply objectionable thought that some women actually deserve to be battered when they "don't listen" to their men. But does it really?

To have a chance of recognizing any funny in this joke requires you, crucially, to hear someone tell it (either in reality or in your mind's ear) with a very specific and measured delivery. You have to imagine the punch line being told by someone in a serious tone, shaking their head sadly and shrugging their shoulders, as if it's such a shame that these women didn't listen, as they could very well have saved themselves a beating if they'd done so, but now there's nothing to be done about it.

This isn't enough to get what we need to answer Cohen's puzzle, though. To get there, now imagine the joke being told this way but in two different contexts, with two different motivations, to people bringing two very different attitudes to the table.

First, imagine it being told by one male sexist to another. Both sexists believe that women are in fact subject to the authority of men, which may sometimes have to manifest in violence when women "get out of line." If they find funniness in this joke telling, it will be in the joke's subversion of their expectations about *jokes*, as a meta-joke. In this case, the subversion happens when they expect a different punch line from a joke setup than what they would ordinarily take to be an obvious answer. In the famous (and stale) joke "Why did the chicken cross the road?" the punch line "To get to the other side" makes a move exactly of this sort. If battered women deserved it because they really should have listened (as the sexists believe), then a joke about battered women—and the setup question clearly signals that it's a joke context—surely wouldn't go on to make that obvious point, would it? And yet—surprise!—there it is. Their expectations about the nature of jokes—that they won't have obvious punch lines—is what's being subverted. The reason the sexists may find it funny, therefore, is not actually due to the exploitation of any sexist stereotypes in the joke; instead, it's only due to their sexist beliefs going into it.

Now consider a different audience. I'm going to assume that you are a goodwilled nonsexist, a believer in the fundamental equal moral status of men and women. I claim that this joke can also subvert your expectations in an amusing way, albeit differently. When I ask you the joke's setup "What do ten thousand battered women have in common?" you may cringe, not being able to help but think, "Good god, battering is terrible! Why are you joking about this? What these women have in common is that they were the victims of domestic abuse, of being the victims of some horrible men in a misogynistic world!" When I say, though, in that sad and sardonic voice, with a "what can you do?" shrug, that these women instead "should have listened," I'm caricaturing what a *sexist* would say, sadly communicating "information" that I (the sexist character I'm playing) think is true in a serious fashion. In doing so, I'm aiming to subvert your nonsexist expectations in a surprising way, offering what actual abusers would think of as the obvious-but-unfunny answer, the answer that would come springing immediately to their own minds. This punch line is a surprising script flip to goodwilled people like you, albeit in the way you actually expect typical joke punch lines to work. The joke (and its funniness), in this case, is on the sexists. When I tell the joke in the voice of a sexist, I'm making fun of—satirizing, cutting down to size, pointing out the idiocy of—the sexist's immoral views of women.

To drive home the crucial role that context plays in wisecracking, we have to think about not only the attitudes that a joke teller brings to the table, but also the attitudes that joke hearers bring to the table. Indeed, to illustrate my point here without the tortured analysis just given, I think that it's possible to imagine one previously battered woman telling this joke to another, again with the "What can you do?" voice, as a way of satirizing and cutting down to size the horrible kinds of men that they and too many other women have encountered. Joking about one's pain and suffering is a powerful way of taking back control over one's life, a way that many psychological studies reveal is a significant source of recovery. In chapter 7, I'll provide empirical support for this point by discussing how and why some people cope humorously with violence and tragedy in their lives. For now, I simply mean to hammer home the crucial significance of recognizing the context, as well as the attitudes of all involved, in such wisecracking exchanges, as it may well reveal where funniness can actually reside in such jokes.

There is this exact same bidirectional subversion of expectations going on in the Stevie Wonder joke. Again, for you to find any funny in it, you have to hear the joke in your head as being told by someone in a very specific and careful way, this time with the punch line being delivered with a *duh!* tone, as if the answer is perfectly obvious and you the listener are dumb for not anticipating it. Now, for you, my nonracist reader, what comes to mind most readily is likely that Stevie Wonder is *blind*. In providing a different answer, though (one cleverly starting with the same two letters), the joke instead subversively gives the sort of answer that a dumb racist might think obvious, and it is delivered in the voice of the dumb racist. To the dumb racist, by contrast, the joke subverts his expectation that it'll provide a punch line appealing to a surprising property, and the fact that it doesn't, the fact that it relies on a stereotype the racist actually accepts as true, is (surprisingly) the reason he finds it funny. "It's funny 'cause it's true," he thinks, "and I didn't expect that!"[16]

Once we recognize the two ways amusement might be found in such jokes (as well as the crucial importance of context and attitudes), we can revisit Cohen's original joke and find the funny even in it. Imagine two old friends, Black women, sitting on a front porch one evening chatting amiably, when they spot a group of Black teenagers following a woman rather too closely down a darkened street. One of the women whispers to the other, "Uh oh, somebody ought to throw those boys a basketball," just before the teenagers thankfully start to disperse. The women may both find this remark funny (as, I think, can we). They aren't wisecracking in anything like a racist or racially worrisome fashion. Indeed, the crack might be offered in the voice of a southern White bigot, in which case the wisecracker is making fun of southern White bigots (making a crack about a cracker), and so exploiting racial stereotypes as a way of satirizing dumb racism. Or it might be made in her own voice, but as a way of playing with the stereotype that her friend will totally understand as mere play (given how close they are and how much they know about the innocent intentions and attitudes of the other person). In neither case does there seem to be anything morally objectionable or discomfiting about it.

But what about the context and attitudes of racists and sexists who make such wisecracks? Suppose two White bigots see and say exactly what the Black women do from their porch, but the bigots mean it. "That's how they are," chuckles one as he calls the cops. If they're amused by the joke for the "obvious" sorts of reasons, are they right to be so amused? Do they actually have the reason they think they have for amusement?

No. They think it's funny-'cause-it's-true, essentially, but what they take to be true—that all Black men have certain thuggish characteristics—is false. If what's necessary for the thing they see as funny actually to be funny is for all Black men to possess these characteristics, and they don't, then the crack in this context just has no funny-making properties. If they are amused for this reason, then they are just wrong.[17]

This is also precisely what's going on with the sexists who see the battered women joke in its "meta" form, thinking that the punch line is obviously true, unexpectedly, given that women are indeed subject to their men's battering authority. That is also the wrong reason to be amused. The belief the sexists have about women is false, so the property they are seeing as funny-making—women's subordinate status relative to their male partners—does not exist. There is no such funny-maker.

Recall one of the key tenets of the human theory of humor from chapter 1: Certain properties make things funny in virtue of their being the sorts of things that would amuse humans with a developed and refined sense of humor *and unobstructed vision.* Among the things that can obstruct our vision are our stereotyping biases, which can prevent us from seeing clearly certain facts about specific people. These may include facts about members of racial and ethnic groups, facts that undermine various stereotypes: Black men aren't, as such, inclined to gang rape, easily distracted by basketball, or illiterate; women aren't, as such, inferior to, and properly subject to violence from, men; Mexicans aren't, as such, inclined to thievery; Catholic priests aren't, as such, inclined to pedophilia; Jewish people aren't, as such, inclined to financial exploitation. If you think punch lines attributing these properties to certain groups of people in this way are "obviously true," though, then your obscured vision has you thinking these jokes funny for the wrong reasons.

And the fact that some of our fellow humans have their moral vision so obscured is what's actually deeply disturbing here.

The battered women, Stevie Wonder, and basketball jokes all do double duty, managing to subvert the expectations of two audiences in two different ways (and I think this view is true for the other two jokes I included as well, although I won't bother belaboring those). Nevertheless, these jokes are morally discomfiting, as Cohen notes, but the discomfort will be felt only by people who do not think the punch lines are "obviously true." Why? It's because nonracists and nonsexists are able to see that such jokes, depressingly, may be found funny by racists and sexists for the wrong reasons.

When our fellows are wrongly amused in this way, it reflects their racism and sexism, and the fact that they continue to exist among the rest of us is deeply discomfiting.

There may be additional discomfort associated with tellings of this sort in the thought that if we nonracists and nonsexists are amused by these jokes, we might be viewed as complicit with the racists and sexists, misperceived as being amused, like they are, for the wrong reasons. Other people may not get that we could be amused for nonracist or nonsexist reasons.

Note, though, that even if these reasons are compelling, the source of the actual discomfort here is not in the joke as such. Indeed, as I maintained in chapter 2, there's just no moral discomfort or immorality to be found in the jokes themselves. Instead, the discomfort and immorality can only be found in the contexts and attitudes of tellings and tellers, that is, as part of their role in making wisecracks.

To sum up, Cohen was in general correct that there can be funny in these jokes when you have access to the right sorts of reasons that their tellings might provide, but they can also be morally discomfiting, not for any immoral properties embedded within them (so it's no wonder Cohen couldn't find any), but rather only because we are aware that some people may respond to their tellings with amusement for the wrong reasons, reflecting their own racism or sexism, or that our own amusement at them may have people mistakenly viewing us as complicit in racism or sexism as well.

Making Stereotyping Wisecracks

Exploitation of stereotypes can be funny, even if it's also morally discomfiting. But so what? The fact that a stereotype-exploiting wisecrack that bubbles up in my brain would be funny may not give me much reason to actually make it aloud to anyone. Indeed, there might be something quite immoral about my doing so, an immorality that easily outweighs any funny there might be in the wisecrack. What might that be?

I think we can all start off on the same moral page by agreeing first to a fairly obvious truth: Being a racist or sexist is immoral. Of course, as I noted earlier, what racism and sexism consist in is hard to make precise. For my part (as I also noted), I think they most plausibly involve having disparaging or disrespectful attitudes toward members of some racial, ethnic, or gender group solely in virtue of their being members of those groups. It is to think lesser of someone simply because of their (racial, ethnic, or gender) group membership. Viewing people as morally inferior for arbitrary reasons like this, taking them less seriously than their moral worth as equals demands, is disrespectful. The fact that an attitude would be disrespectful is a powerful moral reason against having it. Indeed, it seems evident that we have, in general, serious moral obligations not to hold disrespectful attitudes.

Racists and sexists sometimes say things or treat others in ways that express their racism or sexism. They may aim to directly threaten members of the stereotyped group or bludgeon them with their words, and they may publicly disparage or discriminate against them. These actions are all immoral too, not only disrespectful but harmful. So when some of the racist or sexist things they express in talking about or treating others in disparaging ways are wisecracks, then it's obvious that they should not make them. All of this is easy, Morality 101.

More realistic and familiar cases are less easy, and even downright queasy. For example, suppose that racists or sexists circulate racist/sexist jokes in emails only to their racist/sexist friends, so that they don't aim to treat anyone else poorly or to say things members of the disparaged races or genders are meant to hear.[18] Or suppose that people of more enlightened racial/gender sensibilities find some stereotyping cracks funny that, again, they share only with their like-minded friends with explicitly good-hearted aims, simply to provide their friends with a hearty laugh on a cold and gray Monday morning, and not with any racism/sexism in their hearts. Or suppose that people who have successfully striven to eliminate all racism/sexism from their lives and who regularly work for social justice nevertheless make stereotyping wisecracks with each other, sometimes simply to play with stereotypes, and sometimes to subvert them. Or suppose that members of the stereotyped groups themselves share jokes and wisecracks exploiting those stereotypes with each other or with people from outside of their group.

What I've been arguing to this point is that there may be immoral properties that should be added to the kitchen sink list of funny-makers, such as deception and mockery's sting, and that making wisecracks that incorporate those immoral properties may nevertheless be morally permissible as long as the intentions and motivations of the wisecrackers are above board. But when it comes to stereotyping humor, many people explicitly have wanted to reject a view like this, claiming instead that there can be moral wrongs in making racist/sexist jokes and wisecracks that are completely independent of their makers' intentions and motivations. This claim is worth investigating: Where would the moral wrong be, if not in the bad intentions or motivations of the joke tellers and wisecrack makers?

There are two popular answers: Engaging in such humor is immoral because it causes offense, or because it causes harm. Both answers, however, are too simplistic or empirically suspect to do the trick.

Offense versus Harm

What is harm, what is offense, what's the difference, and what does morality say about causing each? Joel Feinberg, in writing about the moral limits of the criminal law, argued that something counts as a harm if it sets back your interests, either your interests in continuing life (which includes your basic physical, psychological, financial, and autonomous needs and desires) or your interests in the pursuits of specific goals.[19] I harm you when I break your leg, steal your money, imprison you, or take a Sharpie to the canvas you've painted or purchased. And I can harm you without you knowing it: I can secretly empty out your bank account, for example. Being harmed isn't a subjective psychological state; it's an objective status.

Something offends you, by contrast, only when you have been put into a widely disliked state of mind, one that (merely) distracts you for a while from the pursuit of your interests.[20] Offensive states of mind are generally caused by nuisances: disgusting sights or smells, or other affronts to your senses (e.g., grating sounds); shocks to your moral, religious, aesthetic, or patriotic sensibilities; shameful or embarrassing events; boring or frustrating things; and fearful or humiliating events (e.g., someone pointing a rubber gun at your head).[21]

This conceptual mapping is helpful to start with, but we immediately run into a problem when we consider the obvious fact that many of us have interests in not being offended, so any offenses we undergo would, by this definition, also count as harms. Feinberg's response to this worry is to offer an ad hoc restriction: Harm, he says, involves setbacks to our interests, with the exception of our interests in not being offended.[22] I think we can do better, though.

To be harmed, I say, is simply to be damaged in some way, physically, psychologically, financially, romantically, or otherwise. It's an objective status of the person, and it can occur without that person's awareness of it (as with some quietly growing cancers). To be offended, though, is to be put into a particular psychological state, that is, to be taken aback, stunned, shocked, or put off. It is a response to shocks or affronts to one's sense of decorum, one's sense of smell or hearing, or to one's moral, religious, or aesthetic sensibilities.[23] It is a thoroughly subjective response. You may not be aware that you have been harmed, but you can't *not* be aware that you've been offended.[24] This is the key difference between the two states.

As a result, you can be harmed through being offended, in a way, but it's typically an indirect or subsequent harm, more a function of the extent to which your affronted state tends to weigh on or is weighed by you. That is, harm may be caused by offense, but it isn't really the psychological affront in and of itself that constitutes the harm; instead, it is a kind of psychological damage caused by how powerful the affront is or by how long it persists. This means that sometimes you can prevent or mediate the amount of psychological damage that the original offended state might cause either by nursing the offense (by replaying the offending event over and over again in your mind, say) or by distracting yourself from it, moving on, or somehow lightening up (using methods to be detailed in chapter 7).

Offense and Offensiveness

So are there moral reasons against offending someone? There is no straightforward answer to this question, as people can be offended by many different types of events, and so sometimes there just aren't any moral reasons in play. When my colleague bores me, he has put me into a disliked—offended—psychological state.[25] I am unharmed, though, by being put into that offended state (that is, he doesn't damage me). And he's actually doing so with entirely good intentions, as he thinks I'll enjoy hearing him drone on about his weekend at the "Watching Paint Dry" convention in Akron, so I see no immorality here.

You may also shock my aesthetic sensibilities without morality being implicated. Feinberg's example is of someone wearing a shirt of "violently clashing orange and crimson" who sits across from you on the bus.[26] You might also be aesthetically offended by an artist who completes her delicately lovely watercolor by painting a thick red blotch over it, or by a favorite musical artist who puts out an album consisting entirely in feedback.[27] Morality is just irrelevant to your offended state.

But even shocks to so-called moral sensibilities don't necessarily conjure up any moral considerations against them. Several years ago, when my then-girlfriend-now-wife and I were playing cards with my very religious parents, she accidentally muttered "Fuckin' shit!" after seeing her hand. It was, by god, a genuine shock to their moral sensibilities (my mom—hilariously—started involuntarily whispering softly, "uh oh, uh oh, uh oh!"). But it neither harmed them nor manifested any disrespect toward them (even if it caused a whopper of a psychological jolt). My girlfriend was enjoying herself and she wanted everyone else to have fun too, but as her competitive juices started flowing, she suddenly became fully herself and accidentally let one rip.

The reason none of these cases implicate immorality, or at least *wronging or blameworthy* immorality, is that that none involve deliberate, intentional offense. My wife didn't mean to offend my parents at all, nor did my boring colleague or the adventurous artists mean to offend anyone.

But what, say, if my wife knew full well that my parents hated profanity, so she maliciously said what she did in order to shake them up, precisely in order to offend them? Now wronging morality is involved, but it's in virtue of her expression of disrespect for them, and not in virtue of her putting them into an offended state as such. She'd be using profanity as a bludgeon, but she could cause the exact same sort of bludgeoning offense with any of several other possible tools, like a casual "Hail Satan," or a comment about how much she loves threesomes. Obviously, if you are motivated by disrespect when aiming to offend someone, then you've wronged that person, and you have as a result made yourself the appropriate target of their angry moral blame. The blame here, though, is exclusively for your malicious intentions and motives. It's the disrespect that's wrong, independently of whether any offense is actually caused. After all, even if my parents weren't offended by someone's cruel attempts to offend them, the disrespect motivating the unsuccessful attempt would still make it both wrong and the correct target of angry blame.

Relatedly, and very importantly, people can be mistakenly or unreasonably offended. As an example of the former, perhaps I attend a meeting in order to object to a city council proposal to cut funding to local schools, and so I conclude my appeal by saying that we "shouldn't be niggardly in our approach to our children's education." Some may well be offended by my use of "niggardly," thinking I'd used a racial slur.[28] They are just mistaken to be offended, however, as there is no etymological connection whatsoever between the words, and I most certainly didn't use a racial slur. It would be like someone getting offended by my "profanity" when they hear me talk aloud about my shih tzu ("shit zoo") or my trip to Norfolk ("nor-fuck").[29]

As an example of unreasonable offense, suppose I think that both interracial marriage and homosexuality are immoral, so that when I see a married Black and White gay couple kissing, I'm doubly offended by the sight. My offense is unreasonable, as the moral sensibilities that give rise to my affronts have no good grounding.

We can't thus simply take the fact that people are offended by some jokes or wisecracks to provide a compelling moral objection to them. These people might be mistaken or unreasonable, or they might be really just (correctly) upset by the disrespect of the joke teller or wisecrack maker. What we might do instead, then, is appeal to what's *offensive* as providing the desired moral objection. This introduces a normative standard independent of any individual reaction, but what does the term "offensive" mean, exactly? It might mean that some people just are in fact offended by it. That can't be right, though, as it would imply that interracial marriage or homosexuality are actually offensive, given that some Neanderthals are still offended by these things. Perhaps, then, to be "offensive" is just to be something that most people are offended by? But this meaning would allow that, in a society mostly dominated by racists or homophobes, interracial dating and homosexuality would indeed be offensive (can you imagine such a place?). But this too is surely false. So perhaps, then, what's "offensive" is just what any reasonable person would be offended by? But reasonable people can reasonably disagree in matters of offense, given different orientations, assumptions, and sensibilities that they bring to the table. Some Black people were, perhaps, reasonably offended by Chris Rock's routine (he was airing dirty laundry, after all), and some reasonably were not. Who's right? Whose responses best represent *the* reasonable person's response? I can't see how to settle this issue.

Furthermore, even if there were a way to determine which or whose responses count as representative of "the reasonable," I still can't see how to determine what moral force reasonable offense should have, if any. The fact that the durian fruit I like to snack on has the most offensive odor of any fruit in the world—a combination of sewage, feet, and rotting flesh—offers no moral reason at all against my enjoying munching on it in private or with my durian-loving friends, even though no reasonable person could fail to be olfactorily offended by it. Nor does the fact that my feedback-filled guitar solo will be reasonably offensive to those with classical musical sensibilities give me any moral reason not to launch into it during my band's rock concert.

It's also worth noting that some (reasonably) offensive wisecracks may be so funny that the reasons they generate for amusement could outweigh whatever moral reasons there might conceivably be against their offensiveness. This is the entire point, I think, of the famous Aristocrats joke. The aim in telling that joke is to be as offensive as humanly possible about the sex acts the family does on stage together, before announcing, incongruously, that the family's act is called "The Aristocrats!" But it's not in the punch line of that joke where its real funniness lies; it's instead in the vile, vulgar, deeply offensive filth that precedes it, and in particular what's funny is in its utter transgressiveness being partnered with the thought of all the "squares" who would be horrified by it. But even if those squares would be reasonably offended by it (they're supposed to be, after all), and even if the genuine offensiveness generated could provide a moral reason against making the Aristocrats joke, the funniness of, say, the late great Gilbert Gottfried's operatic rendition of it would easily outweigh that lonely and square moral reason.

Harm and Harmfulness

Appealing to offense and offensiveness doesn't help us to identify any compelling moral reasons (independently of bad intentions or motives) against engaging in stereotyping humor. Indeed, it seems to me that most people who designate some bit of stereotyping humor to be offensive are doing so because they already view it as morally wrong. But then it's not the offensiveness that's doing any moral work for them; rather, "offensive" is just shorthand for whatever they take to be more fundamentally immoral about it. So what might that more fundamental immorality be? The most popular theory is that such humor causes harm.

I've already tipped my hand in saying that I believe racist or sexist attitudes are immoral in virtue of being disrespectful. But some have urged further that having those attitudes alone, and even merely holding false racist and sexist beliefs (without any associated disrespectful attitudes), may really be immoral in virtue of the harm they cause their targets.[30] I'm inclined to doubt this claim. By god, I hate the Swiss—pick a side!—but I find it difficult to see how my hatred could harm a single Swiss person.[31] But no matter. We are looking to find a harm in the making of stereotyping wisecracks, one that is independent of any racist/sexist attitudes or beliefs in the maker, and is independent of anyone's expression of racism or sexism to a targeted person, because, after all, we need to keep in mind that some of our real-life wisecrackers may not have any disrespectful attitudes or beliefs at all, or, if they do, none of the targets of their disrespect may be exposed to them, or the wisecrackers may not infuse their stereotyping humor with their own racism or sexism, and so on.

David Benatar offers a harm-based objection to telling racist or sexist jokes that we might adopt: Merely racial or gender jokes (jokes playing on racial or gender stereotypes, but perhaps not racist or sexist in and of themselves) can generate harm-based moral reasons against telling them if they were to somehow "inculcate and spread" a negative stereotype, a prejudiced view about people that assumes individual members of a group have certain attributes that are often falsely thought to be essential features of that group.[32] This can occur even when the teller has no racist or sexist thoughts, intentions, motivations, or beliefs. John Morreall agrees, and he claims that telling these jokes plays with objectionable stereotypes in a way that makes them palatable—amusement is fun and feels good—and so they enable "prejudicial ideas to be slipped into people's heads without being evaluated."[33] And importantly (and plausibly), the harm of the inculcation and spread of these stereotypical attitudes isn't all-or-nothing or distributed equally to all stereotyped groups, "but is proportional to the harm those stereotypes are likely to cause,"[34] so lawyer jokes, for example, aren't as harmful (or immoral) as stereotyping jokes about Black people or women.

Is there any evidence for these claims? There's some, but it's unclear what conclusions, if any, we can draw from it. On the side of Benatar and Morreall, there is empirical literature on how some men's exposure to sexist jokes (a) can increase their willingness to be more forthright about their sexism,[35] and (b) can increase the self-reported rape proclivity of those already hostile to women, especially among those who also accept various rape myths (e.g., that some women "are asking for it"[36]). In addition, hearing sexist jokes has been reported to actually decrease *women's* views of the joke teller as a sexist and dampens their motivation to confront the joke teller for his (or her) sexism. This result suggests that sexist humor is more dangerous, and harder to call out, than people may think.[37] (It goes without saying, of course, that all of these studies have been about jokes, not wisecracks. One example used in the studies: "How many men does it take to change a light bulb? None, let her do the dishes in the dark."[38])

But there is empirical evidence on the other side, showing that, for men who are actually averse to such jokes, the jokes simply have no effect at all on their rape proclivity or discriminatory leanings,[39] which suggests that the morally objectionable sexist attitudes of those already hostile to women don't need much nudging to make them more openly inclined toward serious harm (and such nudging apparently can be caused by a variety of other events as well, including just reading rape myths).[40] Indeed, there is an equally plausible interpretation that these attitudes were already in place in the nudged folks, and so all that's caused by their exposure to the jokes is that their preexisting shitty attitudes are brought to bear a bit more explicitly in their thoughts.

Analogously unclear evidential results hold for racial and racist humor. There is some evidence that disparaging jokes about members of some racial groups have the potential to open the door for some people who hear them to more openly express prejudice toward members of those groups.[41] Ironically, though, there's also evidence that so-called confrontational humor, humor about race aiming to subvert racist stereotypes, is often misconstrued in such a way that it has the same effect, the potential to increase open expressions of prejudice toward members of the joked-about group.[42] Indeed, examination of both disparaging and subversive racial humor reveals that effects on people (whether they are harmful or not) actually depend on what people's attitudes and motivations are going in. Are people already motivated toward disparagement or prejudice toward members of some group? Then disparaging and subversive jokes about members of those groups tend to increase their being more open to express their prejudice. But the opposite is true of people motivated against prejudice: they tend to be turned off by the disparaging jokes, and they find funnier the subversive ones.[43] The effect on them is thus away from prejudice. This isn't harm, it's a benefit. Relatedly, there is no discriminatory effect generated in nonracists against racists when the nonracists hear antiracist jokes (e.g., "What do you call a racist's senior year? Fifth grade!").[44]

It's hard to know what conclusions, then, if any, to draw from the empirical work. At the very least, what effect that jokes, in and of themselves, do or can have on attitudes—whether they directly cause harm or not—is fairly unclear.[45] And of course the effects of *wisecracks* on attitudes is so understudied that there's just nothing to say about them at all from the empirical side of the map.

The evidence is far from clear that telling stereotyping jokes harms the tellers, or at least makes people's attitudes worse than they already are. But what about harms caused to potential hearers, in particular members of the disparaged groups? Perhaps the aimed-for audience of your stereotyping jokes is just your like-minded friends, but a member of the disparaged group overhears it, causing a fear or trauma response—"Here we go again"—as they don't know the motivations of the tellers or what they mean by it? Or perhaps someone who heard the joke repeats it in a setting where members of the disparaged group hear it? We can't control how the jokes we tell are heard and then retold, after all.[46]

This is all quite possible, of course. But again, it's not an objection aimed exclusively at the telling of stereotyping jokes or wisecracks as such. It's instead an objection to blithely saying things in public that might be hurtful, whether or not there's funniness involved. Philosophers are notoriously guilty of negligence of this sort, as some think any and all ideas are ripe for mention and critical examination, so they'll talk loudly at public dinners about how fetuses are or aren't persons, about whether one should push a fat man over a bridge to stop a runaway trolley, about whether doctors could carve up five patients to harvest their organs to save one person, and so forth. These topics will be, to some diners who overhear them, horrifying. But that doesn't make the discussion of the ideas themselves harmful; it only makes their discussion in this blithe and negligent way harmful. So too, for all we've seen thus far, with certain joke tellings: That their being overheard by some people will be harmful doesn't necessarily attach harm to the telling itself, only to the telling in a blithe or negligent way.

We haven't yet seen clear or compelling moral reasons against engaging in stereotyping humor in and of itself that stems from considerations of harm, as we just don't yet know enough about the relation between this sort of humor and the actual "inculcation and spread" of various harmful attitudes. Nevertheless, there is an objection in the vicinity that we should take seriously.

Risky Business

While there may be no actual harm caused in any particular instance of stereotyping wisecracks, those who engage in such wisecrackery might be said nevertheless to generate a reasonable risk of harm, and there are moral objections against such risky business. What are the risks? Well, for one thing, the delight they get in making these cracks may tend to paint a patina of pleasure on their racial and gendered play, which might risk introducing or buttressing some racist attitudes or beliefs in them, and that might well manifest in their poor treatment or expressions of disrespect to people of other racial, ethnic, or gender groups down the line. It risks desensitizing the wisecrackers a bit, which risks making them less sympathetic to the oppressed and disparaged. It risks undermining motivations they might otherwise have had toward fellow feeling and the alleviation of suffering. It risks being overheard or misconstrued by members of the disparaged groups. It risks hardening indifference or disdain in the tellers or hearers. And these may be risks that, morally speaking, just aren't worth taking.

It turns out there is some empirical support for these ruminations, some of which were touched on earlier. For people already inclined to sexism and racism, of a hostile sort, the evidence shows that when they engage in and enjoy stereotyping humor, their attitudes do indeed tend to get worse in the harmful ways: Their rape proclivities do risk going up, and the jokes do risk increasing their discriminatory ways.[47] Among these people, the risks of harm would seem to be too great to make their engaging in stereotyping humor morally permissible.

What, though, about people with better hearts who play around with stereotyping humor in their joking exclusively with each other? Suppose two non-Black nonracists are on the porch now, and in witnessing the Black men following the woman, one turns to the other and says, "Somebody ought to throw those boys a basketball." They both know that neither of them is a racist, they both know that neither believes the stupid stereotypes exploited by the wisecrack, and there's no actual harm caused by the wisecrack itself (no one else hears it, they soon forget it and move on, etc.). Is there anything nevertheless morally risky here?

One might morally object to these wisecrackers, not on the basis of their disrespectful racist or sexist attitudes (of which they have, by stipulation, none), nor on the basis of any actual harm they are causing (which, again, is by stipulation none), but instead on the basis of their playful attitudes. There are certain subjects, the objection might go, that are too serious to play with. These include wisecracks that play with racial and gender stereotypes, especially those of the oppressed and marginalized. Achieving social justice is hard, it involves lots of dedication and difficult work, and so to make cracks about these matters by toying with racial and gender stereotypes is to fail to take the injustices of inequality, racism, and sexism seriously enough. It is instead to trivialize issues of great weight. It is to play with fire: "Do not promote a lack of concern for something about which people should be concerned," as Morreall puts it.[48]

When you yell at your kids for playing with fire, you're not objecting to the immorality of fire; you're objecting to what seem to be your kids' cavalier attitudes toward fire's danger. So too this objection to stereotyping wisecrackers is to their cavalier attitudes toward the danger of racial and sexual stereotypes. But what is the precise danger? Morreall says it's that playing with these stereotypes generates a reasonable risk of harm, even in the morally innocent: It can too easily blend into or cause actual racism and sexism: "Mere repeated thinking of groups in negative stereotypes is enough to prompt us to treat real individuals not according to their actual merits and shortcomings . . . , but as automatically inferior because they belong to those groups."[49] And Luvell Anderson writes in a similar vein that the exploitation of some racial stereotypes in humor can contribute to a problematic background ideology, one in which the characteristics attributed to various racial or ethnic groups in the stereotype become viewed as part of their members' essence, and if these stereotypes aren't challenged, they "become part of the common ground, possibly naturalizing the properties being described in the minds of hearers."[50] In sum, this type of playing risks causing people to be more racially and sexually insensitive, less empathetic, less sympathetic, and less concerned to alleviate the suffering and oppression of others, and it would do so via the insidious—and seemingly innocent—pleasures of amusement.[51] Joseph Boskin call this "the complicity of humor."[52]

But what reason do we have to believe the empirical claims being asserted here? The psychological evidence for them is, again, muddy or lacking. As noted already, some psychologists report evidence that people who too cavalierly play with racial and sexual stereotypes (those who have cavalier humor beliefs) are more likely to accept discrimination against women upon hearing sexist jokes.[53] But this is actually true only for those who also already value their own group's dominance and unequal group status (those who have social dominance orientation). Others have reported that engaging in "disparagement humor" increases tolerance for subsequent discrimination against those disparaged. But again, this is true only of those who are already "high in prejudice."[54] Still others have reported results showing that men who hear sexist jokes have increased rape proclivity, but again, this turns out to be true only for those who are already hostile sexists, not for those who aren't.[55] So the risks of harm are really attached just to those who already have bad intentions and motives.

Indeed, it's hard to find any clear empirical evidence of harm risks when those of good (or at least nonbad) intentions or motives play around with racial and gender stereotypes with each other. But this doesn't mean there aren't any such risks. When we mock those in the other political camp, after all, it surely seems to decrease our empathy for them, to increase our schadenfreude at their failures and comeuppances. And it surely seems possible that this correlation is causal, that it's our playing with the stereotypes about our political foes that is what in fact decreases our empathy for them. When we make someone the butt of a joke, we tend (at least for a bit) to take them less seriously as a result. So it does seem quite natural that there'd be a risky causal connection like this at work when people play with racial and gender stereotypes too.

This is all indeed quite possible. So let's just grant it: When playing with these stereotypes, we will say with measured confidence, there's a risk that it will cause harmful attitudinal, empathic, and behavioral changes in the players. Even if this is true, though, it's not yet enough to give us an across-the-board principled objection to telling and making stereotyping jokes and wisecracks, as we haven't yet heard the case in their favor.

What possible reasons could there be to play with this particular form of fire if you're a person of goodwill? There are several. First of all, there is the standard reason: It can be funny. And as it may cause amused pleasure to others, its amusing properties may also generate a moral reason to crack wise. We already know about some of the general interpersonal values associated with engaging in a humor-filled life.

Furthermore, playing with stereotyping humor can be enjoyably thrilling. As with playing with actual fire, there can be fun in the risk, the danger, in successfully finding humor in typically fraught racial and gender stereotypes, in making your way without explosion through a minefield. Chris Rock's routine was thrilling in this way, and was made even more enjoyable thereby, precisely because he performed such a high-wire act so well.

Finally, playing with stereotyping humor can be subversive, in a positive way. It can help to remind us of the idiocy of racism and sexism—by exposing and caricaturing what dumb or bad people occasionally believe about their fellows—and so keep us vigilant ourselves in not buying into those stereotypes. The subversive element of Rock's routine—"We Black people can assert our equality by talking without apology just like White people do about their own bad apples"—was empowering. (That element is likely also what was vaguely disturbing and confusing to many White people.)

So there are reasons, both comic and moral, in favor of some people of goodwill playing with stereotyping humor. Our question, then, is simply this: Do they outweigh the risks of harm that come along with such humor? Possibly, sometimes. Because we do have a much clearer idea of the harms sometimes incurred when people of bad will engage in stereotyping humor, and these harms can be pretty significant (increased rape proclivity!), it seems that what's being risked by those people is way too serious to be morally permitted. But when it comes to better-willed people, these moral risks are too unclear to generate a blanket all-in verdict. Sometimes, when the parties are of good enough will and know each other well enough, when joking around serves to bond them in positive ways, when their attitudes are quite stable, and when the jokes are particularly funny, then it seems that any moral risk of harm caused by stereotyping wisecracking may be outweighed. But the more toward "it's funny 'cause it's true!" they skew, the less settled their attitudes, and the less funny the jokes, the more morally worried we should be about it.

This isn't much by way of practical advice, I admit, but my main points in the chapter have been to offer a qualified defense of the funniness of some stereotyping jokes/wisecracks, as well as a heavily qualified moral defense of occasionally telling or making them. But there are many factors involved here, and because we don't have a clear empirical line on some of them, it's hard to say much more than that. Disappointing, I know, but it's not the first time—and by god it won't be the last—that philosophy has disappointed.

∴

Part Three

FINDING FUNNY

∵

CHAPTER SIX

"I Feel Your Hilarious Pain"

Flawed Senses of Humor, Flawed Senses of Morality

Some immoral features of wisecracks—such as deception, mockery's sting, and stereotyping—can actually make them funny (or funnier), and their funniness is, ironically, what partially contributes to making them morally permissible to engage in and be amused by. That's a major takeaway from the last three chapters. But recall that what makes various properties funny-makers in the first place is just what a human with a good sense of humor would find amusing. So now we have to explore what makes for a good sense of humor. We also need to explore how our senses of humor more generally bear on our senses of morality. If we can get some good answers, we should then be able to figure out some specific ways to improve our senses of humor (and, perhaps, our senses of morality).

Sense(s) of Humor

On nearly every surveyed list of desirable traits in a mate, alongside things like "physical attractiveness," "openness," and "maturity," you'll see the trusty old standby "a sense of humor."[1] What are people asking for when they ask for this? One likely possibility is that they're looking for someone with a *good* sense of humor, where that is often taken simply to mean some-one whose sense of humor is similar to their own.[2] But that doesn't yet tell us what exactly they take a sense of humor to be in the first place, let alone a good one (no one would, with a straight face, assert that a truly good sense of humor is one that simply matches their own).

So what is a sense of humor? Psychologists are the only ones I know of who have had anything at all to say about what it might be. Now while many psychologists are very good at what they do (and some of my best friends are psychologists!), sometimes they operationalize concepts in a way that's rather different from how most folks conceive of them. A prime exam-ple is the way they've written about "a sense of humor." It has, in various psychologists' writings, been operationalized as (a) how often someone laughs or is amused; (b) how many witticisms or jokes a person tells; (c) how well someone understands the content of jokes; (d) how someone expresses her amusement; (e) how often someone seeks out things that amuse her; (f) how well someone remembers jokes and amusing anecdotes; and (g) whether a person uses humor as a coping mechanism.[3] These features are all more or less easily measurable, of course, and that's often what drives such operationalizing. But none of these really captures what most of us have in mind when using the phrase "sense of humor." For example, having a sense of humor surely does require that one is actually amused at least some of the time. But it can't be that the more often you're amused, the more of a sense of humor you have. Indeed, if you laugh all the time, or if you are constantly telling jokes, you are more likely to have a psychological disorder than a sense of humor.[4] The psychological operationalizations also often conflate, as do ads for dates and mates, "a sense of humor" with "a good sense of humor."

In truth, I think we can rather easily give at least a formal definition of both. A sense of humor is in fact a sense, which is just a mechanism of perceptual experience, a way of interacting with and responding to the world, and at least to that extent it is akin to our other senses, starting with the basic five of smell, taste, touch, sight, and hearing.[5] So just as a sense of touch is a nonvisual way of perceiving the tactile properties of the world around us, and just as a sense of sight is a way of visually representing the three-dimensional properties of the physical world around us, and just as a sense of temperature is a way of perceiving the speed of molecule motion around us, a sense of humor is yet another way of perceiving the *amusing* properties of the world we encounter.

This way of putting it might be controversial and irritating to neuroscientists, who, like psychologists, want identifiable and measurable domains of study, and so want to restrict talk of "senses" to cellular responses to our physical environment that correspond to specific, identifiable brain regions where the signals from the nerve-sensory cells are received and interpreted. Things like a "sense of direction," "an aesthetic sense," a "sense of danger," a "sense of self," or a "sense of humor" are instead what they call post-sensory cognitive activities.[6] They presuppose perception by the "lower-level" sensory apparatuses that we then consider and interpret via cognition before responding.

Now it's true that, in order to be amused by someone's clever wordplay, I first have to hear her utterances and so perceive and understand them, or to be amused by someone's slipping on the ice, I have to visually sense and perceive it first as "someone slipping on ice." But the fact that there are cognitive layers or mediation involved shouldn't exclude humor (or direction, and so on) from the helpful list of senses, because, again, if senses most generally are simply forms of perceptual experience, then that's just what our senses of direction, aesthetics, danger, self, and humor are too, so I don't see any reason to exclude them from the list.

If we do include humor as a sense, then we can also define good and bad senses of humor, again formally, as we do the goodness and badness of our other senses, although with some subtly different wrinkles. Here's the basic formulation: Someone who possesses a good sense of sight, for example, is simply someone who sees well; someone with a bad sense of sight sees poorly.[7] Someone with a good sense of smell detects and discriminates well between various odors; someone with a bad sense of smell does so poorly. So too, then, someone who possesses a good sense of humor detects, discriminates between, and responds well to various comic properties, and someone with a bad sense of humor does so poorly.

What do "well" and "poorly" mean, though? Start with our most basic physical senses (sight, smell, hearing, etc.). For these, "well" and "poor" are descriptive grades of our abilities relative to statistical human standards. We humans can't see ultraviolet light, as can ferrets or reindeer, and we can't see the tiniest movement from hundreds of yards away, as can hawks. We lack the ability of hound dogs to detect and discriminate between scents and trails that are half a mile off or a week old. We can't hear the frequencies that moths and bats can. And our sensibilities are vulnerable to being fooled, as we know well from various optical illusions.

Consequently, when we talk about someone having a "good" or "bad" sense of sight, smell, or hearing, we are typically referring to their having a competently or incompetently functioning sensory mechanism for a statistically average human,[8] which is just to say that they can see what an average human with a properly functioning human sense of sight would see, in similar conditions. And when we talk about someone having a "bad" sense of sight (or taste, touch, smell, or hearing), we're typically saying that they can't see—or can't see in as accurate a fashion—the things that those average humans with functional sensibilities can see in similar conditions. In these cases, having a good sense of sight isn't really a praiseworthy matter, nor is having a bad sense of sight a criticizable matter; in both cases, it's merely a true description of the quality of the sensibility itself.

Some descriptively bad sensibilities have available correctives: glasses for those with poor eyesight and hearing aids for those with diminished hearing. And there can be criticizable failures to use those correctives. If my kids want me to watch something on their frustratingly tiny phone screens and I say I can't see it, they'll tell me, with some edge, "Then put on your glasses, Dad!" And the role played by deliberately turned-down hearing aids in marriages is surely well known. But the criticisms here aren't targeting people's sensibilities; rather, they are targeting people's failures to use readily available methods to help make their flawed sensibilities function up to the standards of the statistical norm.

In addition, we sometimes correct or criticize people who claim not to perceive various properties for failing to attend to matters properly or for failing to make other adjustments so that their otherwise perfectly functional senses will work as they ought: "Just hold the image close to your eyes and focus on the middle before letting your eyes relax and you'll come to see it in 3D," we may say to the person who claims to be unable to see the hidden image in an autostereogram. Or perhaps we'll say, "Eat a cracker first before tasting that other wine," or "Clean that wax out of your ears so I don't have to yell all the time!" These are criticisms aiming to get people to clear obstructions that prevent their perfectly functional sensibilities from working as they are meant to. But again, these aren't criticisms for having poor sensibilities. There's no normative bite to claims of "good" and "bad" sensibilities as such.

When it comes to the post-cognitive sensibilities, though, where there's a layer of cognitive mediation between cellular and macrolevel responses, there are additional interpretations of having "good" and "bad" senses that do have normative bite, where what it sounds like we're doing really is praising or criticizing agents for their sensibilities. I'll focus just on the negative cases. "He's got a terrible sense of direction," we may say of someone, "as he gets lost all the time in the city," or "She just has no aesthetic taste, preferring her child's aimless and sloppy watercolors to a Rembrandt," or "He has a completely untutored sense of danger, blithely skipping into dark alleys at 3 a.m. just to stare at the architecture." In these sorts of cases, there is a presumption that people have functional sensibilities that are capable of issuing better perceptual responses to various events than they do, and yet they don't, for a variety of reasons. Criticism in these cases has normative bite, as it aims to get them to see various reasons—directional, aesthetic, and danger-ridden reasons that they are capable of seeing—in a way that will get them to respond better to their world.

All of what I've just said applies squarely to our senses of humor. Calling a sense of humor good or bad is sometimes merely descriptive, making reference to the statistical human average. If you're unamused when encountering and engaging with funny things, you may have a bad sense of humor in the sense that you're simply incapable of being amused by what ordinary humans would be amused by were they in your position. This could be due to many noncriticizable factors, such as macular degeneration (you just can't see the amusing properties in the world) or, as we'll discuss, a crippling depression.

We may, however, criticize you for your failure to use readily available humor correctives. Many of these involve clearing away obscuring factors in your perception of the funny-making properties in various wisecracks. Criticism in these cases, though, isn't directed at your bad sense of humor as such.

Sometimes, however, we do criticize people who deliberately prevent their functional humor sensibilities from working properly. These are people we also refer to as having "bad senses of humor," but with a normative scowl: "They need to get a (better) sense of humor." Such folks tend to come in two bitter flavors.

Prigs

We all know the guy. He shakes his head disapprovingly at off-color wisecracks, hisses at "Your mama" jokes, wags his finger at mockery, gets affronted by insult humor, and tut-tuts at teasing. He's a prig. As Aristotle put it, "The [prig] is of no use in playful conversation: he contributes nothing and takes offence at everything."[9] Prigs have a criticizably bad sense of humor. As I've said, there may a number of ways in which someone's sense of humor might be rightly described as flawed, but there are two distinctive and fascinating explanations for why prigs have criticizably bad senses of humor.[10]

Recall that humorous mockery aims at a sting. If you humorously mock me, therefore, I have a comic reason to be amused, but I may also have a competing reason—a moral reason—to get morally upset with you for aiming to sting me a bit, for deliberately drawing public attention to my embarrassing foibles. These reasons may tug me back and forth. Indeed, we all occasionally feel these competing reasons at work simultaneously when we respond to someone's wicked zinger with both amusement and moral discomfort, a laughing "ooooooohhh."

This structure of reasons sets up the first type of distinctive mistake that prigs may make. They think that if there's any immorality in a wisecrack, then whatever reasons we might have thought we had for amusement actually don't exist (so the wisecrack's just not funny) or they are significantly dampened (so our reason for being amused is powerfully outweighed by our reason for being morally upset).[11] But of course, one of my main aims thus far has been to undermine this inference. Even if a wisecrack includes deception, mockery's sting, or the exploitation of racial or gender stereotypes, it can still be quite funny, and it might even be funnier than it would have been without those immoral properties, even if those properties also provide some reason for angry blame.

There's a second mistake some prigs make, and it's related but importantly different. Suppose a prig walks into a bar, and he immediately hears a group of friends with straight faces seeming to insult each other quite mercilessly. Insults are immoral, thinks our prig, and so he thinks he has a reason to be morally upset at all the immorality he is hearing. But in fact he has no such reason. These "insults," as it turns out, are faux; these friends are just playing with each other via mock insults, and there is no ill intent whatsoever in their banter. Let's suppose we tell our prig this, and yet he persists in being angered at the "insulting" language being used. The mistake the prig makes in this case is to continue relying on a "reason" to be morally upset that simply doesn't exist.

To sum up, prigs have criticizably bad senses of humor in virtue of making either or both of two mistakes: (a) they think that any immorality in a wisecrack eliminates or dampens any and all comic reasons for amusement at it, and/or (b) they may "see" and rely on nonexistent "moral reasons" for being morally upset at funny things that in fact contain no immorality.

Buffoons

Prigs get lots of attention (see Downer, Debbie). No one really likes them, and they ruin the amusement party. However, there's a group of people who are the mirror opposite of prigs who get much less attention, but whose senses of humor are just as criticizably bad. These are buffoons. Here's how Aristotle describes them: "The buffoon is one who cannot resist a joke; he will not keep his tongue off himself or anyone else, if he can raise a laugh, and will say things which a man of refinement would never say, and some of which he would not even allow to be said to him."[12]

Buffoons like the party *too* much, and they make criticizable mistakes analogous to those that prigs make. First, they say that if there's any funniness in something, then any reasons for being morally upset by it are either eliminated (so there's actually no immorality in it at all) or dampened (so whatever moral reasons there are actually weigh very little or are easily overridden by the comic reasons). But again, the point of the previous three chapters was to argue for why the buffoon's attitude is also a mistake: There are indeed reasons to be morally upset built into some wisecracks, and these aren't eliminated or dampened by the fact that they also generate comic reasons for amusement (indeed, sometimes the properties generating moral upset and comic amusement are identical).

Suppose that I mock you in a funny way, and it stings, as I've exposed an embarrassing foible. Perhaps you're about to get morally upset, and when I see this, I respond, "Oh, give me a break, it was just a joke!" What I seem to be saying is that, given the funniness of my mockery (which you recognize as well), you have no reason to be angry. But this is false. Mockery contains a sting, sometimes a really mean sting, and that gives the stung people a reason to be morally upset that remains firmly in place even if there are also reasons for amusement at the mockery's funniness. Indeed, these multiple categories of reasons might well manifest in the twinge of guilt the mocker may feel in mocking someone, as well as the bit of anger that a mocked person might feel toward the mocker, even though both can also appreciate that what was said was still awfully funny.

Buffoons make the analog of the prig's second mistake as well. A few pranks can be, I have grudgingly admitted, funny. Suppose a buffoon walks into a bar, where she sees a couple of people setting up a bear trap outside the door of the men's room, in which there is currently someone they hate. When that guy walks out of the door, he triggers the bear trap, and it mangles his leg. His enemies laugh uproariously at their successful prank. Suppose the buffoon is amused too, as she's seeing a prank and so thinks she is seeing some funny in it thereby. But not all pranks are funny; some are pure cruelty, regardless of whether some troglodytes are actually amused by them. Her mistake is to see this prank in a humorous light, as giving her a "reason" for amusement. But no such reason actually exists.

To sum up, the buffoon's criticizably bad sense of humor comes from making either or both of two mistakes: (a) she may think any humor in something eliminates or dampens any reasons for moral anger at it, and/or (b) she may "see" and rely on "comic reasons" for amusement at something that actually don't exist.

If you think prigs are no fun to be around, buffoons can be *really* no fun to be around. They are often our bullies. They make merciless fun of us and then say, "Oh, give me a break, it's just a joke!" They can be assholes, jerks, guffawing dicks, or worse, and they are often best avoided.

The language of "prigs" and "buffoons" is pejorative. These are terms used to criticize people for their "bad senses of humor," where this criticism has normative bite. When we label these people as such, we are presuming that they have functional senses of humor but are themselves preventing their proper exercise. We criticize them, therefore, as a way of saying that they should stop being the way they are, that they should improve their senses of humor.

But there are some people who have dysfunctional senses of humor, that is, they have bad senses of humor in the purely descriptive sense, due to some impairment (like those with poor vision or hearing), one that renders improvement out of their direct control. Once we understand their impairments, we can also better understand what it takes to have a good or bad humor sensibility in both the descriptive and the normative senses. We can also learn some surprising things about our senses of morality.

Humor Styles

A sense of humor is one among many ways in which we perceptually experience the world. But some people have impaired or dysfunctional sensibilities. If senses generally are forms of perceptual experience, and if some of them don't work properly, then their owners will have a more difficult time navigating some parts of the world than those whose senses work properly. This prediction is in fact true of those with impaired senses of humor.

Many psychologists have, thankfully, given up talking about "senses of humor" in favor of talking about "humor styles." These are also measurable psychological states, but they just refer to the types of humor to which people are mostly attracted (so they can be measured by observation of what people are amused by, what types of jokes they tell or wisecracks they make, and/or their self-reports about their humor preferences, among other things). It turns out that the sorts of things different people tend to be amused by significantly predict their levels of well-being, especially given the relation between different humor styles and coping ability.

There are four humor styles, different uses people make of humor in their everyday lives.[13] The first is affiliative, humor that enhances people's relations to others. Examples include forms of the wisecracks I've built the book around: witty banter, teasing, wordplay, mockery, taking the piss, leg-pulling, ballbusting, and more, at least when they serve to create and enhance friendly relationships. The second is self-enhancing (although this label is a bit misleading). It's a humor style involving amusement at the vicissitudes, difficulties, and absurdities of life in general, generally deployed by people to better enable them to cope with various setbacks, serving to foster strength in the face of adversity. Self-enhancing humor—wryly commenting on life's various absurdities or seeing painful events from a removed and playful perspective—helps keep one's self intact, fortified, and in control.[14]

These first two humor styles are correlated positively with well-being, for obvious reasons. Engaging in affiliative humor contributes to the creation and maintenance of friendships, partnerships, and romantic relationships. Engaging in self-enhancing humor also shores people up, and it's correlated with being more cheerful, confident, and resilient, which are also attractive features. You'll tend to have more and better relationships, as well as be psychologically stronger, when you engage in or are attracted to these humor styles.

The final two humor styles, however, are correlated negatively with well-being, again for rather obvious reasons. The third humor style is self-defeating. This style is unfortunately evident in those who offer themselves up as the butt of jokes, so as to ingratiate themselves to others or to get their approval. It is self-denigrating (not self-deprecating, which is actually a big part of self-enhancing humor, thus the misleading nature of the label), and it may well involve papering over or repressing one's own emotional needs in order to get that approval.[15]

The fourth humor style is aggressive, and it too is familiar, involving the meanest forms of sarcasm, ridicule, mockery, put-downs, derision, and teasing, deployed without much consideration of its hurtfulness or its role in exclusion. The connection to lowered well-being should again be obvious: Why would people want to be around someone who was ridiculing them all the time? People attracted to this humor style tend to have fewer friends, partners, and relationships, as people just want to steer clear of them.

These four styles can of course overlap. Affiliative humor can be aggressive; it occasionally involves sarcasm and mockery, after all. A wisecrack may count as affiliative, then, either because it is benign (perhaps if deployed exclusively within the group) or because it aims to bond members of the in-group by hurting those in the out-group. So too self-enhancing humor can be aggressive (insulting others may help one to cope with their bullying and serve to buttress one's self-image). And self-defeating humor can, again if benign, have some affiliative elements—close friends sometimes allow themselves to be the butt of the joke with each other. But for the most part these are relatively distinct categories,[16] especially if we are thinking about styles that are dominant in people's personalities. We all know people more or less defined by each of these different humor styles, and we often organize our interactions with them around this knowledge.

Autism Spectrum Disorder

OK, so here's where things get interesting: Certain psychological and personality disorders tend to be highly correlated with certain humor styles. Start with autism. Autism is a social communicative disorder combining a cluster of traits that, depending on how they present and interact, place one on a spectrum from high functioning to low functioning.[17] While early on there were some seriously wrongheaded claims that those with autism spectrum disorder (ASD) lack a sense of humor altogether,[18] people who study the condition nowadays know that to be false and instead have come to some fascinating findings about autism's effects on senses of humor.[19]

I have to make a crucial disclaimer first, though, that I don't in any way want to be construed as announcing from on high that "here is what autistic people are or aren't amused by," given that of course there are unique and individual humor styles found in people throughout the autistic community—it's a very wide spectrum. Nevertheless, there are some trends identified throughout the contemporary psychological research, and those are what I'll be focusing on.

Many people with ASD[20] are amused by many things, some recognizable as humorous by neurotypicals (or "allistic" people), some not. Many parents of autistic children report that their kids sometimes laugh at things the parents find utterly puzzling or incomprehensible.[21] But there are also many perfectly comprehensible and shared humor responses. For instance, autistic people across much of the spectrum tend to be amused by pratfalls and slapstick, as well as by simpler jokes ("pre-riddles" and puns).[22] Further, some people toward one end of the spectrum (e.g., those with Asperger's syndrome) love incongruity-resolution humor, where a jarring juxtaposition is resolved in a punch line. For example: What did the kid say when the Statue of Liberty sneezed? God bless America.[23]

There is reduced appreciation across the spectrum for several other types of humor, however. Nonsense or absurdist humor, where there is an unresolved incongruity (e.g., animals talking like humans), aren't generally taken to be very funny by those with ASD.[24] Figure 3 is an example of such humor. Here's another, from Twitter:

"You promise you didn't get me bees again."
[me from a distance] just open it.[25]

Unresolved incongruity, where a joke "takes you on a totally different path from the setup, is disconcerting" to many people with autism.[26] What's wanted instead is a return to order. Indeed, there are workshops that teach the mechanics of writing incongruity-resolution jokes, and they have produced some semi-successful autistic comics, but the teaching can't really include nonsense and absurd humor, as that sort of humor intentionally defies logic and order.[27]

Some people with ASD also tend not to find sarcastic and ironic jokes funny, as they don't wear their meaning on their sleeves.[28] Rather, their

love tip: how to show a girl you are in love with her

FIGURE 3. Absurdist humor cartoon ("Love Tip"). © Chris (Simpsons artist).
Used with permission.

meaning—and their humor—is found in the authorial intent of the teller.
Sarcasm works best when told with a straight face. When Trump offered
$5 million to charity if Obama would release his passport and college tran-
scripts, Obama responded, "This all goes back to when we were growing
up together in Kenya."[29] Said with no wink or "just joking" hint, the listener
has to figure out that the speaker actually means the very opposite of what
she's saying. But this can be tough to do—"I can't tell if you're joking or
not!"—and if you have difficulty sussing out nonliteral meanings because
you have difficulty reading people's intentions—as many people on the
ASD spectrum do—then you're going to have a tough time finding sarcasm
funny. Rather, it will seem like a puzzling, and perhaps seriously misin-
formed, statement of fact.[30]

Relatedly—and importantly—many people with ASD tend to be unamused by socially inappropriate acts, acts that seem to violate social
norms.[31] Included here are wisecracks in the form of faux insults, teasing,
and mockery. These are often seen instead as hurtful and wrongful, and so
as providing reasons to be morally upset. And when such misunderstand-
ings occur, the teasing or mocking person is likely to be amused, which
may then be taken by the person with ASD as shaming or bullying.[32] Further, given that these are also the types of humor that often serve to bond
in-group members, those with ASD tend to score low on the affiliative humor style that can be so crucial to getting a variety of interpersonal goods

associated with friendship. To the extent that affiliative humor styles are positively correlated with well-being, autistic people who are turned off by it may miss out on one important component of a good life.

Prigs tend to make one or both of two humor mistakes: either they wrongly think that if there's any immorality involved in a wisecrack then it can't be funny (or its funniness is seriously dampened), or they mistakenly think they see "reasons" to be morally upset by wisecracks that are actually morally innocent. Those with ASD who get morally angered at some forms of affiliative humor that they think are socially inappropriate may make both mistakes too, sometimes thinking stinging mockery just isn't funny, and sometimes seeing "reasons" to be upset at faux insults and teasing that don't exist. When these mistakes are made, they manifest a flawed sense of humor.

Are autistic people who have these flawed senses of humor prigs? "Prig" is a pejorative term for someone with the capacity not to be a prig. But autistic people have impaired capacities for some social interaction and communication, impairments that are the source of some of their mistaken responses to socially inappropriate or absurd humor. So although some people with ASD may have flawed senses of humor in the statistical sense (akin to older people who can't hear high frequencies), they surely aren't prigs, given their impairments.

This all seems correct to me. If it does to you as well, though, you may not like the dark place where this reasoning now takes us.

The Dark Triad

In personality psychology, the *dark triad* refers to narcissists, Machiavellians, and psychopaths.[33] Narcissists have an overwhelming need for attention and admiration, a craving to have their excellence constantly affirmed. Machiavellians are cynical people who manipulate others for fun. Psychopaths are impulsive and thrill seeking, doing whatever they want whenever they want, regardless of the interests of anyone else. Members of all three groups tend to be callous and manipulative. Psychologists study them together, as their traits predict aggressiveness, as well as workplace, sexual, and financial misbehavior. They are highly disagreeable people. Agreeable people seek social harmony, whereas those in the dark triad are antisocial, described variously as "demanding, clever, flirtatious, charming, shrewd, autocratic; selfish; stubborn, headstrong, impatient, intolerant, outspoken, hard-hearted; clever, assertive, argumentative, self-confident, aggressive, idealistic; and unstable."[34] They tend to have short-term success in some areas, such as relationships, academia(!), and business, as those are areas in which they can easily exploit others' cooperative tendencies while feeling no compunction to provide any expected reciprocation.[35] This suggests they have a shared trait. What is it?

The best proposal is that they all have impairments in empathy.[36] Of course there's significant disagreement, in both the philosophical and psychological communities, on what empathy is, exactly. Although I have my own rather idiosyncratically complicated view of how empathy ought to be characterized, I'll set aside truth here in favor of consensus.[37] On the most commonly accepted view, empathy is understood to involve several neural mechanisms, but it basically boils down to two activities: (a) understanding another's state of mind via perspective taking (called "cognitive empathy"), and (b) responding to that perspective taking via vicariously in-sync emotions, such as anger, distress, or joy (called "emotional" or "affective" empathy).[38] There are many complications here, but the basics ought to be pretty familiar to most of us, as we engage in empathy all the time. Suppose my wife comes home from work in shambles: her boss yelled at her in front of her coworkers for screwing up a job. As she tells me the story, I can easily take up her perspective and grasp what it must have been like for her to be publicly berated, and then I'll also come to feel the burning distress she must have felt. Note that I'm not "catching" her distress, as if it were contagious. Rather, I'm responding to what she is responding to, namely, her boss's public shaming of her, but by experiencing it as an imagined simulacrum of how she herself experienced it, and so responding to it as she did.

One of the impairments of autism is difficulty in what's known as theory of mind, or being able to read the intentions and motivations of others from the types of visual cues that allistic people can read rather effortlessly. This impairment makes it hard for those with ASD to take up others' perspectives, and so it's an impairment in cognitive empathy.[39] But this doesn't necessarily translate into an impairment in emotional empathy, as the emotional responses I've described are only typically generated by cognitive empathy. One can also get at them in other ways. In fact, many people with ASD can experience emotional empathy without engaging in cognitive empathy (that is, without having a fully functional capacity to take up others' perspectives). It's abundantly clear from self-reports that many autistic people experience deep emotions, and it has also become clear that many autistic people experience vicarious emotional responses in sync with other people, and at the same objects as those other people. Indeed, sometimes these vicarious feelings are just too overwhelming for those with autism, given what seems to be a kind of emotional hypersensitivity.[40] They aren't arriving at these affective empathic responses through perspective taking, though (or mere emotional contagion); rather, according to the self-reports of some people with ASD, empathy may be arrived at by conjuring up a visual Rolodex of past facial and bodily movements associated with certain intentions, motivations, and experiences, a Rolodex against which they may check current faces and reactions for similarities, which then triggers vicarious emotional responses.[41]

Some people with ASD are capable of generating some affective empathic responses via nonstandard routes, even though they may have some impairments in cognitive empathy. There is a kind of mirrored condition in members of the dark triad, however. They are capable of some forms of cognitive empathy, but they are impaired for *emotional* empathy. What they can do is take up other people's perspectives, understanding to some extent what people are experiencing or going through. Indeed, they use this information to manipulate them.[42] But what they can't do is properly respond emotionally to that information.

Emotional deficits of various kinds abound in the dark triad,[43] but what its members most have in common is that they are all deficient in experiencing emotional distress in response to the distress of others.[44] They are just emotionally callous. Further, they score higher than any other psychological grouping in schadenfreude: Not only aren't they moved to distress at the distressful plight of others, but they are often moved instead to laughter or delight.[45] They have a topsy-turvy (and scary) emotional makeup.

Because of their deficient emotional empathy, the humor styles of members of the dark triad are utterly predictable: They tend to favor aggressive humor—ridicule, sarcasm, and put-downs—mostly to the exclusion of other styles.[46] They tend to go in for laughing at people, rather than with them.[47] However, they can also be very charming and, as many people report, quite amusing. So they can't just go around insulting people, as insults on their own aren't amusing. As it turns out, they manipulate people with their "charming" humor, by deploying a pretense of a joking style that disarms their victims and greases the wheels to getting what they want.[48] When they are observed unobtrusively, though, it turns out they mostly just smile at and enjoy watching other people's misfortunes (schadenfreude). Also, finally, they dislike, and have a kind of terror of, being laughed at by others.[49] They see laughter at others as a source of manipulation and control; to be laughed at themselves thus indicates a loss of control over the situation, and members of the dark triad hate losing control.

In light of these facts, it's actually unclear to me whether what members of the dark triad have is rightly called a humor style. Yes, they laugh at others, and they can also laugh at themselves when telling charming (manipulative) anecdotes about their own "foibles."[50] But if what they find truly enjoyable are the misfortunes of the others,[51] it doesn't seem to be any humor that they're enjoying; rather, it's just the misfortune.

Regardless of whether this counts as having a "humor style," though, what's clear is that their patterns of amusement or lack thereof reveal a deeply flawed sense of humor. Mere misfortune, all on its own, is just as unfunny as mere insult. What's needed to make these things funny is some additional property from the kitchen sink list, some funny type of incongruity, play, surprise, cleverness, etc. Someone's slipping on a banana peel or stumbling over an unseen root in the sidewalk may seem to have such properties. So too may be the sudden exposure and downfall of nasty people. These can be funny misfortunes. But a little girl who slips on the ice and bangs her head hard, spurting blood out of her skull (sorry for the gruesome image), well, that's not funny at all. Nor is the surprising and deadly heart attack of a kind and beloved person who has been the model of good health. Nor, again, is the Carrie prank. But members of the dark triad just don't discriminate between misfortunes in this way. As long as it's someone else's misfortune, then it's funny, they think. But that means they are responding to some things as funny that just aren't, that is, they are seeing "comic reasons" for amusement in some misfortunes that don't exist. Furthermore, even when some meanness (in mockery, say) has some funny in it that they rightly pick up on, they make the mistake of thinking that the funny cancels out all the immorality, all moral reason for upset: "Oh, c'mon," they may say to someone distressed by the meanness, "that was funny!"

Here's a second general type of mistake they make: They fail to see some actually funny things as funny. Given their almost exclusive attraction to aggressive humor, they often fail to see examples of affiliative, self-deprecating, or absurd humor as funny, as meriting (their) amusement. But surely there is some genuine humor to be found in the wisecracking banter of friends and family.

Because members of the dark triad have empathic deficits, they have a flawed sense of humor. Here's a tough question, then: Given that their flawed sense of humor is the product of an impairment, are they buffoons? Calling someone a buffoon is pejorative, a criticism, and so it seems to presume an unimpaired capacity and a normative demand, as with prigs, not to be the way they are. It thus looks like, if we are to be consistent with our treatment of ASD, we have to say that members of the dark triad aren't criticizable buffoons (this is the dark conclusion I previously warned you was coming). They do have bad senses of humor, but only in the statistical sense, like having poor senses of vision or hearing.

From Humor to Morality and Back Again

One primary source of a flawed sense of humor in some people on the autism spectrum is their impaired capacity for cognitive empathy.[52] Having difficulty reading intentions makes it difficult to know when someone is "just joking," that is, when they are engaged in morally innocent leg-pulling humor or faux insults. Some people with ASD may thus mistakenly tend to see "reasons" for being morally upset by this type of humor that don't exist.

But what this means is that they are also making a *moral* mistake. Normally, if I lie to you or insult you without excuse or justification, I am the appropriate target of (your and others') moral anger. If I'm not really insulting you, though, or if I'm not engaged in morally problematic deception, then if you nevertheless angrily blame me for these things, you are wrong to do so. You're responding to "moral reasons" for being angry that just don't exist. If your mistake is the result of a psychological impairment, then that impairment has made you morally flawed. This is the case for some people with ASD, who may have two impaired sensibilities: an impaired sense of humor and an impaired sense of morality. Both impairments have the exact same source, though: an impaired capacity for cognitive empathy, for taking up others' perspectives.

A mirrored story is true for members of the dark triad. They too have an impaired sense of humor, sometimes mistakenly seeing "comic reasons" for amusement that don't exist in the mere misfortunes of others, and sometimes mistakenly taking funny properties to cancel out all immoral properties (if a wisecrack is funny, they may say, it can't wrong anyone). But this humor impairment is also, crucially, a moral impairment, as they can't seem to see any moral reasons for distress at the misfortunes of others, and they can't see more generally why some moral reasons may severely outweigh any reasons for amusement at wrongdoing. The ultimate source of both flawed sensibilities is the same: an impairment of emotional empathy. While they may be able to engage in a kind of cognitive empathy, they seem incapable of properly responding emotionally to what they see from other people's perspectives.

This is a really important conclusion: The impairments of those with ASD and the members of the dark triad reveal that senses of humor and senses of morality are, in these respects, strongly interdependent, so much so that to have one type of flaw in one is to have a related flaw in the other. To have a good sense of wisecracking humor requires that one have well-functioning capacities for both cognitive and emotional empathy.

Regarding cognitive empathy, you have to be able to understand what things are like for other people from the inside, to have a grasp on what their intentions and motives are, so that you can track the relevant reasons for amusement as well as the reasons against being morally upset when encountering affiliative wisecracking like mockery, teasing, taking the piss, and faux "insults." Regarding emotional empathy, you also have to be able to respond in emotional sync with those upset by various kinds of aggressive wisecracking, to recognize where someone's distress pushes a wisecrack over the line, to know when reasons for amusement are irrelevant to how you should respond in the face of sheer cruelty.

But if you have impaired humor sensibilities of either sort, some of your crucial moral sensibilities will also be impaired, as you will be unable to recognize or respond properly to certain essential moral reasons, namely, reasons for distress, reasons against making certain sorts of wisecracks, and reasons in favor of sympathetic concern.[53] Impairments in empathy thus predict that one will have both a flawed sense of humor and a flawed sense of morality.

Too Much Empathy

Unlike deficits in cognitive empathy, deficits in emotional empathy don't admit of any easy work-arounds: Either you're capable of emotionally responding in sync to cognitive empathy (or its work-around) or you aren't. There's no real way around emotional empathic impairments in either comic or moral life.[54] Too little emotional empathy generates flaws in both our senses of humor and our senses of morality.

But so does too much. This claim may seem surprising, but emotional empathy is a Goldilocks virtue: There can't be too little or too much. It has to be just right in order for its bearer to have good senses of both humor and morality. We can see this point via an exploration of some manifestations of bipolar disorder.[55]

Psychologists again and again find that there's a significant negative correlation between many forms of clinical depression and a sense of humor: the more depressed one is, often, the less humor one can find in anything.[56] This result is both unsurprising and depressing, of course. But here's a second, less predictable, phenomenon: People with some forms of major (clinical) depression often have greater emotional empathy than those without it.[57] Psychologists measure it in terms of personal distress: People with some forms of major depression tend to undergo far greater vicarious emotional distress in responding to the misfortunes of other people than do those without the disorder. Indeed, there's a kind of downward spiral generated by this phenomenon: Greater personal distress in response to the suffering of others, without the ability or motivation to do something about that suffering (as well as a confused, disorder-provoked misconstrual of its cause), just leads to greater depression.[58]

There have been no studies, unfortunately, bringing together these two phenomena. But we can engage in some pretty safe speculation. It makes sense that too much emotional empathy is correlated with a depressed and flawed sense of humor, that is, with not finding much to be amused by. When the suffering of others plays such a major distressing role in one's own emotional perspective, amusement just can't find a psychological toe-hold; it's crowded out by all the distress. It seems quite plausible, then, that their greater empathy is very likely one source of some depressed people's flawed senses of humor. There are likely some other sources, including depression's interference with executive functioning and memory.[59] But empathic malfunction (that is, having too much emotional empathy) is surely a significant factor, especially given the role empathic malfunction plays in depression's polar opposite, mania.

People with mania often seem to enjoy humor too much.[60] They tend to laugh and giggle far more than nonmanic people, and at a wider variety of stimuli. Consequently, to quote one psychologist's jargony way of putting it, "it may be that the manic has overreacted with an excess of humor which continues as a self-stimulating phenomenon which causes perpetuation of the manic state."[61] There can be a kind of hysterical feel to the laughter, manifesting a loss of control.[62] In mania, all positive emotions tend to be "enhanced," experienced more widely and wildly.

And what of empathy in those with mania? Here the bipolar conditions are reversed. Depressed patients' personal distress in response to others' distress is far greater than it is in nondepressed people. Some people in manic states, however, tend to experience too much positive emotional response vicariously in sync with others than do nonmanic people: Manic people may be happier for you than *you* are at your good fortune. But their emotional empathy seems to extend only to those doing well; their emotional empathy with—distress over—those doing poorly is significantly impaired.[63] That is, they tend not to recognize or respond properly to misfortune (and so they are similar in this respect to those in the dark triad, who are the kings and queens of schadenfreude). And they also tend to misconstrue others' emotional states as positive, even when they aren't. They want to see the enjoyable in everything. But this translates into having a flawed sense of humor as well: They tend to be amused by misfortune, seeing funniness where what's needed instead is concern.

Once again, both sets of humor flaws predict moral flaws. Being emotionally overwhelmed by distress and misfortune, as are some people with depression, is itself a moral flaw, as it swamps one's ability to help or respond properly to people in distress. And being emotionally immune to the misfortunes of others, as are some people with mania, seeing only the enjoyable everywhere one looks, amounts to a moral flaw too, as it prevents one from seeing moral reasons for sympathy, concern, and aid for those in genuine pain.

Empathic impairments are the source of serious flaws in senses of both humor and morality. Sometimes, as with some autistic people and some members of the dark triad, these are impairments preventing the generation of enough empathy for others. Sometimes, as with some people undergoing depression and mania, these are impairments generating too much empathy for others. What's necessary for good senses of morality and humor, therefore, is the generation of an amount of empathy that's just right. In the final chapter I'll explore how that might be accomplished.

The Unimpaired

What we can learn from those with various psychological difficulties and disorders is that good senses of wisecracking humor and morality require the same capacity—empathy—so that if that capacity is impaired, both sensibilities will be flawed. A functional capacity for both cognitive and emotional empathy is an essential component of good versions of both sensibilities. Thus when people looking for mates snag those who really do have good senses of humor, they'll also snag a bonus quality, as those people will also have a crucial component of a sense of morality as well.

A finely tuned sense of emotional empathy in particular has to chart a middle course between too much and too little. If you feel too much of the distress or enjoyment of others, you'll tend to be, respectively, unamused by some funny wisecracks or amused by some unfunny wisecracks, and you'll also fail to see or respond to some of the crucial interpersonal moral reasons in your midst as a result. If you can't read others' intentions or you feel too little distress in response to their distress, you'll also tend to be, respectively, unamused by some funny wisecracks or amused by some unfunny wisecracks, and you'll also tend to overlook or misread the crucial interpersonal moral reasons in your midst as a result.

These are the prerequisites for properly functioning humor and moral sensibilities. To avoid normatively biting criticism, though, you must also deploy your presumably functional empathy sensibilities correctly, aiming for the Goldilocks mean, experiencing neither too much nor too little.

Vicious (vice-ridden) forms come from excess on either side. Do you allow yourself to respond with too much distress to those in distress and so not enough amusement to genuinely funny things? You are likely a prig and a moralizer. Do you instead allow yourself to respond with too little distress to those in distress and too much amusement at their misfortune? You are likely a buffoon and an asshole.

Prigs and buffoons, moralizers and assholes are, unfortunately, all around us. The buffoons have less empathy than they should for those in dire straits, for those who are suffering, and for those who are denigrated and dehumanized. They thus too easily detach from distress in favor of amusement. "C'mon, it's funny!" they say. On the other hand, prigs tend to have too much empathy in response to suffering people, and so wherever there is any meanness or pain, even a tiny bit, their overextended distress swamps a legitimate humor response. "That's just not funny!" they preach, and in so doing they moralize, aiming to make people feel bad for being amused at funny things, staking out what they think is the highest moral ground.

Now I imagine that some readers will think there's a false equivalence here. They'll agree that we should avoid the callousness of buffoonery, sure, but they may well resist the claim that priggishness is just as bad. After all, isn't having too little emotional empathy way worse than having too much? Indeed, don't we want people empathizing with real suffering and misfortune generally, and if they empathize too much, well, no harm, no foul? As long as people avoid clinical depression, how could their having more empathy than the norm even be a vice at all? And if their greater empathy comes at the cost of some amusement, who cares? Amusement is a trivial bit of fluff, and its tiny value just pales in the face of human suffering, doesn't it? Don't we want a morally better world, a world where more people care about and are kinder to others? And if that world has less amusement in it than a more callous world would, then so much the worse for humor!

Many people today do believe and say things like this, but they are wrong. A world with less humor and more empathizing would be a much worse world, frankly. There is significant underappreciated value in our sometimes empathizing less with, and being more amused by, pain, suffering, and misfortune. It is a powerfully effective way to cope with life's curveballs, and it's often the most appropriate way of responding to life's ultimate absurdity.

CHAPTER SEVEN

"Always Look on the Bright Side of Death"

How and Why to Find the Funny in Pain and Tragedy

> Life's a piece of shit
> When you look at it
> Life's a laugh and death's a joke, it's true
> You'll see it's all a show
> Keep 'em laughin' as you go
> Just remember that the last laugh is on you.[1]
>
> Sung by those being crucified at the end
> of *Monty Python's Life of Brian*

The last chapter laid out the basic conditions of good senses of humor and morality. Both are about recognizing and responding well to various features of the world. Both have roots in empathy, the proper exercise of which is a Goldilocks virtue: Where there is too much, you may tend toward priggishness and moralism; where there is too little, you may tend toward buffoonery and asshole-ism.

As I noted at the end of that chapter, many will think that if we must err it seems best to do so on the side of feeling too much empathy rather than too little. This is actually an egregious err, though. Yes, the buffoonish jerks of the world can really hurt others, which at least the priggish moralists tend not to do. But priggish moralists hurt themselves: In having too much empathy for others, they actually deprive themselves—and those they empathize with—of a significant source of value and well-being, which can be gotten by finding the funny in, and wisecracking about, misery, tragedy, pain, suffering, and even death. Our task here is to find out why, as well as how, these poor folks might go about finding the missing funny in their lives.

We'll start by taking a cue from those singing our opening hymn.

The Absurd

Thomas Nagel, in a justly famous article, defines the absurd in everyday life as involving "a conspicuous discrepancy between pretension or aspiration and reality."[2] Nagel's examples include a legislator giving a complicated speech in support of a resolution that has already passed; a major criminal who's been made president of a philanthropic organization; a telephone declaration of love to what is actually a recorded announcement; and "as you are being knighted, your pants fall down."[3]

This definition doesn't capture all the kinds of absurdities we encounter, of course. Dali's absurdist paintings don't contain such discrepancies, and neither do arguments reduced to absurdity by some logical maneuvering or someone's absurd suggestion that the Monkees were better than the Beatles. But it does capture quite a bit of the absurd in our lives, and it's a concept definitely worth exploring in detail, precisely because the examples Nagel gives can be funny. Think about being in the audience to witness the knighting, for example. Of course, the examples also reveal humiliations: imagine being the one knighted!

Now ordinarily we can rectify everyday absurdities like these either by modifying our aspirations or by changing reality. We could, for example, simply inform the legislator about the bill's passage and excise the speech from the public record, or we could remove the criminal from office once we find out his past. But there's one type of absurdity we cannot rectify: the absurdity of *life*. That's because our "sense that life as a whole is absurd arises when we perceive . . . an inflated pretension or aspiration which is inseparable from the continuation of human life and which makes its absurdity inescapable, short of escape from life itself."[4] In other words, we can't live life without the pretensions or aspirations that make it absurd, and we can't get rid of the absurdity without suicide.

What are our inflated pretensions or aspirations? That the things we take seriously, the things we value and the life projects we pursue, actually matter, full stop, that they are fully justified, secure, deeply grounded, and worth pursuing. But this edifice of value is shaky upon reflection. The absurdity of life "is supplied . . . by the collision between the seriousness with which we take our lives and the perpetual possibility of regarding everything about which we are serious as arbitrary, or open to doubt."[5]

We find ourselves in a world where we perceive and embrace various values, and those values provide us with the reasons we have to do whatever we do. However, we also have baked into our human nature a very special capacity, an ability to reflect on ourselves, on our projects and values. We thus have the option to take up a distinctive perspective on our lives, to take what I'll call the *step-back move* of self-consciousness. This is to see ourselves from outside of ourselves, by taking up a viewpoint that can pull the rug out from under our engaged, valuing, lived-in perspective. While we are in the throes of our projects and pursuits, we think we are fully justified in pursuing them: They are things worthy of pursuit, they truly matter, and they're on secure foundations. Call this the engaged perspective. But when we take the reflective perspective, we step back and look at our lives from the perspective of the universe, as it were, to see that we are embedded in a very specific and local time and place, with highly contingent features: built in a certain biopsychological way, born into a particular family and society, indoctrinated and educated in contextually located ways, and constructed as a kind of clockwork machine in a universe of cause and effect. Once we step back and recognize these facts about ourselves, we can also then see that our reasons for pursuing our particular projects—as opposed to what could easily have been a wildly different set of projects—are fragile, dubitable, possibly without any true foundation at all. They are borne of commitments and ways of thinking and reasoning that are given to us with our specific construction and station in life, but they themselves have mostly gone unquestioned, and so may well seem shaky or groundless under any kind of reflective critical examination. These are what I referred to in chapter 1 as our "ideological biases," the value commitments we tend to defend most fiercely against any kind of attack, yet also the commitments that the step-back move reveals may ultimately be trivial and arbitrary. To see all this is to see our lives as absurd, to appreciate that there is a vast discrepancy between our inflated pretensions of the deep and grounded worth of our projects and the distinct possibility that they are ultimately groundless and pointless. We have to live our lives by ignoring our doubts about their grounds and point, but those doubts remain unsettled and unsettling.[6]

Interestingly, Nagel thinks this absurdity isn't some great tragedy, to be addressed only by suicide or Buddhism. Rather, it's just a function of the most remarkable feature of our humanity, our ability to reflect on ourselves from outside ourselves, as it were. And if it turns out that, from the perspective of the universe, our lives don't matter, then that fact doesn't matter either. We can thus "simply approach our absurd lives with irony."[7] Indeed, as he notes merely in passing, the step-back perspective on our lives may be both sobering *and comical*.[8]

How can it be both? That it might be sobering is obvious. The sobriety comes out of the realization that our most serious life projects may well have no ultimate foundation: None of the things we've been devoting our lives to may matter one whit in the end. What a waste it all might be! What's comical, though, is how *vast* this particular disparity between pretentions and reality would be. To see our lives from the point of view of the universe is to see them as the crucified singers do. It's to see the downright silliness of all these pointless lives lived with such earnestness. Indeed, it's the bloody seriousness with which these pursuits are taken that makes it all so very comical. It's a reminder of the old joke:

Why are academic politics so vicious? Because the stakes are so low.

From the point of view of the universe, none of our stakes could be lower, which is what makes humans at the same time so vicious and yet so hilarious.[9]

We've thus got lots of absurdity around us, applying to everything from the mundane (the politician's speech, the love declared to a recording) to the most "valuable" human pursuits (perceived via the step-back move). These absurdities all involve a disparity between pretensions and reality, and all of them, it turns out, can be both sobering and comical, depending on where and how you focus your attention. To take an actual variation on one of Nagel's cases (something a friend of mine actually witnessed), suppose Ron is presenting a well-rehearsed and tightly argued keynote address about human dignity to five hundred rapt conference members, doing so without notes and in center stage, with his fly down the whole time. Perhaps the talk is filmed, so Ron watches it back later. He'd likely feel horrified, embarrassed, and humiliated, as he would surely focus his attention on the lack of dignity he himself seemed to embody, the very opposite of what he'd meant to convey with his words. But he may also come to see the hilarity in it all eventually, a hilarity many in the audience likely saw immediately, as long as he can just get himself to focus his attention on the irony of his topic in combination with its presentation, on the absurdity of giving a speech on such high-brow ideas in such a low-brow way. Now that's funny!

Still, it's also easy to imagine Ron just continuing to wallow in his humiliation and never coming to see the funny in any of it. And why shouldn't he? After all, it was humiliating. Indeed, it's also very easy to imagine—too easy to imagine—people who are never amused by the absurdities of life, those who see nothing funny in any of life's humiliations, pains, or miseries, people who simply refuse to lighten up ever. The stereotypes here are familiar. They include:

- *Feminists*: How many feminists does it take to screw in a lightbulb? One, and that's not funny!

- *Germans*: In heaven, they put the English in charge of jokes, the Italians in charge of food, and the Germans in charge of order. In hell, they put the English in charge of food, the Italians in charge of order, and the Germans in charge of jokes.

- *The Woke*:

  Q: Why can't you explain puns to kleptomaniacs?
  A: Kleptomania is a mental health issue, and the fact that you'd laugh at someone with a mental health issue tells me more about you than about them.
  (Ableist punch line: They take everything literally.)[10]

- *Pro-lifers* (from a story on a pro-life website about Chris Rock's latest Netflix comedy special, *Selective Outrage*):

  [Rock] said, "People always say, 'Chris, you shouldn't talk about abortion, it's a women issue.' I'm like . . . *I've paid for more abortions than any woman in this room.* When I go to the clinic, I say, 'Give me the usual.' When I go in there, they give me a punch card. Two more and I get a free smoothie."
  Bragging about how many preborn children you've killed isn't funny—but it does say something about how you view fatherhood and the women that you didn't care enough about to offer support or co-parenting when they conceived your child. This is yet another example of pro-abortion men using abortion as a sick tool in order to use women for their pleasure without any responsibility towards them.[11]

Members of these groups can indeed be very serious. Feminists, to take the first example, care deeply about establishing equality for women, securing women's rights of control over their bodies, and protecting women from rape and sexual exploitation. These are all very important pursuits. Why shouldn't feminists be serious about them? Inequality, abortion, rape, and sexual exploitation are all pretty goddam serious issues! Indeed, how could a horror like rape ever be funny?[12]

These are two more general questions that we can explore in order: (a) Why should we ever focus on the absurdities of life at all? And (b) even if we do, why view them as funny, rather than as merely sobering?

Reasons to Focus on the Absurd

Nagel rightly notes that it's psychologically impossible not to take your life seriously, so we don't need reasons to enter into the engaged perspective. We just are engaged. We're living our lives, they're the only lives we've got, so what choice do we have but to be steeped in them and the values driving them? But stepping back from them is an option: It is certainly possible not to step back, after all, possible to close our eyes to that perspective so as to avoid seeing that we're all just like ants—or Sisyphus—marching up and down a stupid hill, engaged in projects that have no ultimate point. So if it's the step-back move that reveals the absurdity of life, and it's possible not to make that move, why do it? Why not just stay steeped in our serious projects, the pursuits that give our lives its very meaning?

Here's a psychological problem with this head-in-the-sand move: the beans have been spilled. Once the possibility of making the step-back move is revealed, we can't help but make it, just like if we are told not to think about a pink elephant we can't not. But even if we are psychologically compelled to make the step-back move for a bit, that doesn't mean we have to wallow in it or ever take it up again. We all (have to) eventually move back to thoughts of our rents or mortgages, partnerships, jobs, and passions, and we probably won't revisit the pink elephant or the reflective perspective until reminded of it. So again, why engage in the step-back move at all (or for more than a brief bit as a philosophical exercise) if you're a feminist, say, or a social justice warrior or pro-life activist?

Here's another angle on the same point. Let's allow that perhaps you do have a reason to step back, a reason grounded in some value, perhaps that of philosophical curiosity. Given what Nagel says, the ultimate foundation of that value and reason will *also* be open to doubt, quite possibly arbitrary or pointless at its root. Being committed to the pursuit of making the step-back move, therefore, will be just as absurd a pursuit as any other. This means that people who pursue the thoroughly reflective life, always seeing life's absurdity and refusing to commit to promoting or pursuing any particular values (because it's all absurd) are actually living a life that is just as absurd as anyone else's: they are embracing and pursuing the value of the absurd, after all. So in light of this fact, why not just stay serious in your pursuits, whatever they are? You are in exactly the same pickle, from the perspective of the universe, as your absurdity-wallowing counterpart.

The answer (finally!) is as boring as it is true (or boring *because* it's true): You need to regularly take up both perspectives, engaged and reflective, in order to have a good, well-rounded life. I am not urging a well-rounded life as somehow intrinsically or objectively morally valuable, as some might, because that would simply invite another step-back move to see how even that value is ultimately dubitable or pointless. Instead, I am urging the pursuit of a well-rounded life as ultimately the most beneficial one for you.

There are obvious benefits to embracing and promoting values, to pursuing lives we take to be of genuine worth, to living as if things matter. Doing so provides structure to our days, it motivates us to get out of bed in the morning, it can be richly rewarding when the pursuits are successful, and, depending on how other-focused our pursuits are, it can help other people live far better lives, which can also generate personal gratification.

But there are benefits to embracing the absurdity of life through the step-back move as well. It keeps things in perspective, as it were, to see that none of it may really matter in the end. It encourages humility. This attitude enables us to see our common humanity: We're all in the same absurd boat together, it turns out, regardless of our significant value differences. We all have our pretentions undercut by reality. Retreating from the engaged pursuit of our pretentions can salve our own wounds when reality interferes, allowing setbacks to bounce off us more easily, and it may also increase our sympathetic concern for the plight of our fellow humans going through the same setbacks.

Both perspectives, the engaged and the reflective, can generate benefits. So why should you strike a balance between them, rather than just picking and sticking with one or the other perspective, the one you deem to reap the greatest rewards of the two? It's because there are also serious burdens attached to an exclusive focus on either one. Pursuing the single-mindedly engaged life may tend to leave you stressed out, setbacks to your pursuits will hit you harder, working closely with those who suffer will crank up your own personal distress levels, your anxiety about failure is likely to be high, and you'll tend to have more physiological problems (inflammation, headaches, ulcers) associated with these psychological traumas.[13] You also probably won't be much fun to be around, so you will have a harder time making and keeping good friends. These are real costs.

Alternatively, those who (seriously) pursue nothing but the absurd are no fun to be around either—nothing matters to them—and in the end they too are committed to promoting what they take to be the truly grounded values of the absurd lifestyle, pretentions reality can undercut as well. And if they don't think any other pursuits or people matter, well, then, they're likely to take moral pursuits less seriously too, so the rest of us will have a powerful reason to watch out for them. They are as likely to wrong us as to amuse us. The absurdist, in the end, will tend to be pretty lonely too, because who wants to be around someone who never views anything—including you and your pursuits—as mattering? Again, these are genuine and significant costs.

The best overall payoff thus comes from living a balanced life, a life involving serious pursuits that are regularly tempered by retreat to the reflective, absurdist perspective, the perspective from within which nothing really matters. These benefits give us good reasons to engage in the stepback move on a regular basis. The best balance between engagement and reflection will of course be different with different people, and I can't articulate the line for us all because there isn't (just) one. But there does need to be some kind of balance in order for people to get the richest overall package of lifetime benefits.[14]

Here's what we've got thus far. We've got reason to live a life balanced between taking up the engaged and reflective perspectives, between living our value-laden lives and seeing those pursuits as absurd. But recall Nagel's point about how we might respond to recognizing the absurdity of life: we can see it as sobering or as comical. I'm of course going to urge that we see it, at least sometimes, as comical. Why? Why not go with Camus instead? The answer again appeals to prudential reasons, and it's modeled on . . .

The Coping Mechanisms of First Responders

> The secret source of humor itself is not joy but sorrow. There is no humor in heaven.
>
> Mark Twain

Some paramedics and other first responders have sick senses of humor. They tell jokes about the dead or gravely injured while tending to them or investigating how they were killed. Their morbid senses of humor, as it turns out, enable them to cope with, and gain some psychological control over, the ongoing miseries and tragedies they have to deal with on a regular basis, which might otherwise emotionally overwhelm them.[15] To go about their business with a grim seriousness, fully emotionally engaged with their charges and responding as many of the rest of us would—with severe distress—to every single killing and maiming they experience would prevent them from doing their jobs, and it would likely psychologically break them. Indeed, there are several well-documented benefits to this sort of humor style (known as self-enhancing):

- It can moderate stress and its physical symptoms.[16]
- It has a greater anxiety-reducing effect than, and has an equal distress-reducing effect as, physical exercise.[17]

- It can enable the cognitive reappraisal of threats, which better enables coping with them.[18]
- It is an effective strategy when deployed in psychological and physical treatment or therapy, by, for example, increasing pain tolerance.[19]
- It increases one's sense of self-esteem, correlated positively with optimism and negatively with depression.[20]
- It is associated with a stable positive outlook, which increases resilience and overall psychological well-being.[21]

It is no wonder, then, that this humor style correlates highly with well-being, as it is the humor style enabling people to deal with the inevitable grotesqueries, miseries, pains, and tragedies of life, to gain some control over those events, and to keep a level head through trying times.

But how do these first responders do it? How do they greet misery, pain, and death with humor? They distract and detach. That is, they withdraw their ordinary emotional engagement so as to better treat the patients and victims and render themselves better able to cope with the suffering they face. Humor is perhaps the most effective method of emotionally distracting and detaching people from serious things like this. Humor is a powerful form of cognitive distraction, as it focuses one's attention on just some features of a situation in a way that can block negative emotional responses to other features of the situation.[22] Ordinarily, when you're in a bad mood or dealing with some difficult stressors, your thoughts focus on and reinforce your mood or stress. But when you are cognitively distracted—in some experiments by math problems, but in other more recent experiments by humor—the cognitive attentional spotlight that typically grounds or amplifies your negative moods or emotions is now focused elsewhere, allowing those negative moods or emotions, which crave nurturing through attention, to recede or dissipate. This is a very familiar psychological phenomenon, occurring, for instance, when we try to josh our significant others out of a bad mood, or when we try to distract our kids from their anxieties before a test with a dad joke. Humor is a great coping mechanism, and self-enhancing humor like this has obviously been found to produce numerous benefits to jokesters and wisecrackers.

It's crucial to note that the distraction provided by the first responders' dark humor does not at all mean they are distracted from other cognitive tasks, like providing the right fluids to a bleeding patient, or noticing evidence at a crime scene. It also doesn't mean they don't have a cognitive grip on what the patients or victims are going through. Their gallows humor is instead just a mood and emotion regulator, which, again, plays an extremely important role for them during the most stressful moments of their jobs. Thus do our heroes in the movies try to flick away fear, before they go on to do their jobs, with a lighthearted quip: "Snakes! Why'd it have to be snakes?" or "Yippee-Ki-Yay, motherfucker!"[23] Dark humor in the face of harrowing events can dampen emotional engagement without affecting cognitive engagement in the least.

So now we've got two different categories of reasons in favor of making light of these dark situations. The first category appeals to its prudential benefits, as such humor seems to better enable coping and increase well-being (or prevent a downward emotional spiral). But what these wisecrackers are doing has moral benefits as well, as it better enables them to help the people who have been hurt. Those in pain and misery are actually made better off by the lighthearted attitudes the responders have about their pain and misery.

Obviously, then, these reasons can generalize to the rest of us. In the face of misery, tragedy, suffering, and death, we may well have good prudential and moral reasons not only to see the absurd disparity between pretentions and reality, but also to see that disparity as comic, to see it in a lighthearted way. Doing so will enable us to cope better, to deal with these miseries in a more measured and functional fashion, and it may also enable us to help people going through those miseries in a more focused and effective way.

But how can we do so? Just like the first responders, we too must detach, withdrawing or dampening our ordinary emotional engagement with or distress for those who are affected. But here we need more details.

Putting on the Right Glasses

Here's the story thus far. Absurdities abound in our everyday lives, little disparities between pretensions and reality. These disparities are often comic. They can also be eliminated, in a way that also eliminates their funniness. But we humans have a distinctive capacity, borne of reflective self-consciousness, that enables us to glimpse the ineliminable absurdity of life and everything in it: From the perspective of the universe, it's all a vast disparity between pretentions and reality.

We can view this absurdity in two ways, soberly or comically. To be sobered is just to have your saliva dry up, to have the wind knocked out of you, to have your emotional buzz disappear, upon recognizing that all your earnest striving may be for naught. How to respond? One option, as Nagel notes, is suicide, but that's no solution; it's just an escape, and it renders one's entire existence absurd. Another option, as Nagel also hints, is to grasp for meaning that transcends the absurd in some kind of religious belief, Kierkegaard's "leap of faith." But this is no solution either, it's just a gasping grasp at a guess, what Camus called "philosophical suicide," a pretty nice zing. Camus's own solution was to rebel in the face of the absurd by pursuing meaning in life anyway, which Kierkegaard called "demoniac madness," not a half-bad zing as well.

I'm interested in a fourth response: amusement.

Nearly all emotions appraise things as mattering. Fear appraises threats, angry blame appraises slights to me and mine, admiration appraises good character, contempt appraises nasty character, pride and regret appraise personal accomplishments and failures. These emotions get off the psychological ground only when the appraised targets are taken to matter. I may not fear a threat if I'm suicidal; if I have no self-esteem, then I probably won't get angry if you disrespect me; if you're beneath my contempt, I won't be roused to feel it in response to your contemptible behavior.

Amusement isn't like these other emotions. It very often appraises things as funny insofar as they are taken to *not* matter. Your slipping on the banana peel is hilarious when only your ego gets bruised, but if you've cracked your head wide open too, the whole thing stops being funny. So while life's absurdity may undercut all the other mattering-based emotional appraisals, it actually enables the psychological conditions for amusement. But why and how should we respond to life's absurdity in the amused way, rather than in the sobered way?

The sobered response seems apt if we focus exclusively on the absurdity, the disparity between pretentions and reality. But this disparity could be tiny. Suppose I care only a little bit about most things, so that values play only a small role in my deliberations (instead I do most things in accordance with whatever impulses crop up). Were I to recognize from the reflective perspective that nothing really matters after all, it could be sobering, but it wouldn't be that funny. Where we find humor in life's absurdity, then, is not in perceiving the disparity as such, but in perceiving the *vastness* of the disparity, the fact that nearly all of us aim, with such earnest striving, to promote and pursue our "solid" and "well-grounded" values, and that these things matter so much to us. But when their potential meaningless or groundlessness is revealed, well, then, my god, how could it be that so many people have been so very, very wrong in such a spectacular way? The human condition is one big moron joke.

When the disparity between pretentions and reality is this vast, its humor is revealed, and it opens the door to a quite familiar response: "What can you do but laugh?" This is the response you might have when you and your friend think that you can move your pool table from one room to the other, but when you try dragging it the table's legs snap and it collapses, destroying both the table and the floor beneath it. As you sit there looking at each other in the quiet that follows, through the cloud of dust and debris, you might both just start laughing.[24] It's the response you might have when you trip over your wedding gown while walking down the aisle. It's the response you might have when you try to let loose a sly fart at the dinner table and wind up shitting your pants. And it's the response you might have when the radiation you've been undergoing for cancer actually gives you another form of cancer.

I know full well that not everyone (perhaps hardly anyone) will think there's any humor in some of these events, especially the last one. Everyone can see all the relevant properties here—the destroyed pool table, the splayed bride, the shart, the new form of cancer—but many may not yet see any comedy in them. Here's an analogy, then, to illustrate how to get there. During the American Civil War, depressed soldiers were sometimes prescribed glasses with rose-colored tints.[25] Seeing their world through "rose-colored glasses" significantly raised their spirits (thus the phrase). Today we know that a variety of colored tints on glasses have different effects on the moods and emotions of the people who wear them. Different tints produce different responses in people viewing the same pictures.[26] We see all the same properties, but we have different affective responses when viewing them through different colored lenses.

The relevant "lenses" for what I've been talking about have to do with emotional empathy and its expression. We may see the very same properties from our different perspectives (engaged and reflective), and yet have wildly different responses to what we see, depending on whether we have our "emotional empathy lenses" on. When we're emotionally engaged with and vulnerable to those we know and love, and they go through something distressing, then we'll see reason to respond to their pain and suffering with distress ourselves. If we take the step-back move, however, and we focus instead not just on the sobering disparity between the earnest and pointless pursuits of all those human ants but on its vastness, then the comic landscape becomes visible to us as well and our responses are open to change. What we humans start to resemble in that instant are essentially cartoon characters—Elmer Fudd, Wile E. Coyote, or Scratchy—and if we distract or detach from our emotional engagement with those "characters," then the misery, tragedy, and suffering they undergo can be enjoyed as downright hilarious. That's right, to get there, we may need to take off our "emotional empathy lenses," and put on our "psychopath lenses." Recognizing the comedy in the absurdity of life may require emotional detachment, even downright callousness, at least for a bit, what Henri Bergson called "the momentary anaesthesia of the heart."[27]

A good sense of humor is one that can—ordinarily, ably, and appropriately—toggle back and forth between engaged emotional empathy and its detachment. But you might well wonder how easy it could be to turn our emotional engagement with others on and off like this. Aren't we just stuck in our emotionally engaged ways with one another? As it turns out, no, we aren't. Psychologists easily induce the dampening of empathy in laboratory conditions.[28] In such conditions, people can turn on their empathy in response to incentives.[29] But in the real world this ability is widely evident as well. Medical professionals tend to turn it off while at work and then turn it on at home.[30] Managers of large companies turn it off when planning large-scale cutbacks and layoffs. Military generals turn it off when planning large-scale battles where they know that significant numbers of soldiers will have to die in order to secure the victory (imagine feeling vicarious distress for every wounded or dying soldier under one's charge).[31] Workers at insurance companies do it when engaged in risk assessment and determining the relative worth of people's lives. And people switch off their empathy when they cross the street so as to avoid the eyes of a panhandler or homeless person. Indeed, to simply quote the title of one article on this topic, "Empathy Is Hard Work: People Choose to Avoid Empathy Because of Its Cognitive Costs."[32]

This is a special resource we have.[33] We can withdraw our emotional engagement with others when it just gets too exhausting, or in times of stress and strain. This may seem like a bad thing, and sometimes it is (people cry out for more emotional empathy from their doctors, and many medical schools implement empathy training as a result[34]). But sometimes, as with the first responders, generals and presidents, and managers and insurance companies, it can be a good thing, as it's the only way to get tough jobs done, jobs that by their very nature require that we think of others, in a way, as objects, "to be managed or handled or cured or trained."[35]

It can also, surprisingly, be a good thing for *others* when we withdraw our empathy for them. The surgeon focused on how her patient feels about the cancerous organ she's removing will be distracted from the job needing doing. And refusing to empathize any more with someone truly stricken by grief may better enable them to move on with their lives.

But it may also be a great kindness to someone if you withdraw or dampen your emotional engagement with them and wisecrack about the absurdity you can see in their painful or traumatic situation. It may get them to see the humor in it as well, which could serve to distract them from it in a way that enables them to cope more effectively with it. I'll provide some illustrations later.

Nevertheless, one might still think that some tragedies and miseries just aren't funny, no matter how you look at them. Or, at the very least, people of goodwill ought not be amused by them. I disagree with both sentiments, and I'll argue against them by stupidly discussing one of the most powerful examples in their favor.

Finding the Funny in Rape?

"There's nothing funny about rape," goes the oft-heard saying. And of course many professional comedians have taken that to be a thrown gauntlet: George Carlin, Ricky Gervais, Dave Chappelle, Sarah Silverman, and Joan Rivers have all made jokes about rape, just to try to prove that saying wrong.

Or have they? Actually, while they use the word "rape" in their jokes, they aren't really jokes about rape. Instead, they are jokes about cartoonish images (Carlin asking us to imagine Porky Pig raping Elmer Fudd);[36] hypocritical religiosity (an ultra-religious critic told Gervais he'd be laughing at him when the devil raped him in hell, oblivious to the fact that it meant the critic would be in hell as well, and the devil would likely prefer to rape him over the "fat old comedian"[37]); restrictive gender or ethnic roles (Chappelle's joke about a serial rapist in Houston who was only raping men: seven men had actually come forward to report it, which meant, according to Chappelle, that there must have been *thousands* of men who'd actually been raped by the guy; and also Silverman's famous joke in *Jesus Is Magic* that "I was raped by a doctor, which is so bittersweet for a Jewish girl"); or self-deprecation (Joan Rivers joked that a would-be rapist had asked her if they could just be friends).[38] It's not the act of rape itself that these comedians are joking about; rather, they are using transgressive language about rape and rapists to focus our laughter on other laughable items.

Once we focus on actual rape, though, many will insist that it's impossible to find anything funny at all about it. My main focus in the book has obviously been on wisecracks, not on the prepared routines of professional comedians, so the question for us is whether something as heinous as rape could in fact ever be the subject of a funny wisecrack. And even if it could, what reason could anyone ever possibly have to make such a wisecrack in the first place?[39]

Good questions. To answer them, I want to start by considering funny anecdotes we often tell about our own past (nonrape) pains. We often relay stories about humiliation and suffering we've gone through, but in funny ways, by making light of them and, in so doing, ourselves—sort of. Let me illustrate. When I slipped on the ice and broke three ribs one morning about ten years ago walking down the driveway to bring in the paper, it was awful:

horribly painful and downright humiliating. I couldn't do much of anything for a good three weeks, and after that for several months I could only very painfully breathe and hobble about. But in recounting this story to others, I tried to make it into a comically exaggerated failure. I told people that, as I was flying through the air in slow motion, I could see my feet above my head, I shouted in a deep and slowed-down voice, "NOOOOOOOOO!" and right before I landed, I thought, "Man, if I were watching this happen to someone else, it would be hilarious!" My "oooofffff" upon landing stirred the shrubbery, and as I lay there in stabbing pain, I could hear echoes of the Tom Petty refrain, "Now I'm freeeeee! Free fallin'!"[40]

We tell such anecdotes as a way of presenting a particular self to others, and when others tell such stories to us, we are able to gather data about them to understand, and perhaps ratify, their presented selves, to find out who they are and what they care about.[41] Telling anecdotes (tailored to fit the conversational context) can create rapport with others.[42] Indeed, the most successful forms of rapport building are the self-deprecating versions of personal stories, as they reveal vulnerabilities to which others tend to respond with sympathy and affection.[43] These personal anecdotes

> present a self with an ability to laugh at problems and overcome them . . . an admirable character trait. Self-effacing personal anecdotes redound to conversational rapport and positive face for the teller in several ways at once.[44]

Neal Norrick, the linguist who made this point, goes on to relay several recorded conversations between adult friends that illustrate them. One involves the familiar sort of story about the acquisition of information about sex:

JIM: When I was in the seventh grade somebody sold me . . . one of these soft *art* erasers under the pre[tense of] telling me it was a *condom* y'know hahahahaha. And I was [*curious*] y'know to see what it was like. And uh "I don't see how you *use* this."
VERA: What was it? It was an eraser?
JIM: Yeah, a real *soft* eraser. Y'know the kind that you can . . . that's malleable?
TEDDY: But not *that* malleable.
JIM: Right. Right.
VERA: Your parents never *did* tell you anything though, did they?[45]

Jim is telling a story that reveals his total sexual ignorance as a kid (while also allowing innuendos to run freely). It's embarrassing, but he can laugh about it now, and it endears him to his friends, providing an opening for them to add a few more wisecracks as well.

Telling personal, self-deprecating anecdotes about past pains in a light-hearted, humorous way has clearly positive bonding power. But these are, in the long run, relatively low stakes examples, my fall and Jim's sexual ignorance. Could something as horrific as rape, whose effects can be profound and lasting, and whose very occurrence manifests misogyny and psychological and physical trauma, as well as a systemic power imbalance between men and women, ever be the topic of a humorous personal anecdote like this?

It's not only possible but actual. In recent years, some rape survivors have begun talking about their experiences comedically on stage, both in theaters (as one-woman shows) and in stand-up venues. Kelly Bachman and Dylan Adler put together a comedy musical revue called *Rape Victims Are Horny Too*, which aimed to show, as Bachman put it, that "survivors are not just, like, wilted flowers, who are sad, suffering, victims all the time," that they can be silly, defiantly joyful, and, yes, horny.[46] In 2019, several women performed stand-up about their experiences in a show called *Rape Jokes by Survivors*, hosted by the Upright Citizens Comedy Brigade.[47] And a slate of comedians, under the group name "Rape Is Real and Everywhere," sold out comedy shows across Canada in 2017 and beyond.[48]

Performers in this last group, discussing why they do what they do, cited many of the reasons I've already given in favor of finding the funny in trauma: It invites support and solidarity from sympathetic audiences, it communicates a powerful experience (inviting empathy), and it attacks or undermines "rape culture." But they note an additional and powerful reason: To insist on the mantra that "rape jokes are never funny" is to reinforce the silence, shame, and secrecy that surround rape. Their jokes aim to thwart those bad effects:

The show tackles rape myths in hilarious and heartbreaking ways, really illustrating how cultural perceptions of rape affect survivors. One comic has a hard-hitting joke about feeling guilty she wasn't "raped enough." There was no stranger down a dark alley, no assailant hiding in the bushes. If only she'd been a little more raped, she said, then she'd feel like she had a right to talk about it. Part of the power of the show is that it exposes just how ridiculous rape myths like this are, and begins to create a new narrative.[49]

There have been complaints about the show—of course!—but they've mostly come not from other rape survivors but from people who are concerned on their behalf. Nevertheless, the atmosphere at these shows has been "one of solidarity and support." And they are evidently enjoyable. As one person in the audience described the show, "I found it 100 per cent more funny than being raped."[50]

These are wisecracks about rape, and they are funny. They also empower their makers and bond them to their fellow survivors and audience members. They are a powerful strategy for coping with trauma, of restoring control—authorship—to the narrative of the wisecrackers' lives. These all strike me as incredibly compelling reasons in favor of their making such wisecracks.

We've now seen why there might be good reason to make a wisecrack about rape, albeit only for those who are survivors. In their voices (and only in their voices), these wisecracks are personal anecdotes, funny ways of describing their own traumas. But how can there be funny in them? Where indeed could it be located? And how might others find it too?

The key to finding the funny in personal anecdotes of past pain is that those who tell it and those who hear it have to interact with one another in distinctive and complicated ways, both cognitive and emotional. Go back to my broken ribs story. When I exaggerate its features in the way I do, I'm basically telling a story about a character. Sure, that character is "me," but it's an exaggerated version of me, one whose head space I'm inviting you into through my detailed descriptions. That is, my descriptions of the events as I saw them invite you to see them through my eyes as well. But as I do so, I detach myself emotionally from the actual pain and distress that I underwent, which enables me to make the character I'm drawing more like a cartoon character, someone whose actions and experiences are made more fantastical in a way that generates comic effect. And when you pick up on the fact that I'm telling a funny anecdote, you recognize that I am encouraging you to detach emotionally from the pain of me-the-actual-person in the same way as well. When you do so, what you'll see is just the comic absurdity I aim for you to see: the significant disparity between my pretensions (walking purposefully down the driveway) and reality (a spectacular failure at walking down the driveway). My comic exaggeration in telling the tale draws attention to, and aims to heighten, that disparity.

What's necessary, therefore, for you to find the funny in my story is that (a) you have to be able to take up the perspective of me-the-character, that is, you have to be able to relate in some way to me and how I experienced things; (b) you have to block yourself from emotional vulnerability to the painfulness of my actual experience (as that'll just cancel the comedy); and (c) you have to attend to—as I intend for you to—the heightened disparity between pretensions and reality. If you can do all of this, our shared amusement can bond us.

These factors help explain why attempted wisecracks about the experience of having been actually raped or tortured or otherwise gruesomely attacked (if survivors even try to make them) to nonsurvivors are tough both to make and pull off, and why some people refuse to find them funny or they become upset on behalf of the performers. Some audience members are either unable or unwilling to share in the perspective of someone describing her rape; even if they are able, they just won't emotionally detach from the performer's experiences; and even if they do that, they won't attend to the disparity between pretentions and the reality of victimhood as applying in a heightened (and so funny) way to a victim, who was, after all, a passive recipient of cruelty.[51]

The conditions I've given thus far for finding the funny in pain and trauma aren't yet enough, however. That's because sometimes we tell personal tales of woe quite seriously. I may tell you the ice-slipping story as I lay in the hospital, wheezing, like this: "I was going out to get the morning paper, and I didn't see the ice, but as I planted one foot, it just lost any traction. Both legs flew up, everything was in slow motion, but I landed hard on my back, losing my breath. I knew it was bad as soon as I hit the ground, but I didn't know how bad. Three broken ribs!" When I tell you this story in this way, you'd better not laugh! Sympathy is what I expect instead of amusement. What matters for your success in navigating this terrain is your ability to determine what context we're in, Camus or comic.

Delivery style may do the trick, but even that may not be enough, as some people use the same delivery in both contexts. Think of the dry wits you know, capable of delivering the funny in a completely somber or sober way. When done well, this delivery can actually increase funniness. These folks risk regular misunderstanding, however.

The contextual determination cannot necessarily be found in content or delivery. It can only be found in the wisecracker's, yes, intentions and motivations. This is why it can be so hard for people with deficits in theory of mind to detect the funny in the exaggeration, sarcasm, role playing, and theatricality of some humorous anecdotes. This includes those with autism, Williams syndrome, and right hemisphere brain damage.[52] And a failure to detect which context you're in can lead to genuine hurt, as when you take someone seriously who is in fact joking about their experience, or worse, when you don't take someone seriously who *isn't* joking.

All of this is of course incredibly subtle and complicated, but the complexity helps explain why some people have a really hard time ever finding anyone else's distressing experiences funny, and it also explains why they find some distressing things funny that aren't being shared as such. First off, appropriately sharing in the humor of a painful experience requires some sophisticated empathic skills, of both the cognitive and emotional stripes. You have to be able to know what context you're in, which requires the ability to discern the teller's intentions, to know whether they're being serious or playful, and you have to be able to take up their perspective through the telling of the anecdote, to see what things were like for them. This is all just cognitive empathy. You then have to be able to feel their pain, but only in the hilarious way! This is the most delicate of empathic dances. Ordinarily, when you describe to me a distressing experience, I emotionally empathize with you, which means I render myself susceptible to feeling "your" distress alongside you, for the reasons that you feel it. But what if you describe to me an experience that would ordinarily be distressing, yet it's something that you're wisecracking about instead, given that you are emotionally detached from its distressing features? Then for me to emotionally empathize properly with you, I have to not feel distress at those distressing features. That is, emotional empathy in such circumstances requires, ironically, that I emotionally detach from your pain or trauma along with you. And this is what's necessary for me to attend to the absurd disparity between your pretentions and reality, and so to find the funny in your pain.

As I say, this is awfully sophisticated stuff. And the different ways people fail at it can be predicted, if I'm right, as manifestations of different empathy-related impairments or failures. Those who have a tough time with cognitive empathy (theory of mind) are predicted by my model to have a tough time determining whether people who tell personal anecdotes are in serious or joking contexts, and they will also have trouble taking up the perspectives of, and so identifying with, those who are relating their cartoonish tales. Indeed, this is in fact the case. Sarcasm, in particular, can be tough for people with autism or right hemisphere damage, among others, to pick up on.[53] Alternatively, those who have a tough time with emotional empathy— such as those in the dark triad or with fronto-temporal dementia—also have a tough time not being amused all the time by serious tales of tragedy and woe. While they can take up other people's perspectives to a limited extent, and so tend to be able to determine whether the storyteller intends to put it in a playful or serious context, and they can also see what it was like for those relating such painful events, they just don't care about the distressing or painful bits because they are in a constant state of emotional detachment from others, so someone's tale of woe will always seem to them to be an occasion for amusement, regardless of whether it's meant as such. When I'm telling my painful tale in a wisecracking context, I'm inviting you to be amused with me. When I tell it seriously, I'm inviting you to sympathize with and be distressed alongside me. When I tell it seriously, as a tale about me and not my cartoon character, and you laugh, then you're laughing at

188 ‹ CHAPTER SEVEN

me. That is, you're amused by my idiocy or inferiority, and not my cartoon character's idiocy or inferiority, as would be the case when I tell the tale humorously. This is how those impaired in empathy of both sorts are correctly predicted by my model to respond.[54]

What the model predicts for those with bipolar disorder depends on the pole. If you have an excess of emotional empathy in response to other people's distress—that is, if you feel too much distress in response to the painful or traumatic experiences of others—then you'll likely find very little, if anything, funny about someone's meant-to-be-funny personal anecdotes about painful episodes. In other words, you're likely to have a tough time emotionally detaching from other people's distressing experiences, even when those who have gone through those experiences are doing so and are inviting you to do so as well. This prediction accurately describes the dampened amusement of many people with clinical depression. However, if your empathic capacities become deeply impaired, as is true of those in manic states, you are likely to find (as do those in the dark triad) lots of distressing things funny, given that you are emotionally detached from the distressing experiences of others generally, regardless of whether the tales of those experiences are told seriously or jokingly. And this is in fact also what occurs.

I've been talking about those with impairments in cognitive and emotional empathy. But what about those who have unimpaired capacities but don't properly exercise them? I'm referring to those who are capable of reading your intentions and sussing out that you're in a playful wisecracking context, but when they hear you tell your hilarious tale of woe, they nevertheless respond to you with concern, sympathy, or distress instead of amusement. They refuse to emotionally detach alongside you. They refuse to *play*. Instead, they treat you like a hurt child. "Oh, that's not funny!" they may say, "Oh, you poor thing, that's horrible! How can you laugh at that?" They make you feel like a naive and insensitive buffoon, when you are nevertheless trying like mad simply to cope with the pain you underwent. They want to drag you down to their glum level. They have bad senses of humor.

These people's empathy—the feature they often most prize in themselves—is actually generating the wrong responses, and it prevents them from amusement, closer affiliation, and human growth. When we wisecrack about our pains, we are emotionally detaching from our distress, yet these people remain focused on it, and not on us. They are the so-called kind, caring, and "just concerned for you" people in our lives. But these so-called morally good traits actually prevent them from being our fellows, those with whom we can be most deeply and genuinely interpersonally intertwined.

Indeed, I think, they aren't even that morally good. That's because true kindness and caring, for example, occasionally require empathically driven emotional *detachment* from the distressing pains of our actual fellows, so that we might revel together instead in the affiliative and bonding amusement that's available to us once we focus on the absurdities of our lives. It may be that in our darkest hours all we want is to share some amusement with others at our plights, where actual kindness and empathy require the sputteringly uttered, "What can you do but laugh?" And having a close someone with whom we can share in that amusement, well, that can be heartwarming and empowering, better enabling us to cope with that darkness, serving as well to bond us even more closely. Those who refuse to engage in such humor out of a sense of "kindness," "sympathy," and "concern" may actually be withholding true kindness, sympathy, and concern. Their moral sensibilities may be just as stunted as their humor sensibilities.

I've had to practice what I preach. A few years ago, I was diagnosed with aggressive prostate cancer, and I had to have surgery to remove the betraying beast, a radical prostatectomy.[55] When I told my closest friends about what was going on with me, I could stand a wee bit of sympathetic concern for a wee bit, but what I most craved were good wisecracks. And I finally got a few: "Leave it to you to get the weakest, most treatable cancer there is," said one friend. "C'mon out for a drink," said another, "you're not dead yet." "That's a radical strategy to get a break from your administrative duties," said a third. These people aren't just assholes; they are my dearest asshole friends. And my gratitude for their emotionally detached wisecracks about my diagnosis was enormous. Just like my cancer-riddled prostate.

Conclusion

My aim in this chapter has been to show how and why to find the funny in—and wisecrack about—pain, distress, suffering, misery, and death. We can get there through the judicious deployment and detachment of the various features associated with empathy. The relevant kind of humor here is absurdist, located in the vastness of the disparities rife in our lives between pretentions and reality, disparities applying to everything from everyday falls and failures to our very existence. We can get to this amusing spot with one another, ironically, by an empathically sourced emotional detachment, where we focus on cartoonish accounts of our pains and miseries. Being amused by absurdity of this sort can contribute significantly to personal coping, interpersonal affiliation, and moral bonding. But the bottom line is that such absurdity is funny. Amused enjoyment of the absurd can generate far greater value in our lives than it's been given credit for. So lighten up!

But don't lighten up *too* much. Don't become a full-blown psychopath! Too little emotional empathy for others may leave in you in a heightened amused state, true, but a lot of your amusement will then wind up being at actual people, not with them, and that too is a surefire recipe for missing out on the fullest interpersonal values that the Goldilocks version of emotional empathy can deliver.

Conclusion

To conclude the book, I'll bring together its various arguments and themes into an interwoven payoff, a punch line to this wisecrack, if you will.

I have focused throughout primarily on wisecracks, of course, those typically improvised bits of spontaneous, conversational, and interpersonal wit that make up the bulk of our humor lives. Previous work on humor in philosophy and psychology has focused on jokes, those canned bits of material we interrupt our conversations to tell or perform for one another. Both wisecracks and jokes can be funny. But only wisecracks really generate the kinds of moral trouble that can hurt feelings, stir up angry blame, corrode friendships, and lead to cancellations or worse. Wisecracks are ways of interacting with other people, but they are distinctive because what makes wisecracks aesthetically good—amusing—is often the very same thing that can make them morally bad. They tweak or ignore some of the norms that sustain our interpersonal lives, such as our expectations of trust and honesty, our desires for respect and equal worth, our concern to be viewed as the particular people we are (rather than as members of some group). These features make them very different, and far more interesting, than jokes.

I haven't said much about professional comedians in this book, as they are mostly joke tellers. But some, quite interestingly, are better construed as wisecrackers, on my formulation. Dave Chapelle is perhaps the best and most famous of the professional wisecrackers, someone who weaves anecdotes and arguments in a conversational style with his audience that feels deeply (inter)personal (and hilarious). He built up a powerful and intimate relationship with that audience over the years, with no recognizable difference between him and his comic persona, so that people thought (and think) that they were sharing intimate moments with him through the revelations, vulnerabilities, arguments, and downright empathic concern he extended during his many brilliant comedy specials. But this sense of intimacy was also the source of much anger upon the release of his 2021 special *The Closer*, as he seemed now to some of his audience as if he were hypocritically undercutting the empathy he so often demanded in his humor on behalf of members of the Black community by doubling down on mockery of members of the trans community, people with whom it seems he ought to have shared a close bond, people who have also been the victims of violence, oppression, and marginalization. It was, to many fans, a betrayal, and this perceived immorality seemed to make his attempts at humor in that special gut-punching to them, and so just not (very) funny.

Whether or not this was the right reaction to that special, or to Chappelle in general, my point here is simply to draw attention to this angry response as the risked outcome of many wisecracks. It was one important aim of this book to make explicit the moral source that many of those risks have, in deception, stinging, and stereotyping. But it was also another, more important aim of the book to argue for why it's very often nevertheless worth *taking* those risks. Wisecracks also "risk" bringing great joy and value to our lives. They can forge and reinforce our very best relationships, give us strength, help us cope, and get us to empathize with each other. Indeed, I think wisecracks are a key to recognizing our common humanity. But let me back up and review before returning at the end with some actual support for that last pretentious remark.

Here are the primary takeaways of the book:

- Wisecracks can make moral trouble. That's because their funniness sometimes comes directly from their wronging properties. But if wisecracking can wrong people, then who cares if it's funny? It's all just a bit of trivial fun, isn't it, so if it is immoral, it's got to go! My primary motivation was to explore whether there was an adequate defense of some wisecracking that could overcome this familiar moral complaint.
- First things first: If wisecracks could be funny, we had to find out why, and that required a detailed exploration in chapter 1 of what makes things funny in general (which includes jokes and inadvertent humor as well). After investigating radical subjectivist, intersubjectivist, and objectivist theories of the funny, I came to the conclusion that the world of humor is wildly pluralistic: many, many properties can be funny-makers, in many, many different combinations and weights. I listed as many of those as I could under the kitchen sink theory. The radically disparate nature of this list, however, led to the more pressing questions: Why are these properties on the list together? What unifies them as funny-makers? And the answer made reference to our sense of humor (suitably scrubbed) in the human theory of humor: These are the properties that a developed, refined, and unobstructed human sense of humor would respond to with amusement. Only this

theory makes sense of the kinds of humor disagreements we have and the kinds of reasons to which we point in trying to resolve them. And only this theory recognizes our sense of humor as a human universal, something we share in common, something distinctive to our species.

- Wisecracks are made funny when they contain certain properties, in certain amounts and combinations, on the kitchen sink list. But if some of those on the list are immoral properties, why doesn't that just disqualify their wisecracks from being funny? This was the question motivating chapter 2, in which I investigated the general relation between the funny and the moral. And here again we saw reinforced the value of focusing on wisecracks over jokes, as jokes in and of themselves can't wrong people, at least in the sort of way that makes blaming anger appropriate. Not even joke tellings are that relevant to morality in this way, as their funniness is mostly determined by performance standards, and not from interpersonal relations as such. Wisecracks are morally troubling because they are made by moral agents to other moral agents, and because these are ways of interacting with others, they can go morally wrong. So what is the correct view of the general relation between immorality and the funniness of a wisecrack? Does immorality always kill or reduce humor? No. The Correct View, I argued, was much more nuanced: Sometimes immorality can reduce the humor of a wisecrack (as in the Carrie prank), but sometimes immorality can make wisecracks funnier. Indeed, sometimes, wisecracks can't be funny at all without their immorality. This is because some wisecracks have as their funny-makers the very same properties as their immorality-makers, and it's in these cases that we need to decide which is the right overall response to have: amusement or anger?
- To illustrate and vindicate these points, I took us on a guided tour of specific funny-and-immorality-making properties found in familiar sorts of wisecracks: deliberate deception, mockery's aimed-for sting, and stereotype exploitation. Chapter 3's task was to show how the deliberate deception in leg-pulling and pranking humor is actual (and not faux) deception that shares the same immorality-making property as all other cases of deception, namely, it risks damaging people's exercise of their autonomy. When I block you from seeing some truth, no matter whether my aim is to be funny or not, I risk causing you to fumble ignorantly about in the world and hurt yourself. That is a moral reason against deliberate deception, period. But that very same feature, deliberate deception, is what makes (some) leg-pulling and pranks funny, as it's what reveals people's gullibility in believing ridiculous things. In many cases, this sort of humor can be justified in the face of its

immorality-making properties, as the risks of damage are so very tiny, and the rewards (to both leg-puller and leg-pulled) may well be worth it (for example, they may promote the values of becoming a more critical listener and talker).

- The second illustration came from stinging mockery in chapter 4. Mockery aims to publicly highlight someone's flaws, and so it aims at a kind of sting in the mocked person, ranging from embarrassment to humiliation. Aiming at such a thing is typically immoral, though, so mockery has to be funny in order to generate any kind of defense against this moral complaint. And indeed, mockery can absolutely be funny. Further, we engage in it all the time, especially with friends and family. These affiliative forms of mockery, where we are all mutually vulnerable to it, are interpersonally valuable, generating a host of moral and prudential benefits. And these benefits, along with mockery's funniness, can sometimes easily be enough to outweigh the moral weight of its sting. And yet, one might well think, given mockery's horrifying human history, where it's mostly been directed at those who have disabilities or who have undergone various misfortunes, mockery at such people should be ruled out, permanently left off the moral table. There are three ways to characterize and ground this objection—appealing to desert, punching up/down, and piling on—and while only the last objection to mockery is compelling (and counsels heavily against a certain sort of cancel culture), it didn't actually support the sweeping moral worry in question, that certain people can never permissibly be mocked. And indeed, once I explored and endorsed the social model of disability, its spirit of inclusiveness actually seemed to counsel that not only is it sometimes permissible to mock people of disability or misfortune, it may actually (sometimes) be morally required. To fail to do so might well deprive such people of genuine interpersonal and personal benefits, which itself would constitute even more disabling and discriminatory treatment.

- The third illustration came from stereotyping humor, in chapter 5. Here, due to the previous literature on the topic, I expanded my range to include not only stereotyping wisecracks but also the telling of certain racial, ethnic, sexual, and gendered jokes. Again, what makes these jokes and wisecracks funny, when they are, is the exploitation of stereotypes, which is also what's morally objectionable about them. So how are we to view the relative weight of these two appraisals? Should we angrily blame stereotyping wisecrackers or join in on their amusement? The answer I gave couldn't have been a more weaselly response: *It depends.* But there's no other answer to give, given the wildly varying contexts in play. Sometimes racists and sexists direct these jokes at the targets of the stereotypes, but sometimes they just share them with each other. Sometimes people of goodwill share them quietly with each other to play with the thrilling danger, but sometimes they do so as a way of making fun of racists and sexists. And sometimes the targets of racism and sexism share the jokes with others as a way of subverting those stereotypes. What matters most for moral purposes in each case, I argued, are the intentions and motives of those engaged in the exchange. And while there may well be risks of harm involved, even among those with the best of intentions, wisecracking in this vein might still be justifiable, given (a) its funniness, (b) its degree of risk, and/or (c) the possible moral and prudential benefits of doing so (including subversion of the stereotypes). This is an issue of enormous complexity, though, and I don't pretend to have dealt with it adequately.

• Having surveyed the three primary immoral properties that can serve double duty as funny-makers, and having tried to make a case for why engaging in such wisecracks even so might sometimes (or often) be justified overall, the final part of the book turned to a broader investigation into the value of humor in our lives, for why we should probably seek it out more than we do, as well as where to find it. The human theory of humor made essential appeal to the human sense of humor to explain the existence of the funny-makers on the kitchen sink list. It was the best way to explain the difference between what's funny and what's not. But senses of humor also come in good and bad forms. Some of these evaluations are purely descriptive: Just as I have a poor sense of sight (having worn thicker and thicker glasses since the age of six), so too I may have a poor sense of humor, where these both simply refer to my abilities to perceive the world around me relative to the average human. Many people with descriptively bad senses of humor have them because of various empathic impairments. Their difficulties with empathy make it hard for them to appreciate certain types of humor, and it also occasionally has them responding to "comic reasons" that actually don't exist. As it turns out, their empathic impairments are precisely what also tend to cause them to have poor senses of morality: they either take too seriously, or not seriously enough, the immoral properties of wisecracks, and they sometimes respond to "moral reasons" that don't actually exist.

These results bring together and support many of the themes of the book. Most importantly, they highlight yet again why studying wise-cracks is so important (and why the lack of previous work on it is rather surprising): Wisecracks are the arena in which the funny interacts with the moral in virtue of the way they both tap into empathy. A flawed sense of empathy predicts both a flawed sense of humor and a flawed sense of morality. This isn't to say that there aren't funny psychopaths: the Joker comes to mind as an easy (if fictional) case. But psychopaths tend to have, overall, generally bad senses of humor, insofar as they totally miss out on a wide range of incredibly valuable funny-makers, namely, those in the affiliative and self-enhancing camps. Good senses of humor need to recognize and respond to these as well, but to do so, they need to be attached to a well-functioning sense of empathy.

- These people with empathic impairments who have descriptively bad senses of humor aren't criticizable, it's important to repeat. But some people with bad senses of humor are criticizable, namely, prigs and buf-foons. Their empathy is perfectly functional, but they resist its deliver-ances. Prigs overweigh the immoral properties in wisecracks, whereas buffoons overweigh the funny properties. Failing to take immorality sufficiently seriously can be bad, for obvious reasons: people matter, and buffoons don't fully appreciate that fact. It may seem that prigs' re-fusal to respond with amusement where immorality is in play isn't such a bad thing, but it is as well, because they are actually refusing to en-gage with people on an important and deeply human level. Sometimes our humanity and psychological health demand a shared detachment from all this mattering, from the overweening seriousness of the world, so that we can come (together) to see just how absurd all of this earnest striving is, how the high and mighty pretensions that structure our lives may mean nothing at all. What we should do in such cases is just lighten up and *play*.

Which brings us round, finally, to our common humanity (preten-tiousness trigger warning!). It's widely known how many jokes just don't translate well in various parts of the world. Even when all the language and idioms have been cleared up, and even when all the relevant background in-formation has been brought to the fore, some jokes just can't be found to be funny by some people. The funniness of jokes isn't universal, it seems. If you don't find a joke funny, that's all there is to it sometimes. Once you've rec-ognized all the properties of the joke itself, and you're not amused, there's nowhere else to look for any funny.

But there is an additional place to look when it comes to cracking the code of wisecracks, and that's because, in addition to all the facts about the crack itself, there are facts about the crack-*maker* that matter as well. These properties also contribute to how one should respond, overall, to wisecracks. So even though the crack itself may sound like an insult, a quick determination of the maker's intentions and motives may reveal otherwise. Even though the crack may be deceptive, or a stinging mock, or the exploitation of some stereotype, the maker's intentions and motives may reveal the full story, that this was simply meant as a bit of fun, or as a way to get you back on the right path, or as a method of subverting the stereotype at issue. Wisecracks have a much richer stew of properties than jokes, and that richness comes from their ultimate reliance on empathy to make it all work. Just like much of morality.

Recall the point in chapter 1 about what role a recitation of the properties of a wisecrack plays when we're challenged to explain its funniness. It's not an argument, per se. It's not as if, once you come to recognize all of the properties contained in my wisecrack, they'll suddenly have the logical or practical force to issue in an obligation for you to be amused. Rather, my recitation is instead at most an invitation: I want to describe as best I can how I saw the various properties of the wisecrack, how they struck me, so I'm inviting you into my mind in order for you to experience it as I did, as funny. This is explicitly an invitation to empathize. And that invitation (made by wisecrackers, not jokers) is what taps into our common humanity, our ability to take up our fellows' perspectives, to try on their orientations to the world, and to see the funny-making properties through their eyes. And because empathy is also the primary source of a lot of our interpersonal moral norms, the extension of empathy required in a wisecracking invitation of this sort also serves to extend our empathic moral connections with one another. We come to appreciate and perceive other people's interests in the way that they do, and so we become emotionally vulnerable to their up-and-down fortunes and to take more seriously their interests in our own deliberative lives. It is thus no wonder that wisecracking can generate the incredible bonding that it does. It is also sealing moral cracks.

I know, I know, these are grand and, yes, rather pretentious claims, and they haven't been fully vindicated by the book that has preceded it. What I think the book has vindicated, though, is its own invitation: *Try it for yourself.* The wisecracking life is far more valuable than it has been given credit for, and the moral complaints against it are often unwarranted. Wisecracking has gotten a bad rap, and I hope I've cleared it of the most serious charges against it. I haven't, of course, cleared it of all charges. But at least there's a lesson for any buffoons out there: There are some moral limits to your wisecracking, and you'd best learn what they are. And yes, doing so requires the proper deployment of empathy too.

"OK, OK, Shoemaker, enough is enough," I can hear you complaining, "Let me go now so that I can spread the gospel about the wisecracking life!" Great, I'm pleased to say to you at last, go forth and spread that gospel— although, that assumes you know something about it.

Acknowledgments

Writing a book about humor while living through a cancer diagnosis, major surgery, and a global pandemic has been the most joyful experience of my academic life. I was, by these events (and tenure), granted a total exemption from the typically dreary and restrictive norms of academic writing, which recommend carefully hedged—one might say janitorial—articles, making the tiniest of points, stolidly situated within existing literature, and written with language as dry as a Mojave martini. I've written my fair share of such articles. Indeed, they made my academic career. But something unexpected happened when I became a full professor in 2016.

I had by that point published several articles at all the right journals, on topics well-worn in academic philosophy. Don't get me wrong: I always cared about the things I wrote—I wasn't just engaged in academic wanking, the puzzle-solving minutiae some people in my profession unfortunately get off on. I actually did think I was establishing a solid record of TRUTH. But when I got that final promotion, I realized that what I no longer cared about were the brand norms of the profession, where the most well-known philosophers get labels for mining the same topic over and over. "Oh, she's the one who writes on forgiveness," or "yeah, he's the guy who writes on personal identity," or "they're the one who writes on trans-exclusionary radical modal logic." If you've written enough on one topic, you get pegged with such labels and put in their associated boxes, which provides conference organizers or book editors handy go-tos when looking for contributors, and it boosts citation rates for those labeled whenever anyone else writes on "their" topics. (I used to write a lot about psychopaths and moral responsibility, so I got pegged as "the psychopath guy," which had its advantages, I won't lie.) That's all fine and dandy, and it makes the profession thrum along.

What's not fine is that many in the field feel a serious pressure to continue polishing their brands, publishing articles defending their views endlessly against critics, expanding their views with only the tiniest of ad hoc amendments, and then training students to continue writing about their views in fawning ways. And that's the treadmill my promotion made me finally feel liberated enough to get off of. It was time for something completely different.

The seeds of this book were planted on a hike in 2017 through the sand dunes of western Michigan with two Daniels: my good friend Daniel Jacobson and my good brother Daniel Shoemaker. We were cracking wise throughout that walk, breaking each other up with quick quips, when I killed the amusement party by wondering aloud if there'd been any TV shows focusing on characters engaged in the kind of banter we'd been having. The funny in most sitcoms is found in, well, the sits, as well as how the characters react to them, often quite seriously. We the audience laugh at those things ("Tonight on *Friends*, there's a misunderstanding!"). But there didn't seem to be (m)any shows where the audience's laughs were targeted at precisely the same things the characters themselves were laughing at. (There is a great one now, Max's *Somebody, Somewhere*, which brilliantly portrays good friends just hanging out together and cracking each other, and us, up.)

The Daniels tried to ignore this meta-grasping as the party killer it was, but I doubled down: And furthermore, I wondered, has anyone in academia written about it? The deafening silence in response was, as they say, pretty silent.

I started paying attention to this phenomenon regardless. It was the back-and-forth witticisms of friends and family I found myself amused by the most in my life, not comedy specials or jokes, and I realized that how much I enjoyed being around different people depended precisely on how amusing they were in this unscripted way. I also realized that some of the worst people I knew were those presumably upright moralizers who were amused by very little and who morally policed some humor quite a bit. There's something happenin' here, I thought—originally and non-copyright-permission-needing—and what it is ain't exactly obvious.

The more research I did, the more I realized just how little had been written on this topic. All—and I mean (nearly) all—of the philosophical literature on humor (some of which is quite good) is on jokes, as I've noted many times. But it became quite obvious to me that the real moral action had to be in the interpersonal interplays between people, the ones that tickled me most. But these were also the ones that got people really pissed off. Yet why should humor, of all things, piss people off? Why did people get so royally upset at this trivial nonsense?

It's because it's not trivial. Humor matters. It matters aesthetically, prudentially, and yes, morally. We just haven't yet taken sufficient time to notice how it does so and to explore whether we should keep on playing in its sandbox. To investigate this topic was the incredibly pretentious motivation for this book. I at least hope I've succeeded in vindicating the worth of investigating it, even if I've gotten the conclusions wrong. I did have a ton of fun writing it, if that means anything.

There are so many thanks to give. I started writing an outline while a visiting scholar at the Lund/Gothenburg Responsibility Project, in Lund, Sweden, during fall 2019. But I began writing in earnest when the pandemic started, in spring 2020, and I proceeded to write the first three drafts of the book over the next year. I was hired at Cornell sometime during this hazy and highly contagious period, and when I arrived in upstate New York in the summer of 2021, I thought I had a fully polished and powerhouse draft in place. I was woefully mistaken.

In July of that summer, I had my radical prostatectomy, and during the next several months (fortunately), I was on leave to recover, so I reached out to my moral philosophy friends to see who'd be willing to read the manuscript and give me feedback while I sat awkwardly on my prostate donut. Many, out of pity or faux friendship, were willing. Indeed, there were two reading groups formed, one on Zoom with friends around the country, and the other at Cornell with my new moral philosophy and psychology peeps. Both were incredibly valuable. Because these people were my so-called friends, they didn't hold back, on any of the philosophy, humor, or presentation. Many were very concerned about how the book would read, as well as about whether people would pull various ideas and sentences out of context and cancel me. Good lord, these people actually seemed to care about me, or at least they faked it well.

I take criticism very seriously. Indeed, my only decently good quality as a philosopher is that I am utterly unafraid to kill my darlings, as they say, in the service of getting it right, or as close to right as I'm capable. After going through these reading groups and workshops, I rewrote the entire book twice more. These people saved me from humiliation. Or at least they saved me from some humiliation, if not all. I asked them if I could name them, given the controversies courted in the book. They agreed. Here are their names:

- John Doe
- John Dough
- Jane Deaux
- Doja Jane
- Sir John of Doe
- Janelle Doughstein
- Martha Nussbaum

Just kidding! Here are their real names:

- Santiago "Atomic" Amaya
- Olivia "No Empathy for You!" Bailey
- Elizabeth "Boss" Brake
- Eric "Family Man" Cave
- Justin "D'Ark L'Ord" D'Arms
- John "Babyface" Doris
- Dan "Irrational Sentimentalist" Jacobson
- Rachana "Kan We Talk?" Kamtekar
- Simon "Mandela Jokes Are Never Funny" May
- Jeff "The Hammer" Moriarty
- Shaun "Record Knight" Nichols
- Derk "Boom Boom" Pereboom
- David "The Baddest Wizard Ever" Pizarro
- Doug "If and Only If" Portmore
- Connie "The Ringleader" Rosati
- Daniel "The One Mom Loved More" Shoemaker
- Tamler "Somehow an Even Badder Wizard" Sommers
- Bas "Van Der" Van Der Vossen

No way—none—that this book comes to fruition without these people. I actually love some of them, but I'm seriously grateful to all of them.

I also had informal conversations about the book with a distant acquaintance, David Sobel, who is, I hate to say, one of the funniest people I know. (He also came up with Pereboom's nickname.)

In spring 2022, I had the great good fortune to discuss a lot of the material in this book in a graduate seminar at Cornell. The students were terrific, and the book benefited quite a bit from discussion with them. They included Migdalia Arcila Valenzuela, Maria Camila Castro Maldonado, Ruju Dani, Geoff Weiss (from whom I also stole an anecdote relayed in the book), Joseph Orttung, and Gus Turyn. I'm also grateful to the students in Neal Tognazzini's undergraduate class at Western Washington University, who in 2021 discussed an early version of chapter 4 on mockery and gave me some great (and hilarious) feedback.

The Mark whose wisecrack about my lack of humor knowledge sparked the introductory chapter is Mark Coleman, an excellent New Orleans pianist, teacher, and barfly, who is also a longtime friend. We have had a ton of hilarious wisecracking evenings with each other, over many games of pool, 87.6 percent of which I won. But he doesn't need my accolades . . .

I'm seriously grateful to the members of the team at the University of Chicago Press. These targets of gratitude include my editor, Kyle Wagner, who was an advocate of the book from the get-go; Kristin Rawlings, who walked me through the many technical aspects of getting the manuscript in shape; Nathan Petrie and the promotions team for spreading the news; and Mark Reschke, who copyedited with a light touch and an eagle eye.

A special thank you goes to Caitlyn Lodge, who volunteered to help me with indexing the book, a task I find as onerous and painful as plucking leg hairs and ordering them by length.

Finally, and most importantly, there is my family. The empirical research I've cited about the value of mockery, teasing, and ballbusting in families felt like it came straight out of my own family, as this is just what we do whenever we get together. We love each other fiercely. My oldest daughter, Kristin, has a wickedly clever wit, and she can bring people down to size in a blink, but she can also shore up with a quipping compliment too (this is an incredible gift, which I haven't talked enough about in this book). My younger daughter, Ashley, has a truth-sensor in her mockery that is unerring, unnerving, and hilarious. My son-in-law, Nic, has a knack for the driest of sarcastic takedowns—if you get it, good on you, but if you don't, he'll be amused about it all by himself. My two now-teenaged grandsons, Parker and Cohen, crack me up constantly. Parker's current favorite humor style is to play the offended upright moralist: "Wowwww," he'll say, shaking his head in response to some innocent quip about his off-line golf drive, "so you're saying I'm a bad driver because I'm Asian? Wowwww." (He and his brother are half Filipino, did I not mention that?) And Cohen basically infected our family with his humor style, which involves responding to some sincere claim by repeating it with a question mark at the end and a concerned tilt of the head. For example, were I to weakly compliment his brother for some moves in a losing chess game, in an obvious ploy to shore up his spirits, saying, "Moving your queen out so early, at least, was pretty creative," Cohen may quizzically respond, with faux sincerity, "Was it, though?" Maybe you have to be there, but these rejoinders I find hilarious, and they've made their way into my own wisecracking with others.

So too, my marriage of nearly thirty years to Marie Lantz has also been hilarious. Oh wait. What I mean is that there have been many moments of hilarity within it, as Marie and I get each other, and we make each other laugh on a daily basis, sometimes in heartily goofy guffaws. She has championed my writing of this book from the start, and she has also mocked me for my disappointment at the critical reactions of some people as I workshopped it, which actually shores me up. She keeps my feet firmly on the ground, but she's also the first to tout (to others only!) my successes. I'll always be grateful to her. She's a great friend, a remarkably resilient person, and the love of my life. Which makes it all the more difficult to have to tell you, sweetheart . . .

Written under the influence of properly
made Sazeracs, Ithaca, NY, April 2023

Notes

INTRODUCTION

1. Hat tip for some of these points to the one person I've read who takes this distinction seriously, John Morreall (2009, 83–89). I should also make clear that jokes and wisecracks together aren't the whole of humor. There are also funny events or states of the world that are neither. Real-life slapstick—accidental slips and falls of various kinds—can be funny, as can the behavior of various nonhuman animals, the shadow shapes of trees, overly earnest student essays, conversations between clueless people, and many other events. Call this third category "inadvertent humor," as it is about occurrences in which no one is aiming to be funny.

2. Dwyer 1991.

3. Wu et al. 2014.

4. Wu et al. 2014, 1392; see also Samson et al. (2011, 480).

5. Ford et al. 2020, 698.

6. Rachel Dratch played this character several times on *Saturday Night Live*, someone who was always pointing out the downside of every single fun activity people tried to engage in (accompanied by a sad trombone sound), until they couldn't take it anymore and left her, as usual, sitting alone, bemoaning climate change or the terrifying symptoms of SARS.

7. See, e.g., Martin et al. (2003); Ruch and Heintz (2013).

8. Morreall 1983, 115.

9. Graham 1995.

10. Yip and Martin 2006.

11. Hay 1999, 720–21.

12. Brad Wendell, a Cornell law professor who plays drums in a band, also noted to me the way in which the ability to take various wisecracks in a group setting like a band reflects other valuable virtues: grit, resiliency, taking criticism well, being a team player and not a prima donna, understanding when it's not about you, and more. Wisecracking is a way of sussing out these qualities.

CHAPTER ONE

1. David Sobel was the chair, Daniel Jacobson the wry wisecracker.

2. I have John Doris to thank for this sentence.

3. See also Morreall (2009, 39).

4. For points like this, see D'Arms and Jacobson (2010).

5. In the documentary *Comedian*, this is how Jerry Seinfeld treats new material he hears from a fellow comic: "That's funny," he says, nodding slowly, without a hint of a smile or laugh.

6. See this and other examples of Gandhi's humor in this article by PTI, "Meet Gandhi, the Man with a Great Sense of Humour," *New Indian Express*, October 2, 2014, https://www.newindianexpress.com/nation/2014/oct/02/Meet-Gandhi-the-Man -with-a-Great-Sense-of-Humour-667518.html.

7. There is a lot of philosophical controversy right now about how best to understand what it is that normativity fundamentally reduces to. Is it at bottom about *merit* (or "fit"), *reasons*, or *values*? I won't take any stand on this in-the-weeds issue here, but I hope what I say doesn't run roughshod over some of the careful distinctions and arguments that many good philosophers have made. I think the most compelling and natural way of talking about normativity, though, is with the language of "reasons," and that's the language I'm going to adopt here and in the rest of the book.

8. This makes it what philosophers call a *pro tanto* reason.

9. For one source, see Cristin O'Keefe Aptowicz, "Could You Stomach the Horrors of 'Halftime' in Ancient Rome?," *LiveScience* (updated July 21, 2022), https://www .livescience.com/53615-horrors-of-the-colosseum.html.

10. Specific examples to be discussed in chapter 4.

11. In Hannah Gadsby's famous monologue *Nanette*, she seems to view the relief theory as the correct theory of humor, claiming "I make you all tense and then I make you laugh, and you're like, 'Thanks for that. I was feeling a bit tense.'" And later, "Punch lines need trauma, because punch lines need tension and tension feeds trauma." Again, perhaps this is true of (some) laughter, but it's not true of what's amusing generally by a long shot.

12. See Morreall (1987, 19).

13. See Carroll (2014b, 11–12).

14. See Carroll (2014b, 12–14); Roberts (2019, 87–88).

15. Most humor theorists these days adhere to one of many varieties of incongruity theory. For just a partial list, see Raskin (1984); Clarke (1987); Martin (1987); Hurley, Dennett, and Adams (2013); Carroll (2014b); McGraw and Warner (2014).

16. See Olin (2016), who notes this and points as examples to Morreall (1987) and Martin (2007). See also Hurley, Dennett, and Adams (2011) and Carroll (2014b, 48–54).

17. You aren't just "catching" their hilarity, as if it were contagious. You're amused by their hilarity, and in virtue of their hilarity, which contains no incongruity.

18. Schultz 1972; Raskin 1984; Hurley, Dennett, and Adams 2011.

19. Morreall 2009, 13–15.

20. Olin 2016.

21. See Morreall (2009, 34; 2020), as well as Santayana (1986, 27). These authors don't put their view in the "exclusivist" terms I have, however. Indeed, one problem is that it's tough to find a clear formulation from these theorists of what the precise relationship *is* between play and the funny.

22. See Raskin (1984) for this line of thinking about humor and language.

23. Morreall 2009, 36.

24. This is a wisecrack many have attributed to Sidney Morgenbesser, a brilliant Columbia philosophy professor in the last part of the twenty-first century. I have added in the windbag linguist to make my point.

25. Hurley, Dennett, and Adams (2011, e.g., 46) make a similar point.

26. It could also be called the *Humean* theory, as it draws quite heavily from David Hume's general discussion of aesthetics, in "Of the Standards of Taste." I depart from Hume in my discussion of the role of reason giving in normative disagreements, to be discussed later. The view is also quite close to what's known as rational sentimentalism (see D'Arms and Jacobson [2023]). Finally, it's important to note that I'll discuss neuro-atypical humans and their humor sensibilities at length in chapter 6.

27. Hurley, Dennett, and Adams (2011) are basically the only theorists I've seen who attempt to say why their favored property is a funny-maker. They defend an incongruity theory of humor, but they also attempt to show why their version of incongruity gives us the humor-pleasure (what they call "mirth") that it does. Very roughly, mirth is a kind of "pleasure in unearthing a particular variety of mistake in active belief structures. And . . . humor is any semantic circumstance . . . in which we make such a mistake and succeed in discovering it" (117). So these incongruities generate pleasure akin to what we get when gaining some insight into the world.

Of course, they are really just after an explanation of the funniness of *jokes*, not wisecracks (their book is called *Inside Jokes*), so they miss out on the contributing properties of the wisecracking kinds of humor that include cleverness, motive, intent, and so forth. But even on their own terms the account can't explain a variety of coun-terexamples, including (a) so-called observational jokes, which draw our attention to previously underappreciated ordinary events and connections between things, and are "funny, 'cause it's true!"; (b) jokes whose predictable punch lines people find as or more funny than those that are unpredictable (Pollio and Mers 1974); and (c) pranks (while their humor depends on the butt being fooled and maybe gaining insight, the pranksters are amused precisely because they are already fully aware of everything that's going on, so their amusement is a function of how people can quite predictably be rendered foolish).

28. There is some similarity here to the dispositional theory of humor offered by Levinson (1998). However, Levinson's theory is pretty underdeveloped, and he unfor-tunately connected up the human disposition to amusement with a necessary inclina-tion toward *laughter*. Carroll (2014b, 46–48) picks on the latter element in dismissing the view. That's an unnecessary component, though. I aim in what follows to develop a view like this in much greater detail than does Levinson or anyone else.

29. This is precisely the complaint of Hurley, Dennett, and Adams (2011), who say

that appealing to a "sense of humor" to explain the funny is "no explanation at all" (159). My aim now is to show just how wrong that complaint is.

30. Ashley Fetters relays the one she would repeatedly tell her family when she was four: "Knock, knock." "Who's there?" "Guitar." "Guitar who?" "Guitar if you don't have a house!" See Ashley Fetters, "Knock Knock. Who's There? Kids. Kids Who? Kids Tell Terrible Jokes," *Atlantic*, January 5, 2019, https://www.theatlantic.com/family/archive/2019/01/why-kids-tell-weird-jokes/579472/.

31. I'm not going to pass up an opportunity to share a great joke my then-ten-year-old grandson Parker swore he made up: "If you're bad in life, but not *really* bad, do you just go to heck, not hell?"

32. This "by your own lights" strategy is Hume's (1757), and it is also exploited in application to humor in D'Arms and Jacobson (2010).

33. When my daughter Ashley was first exposed to some kick-ass down-home New Orleans food (having come from the palate-dulling Midwest) she had no idea what she was eating and couldn't identify any of the flavors. When repeatedly asked "Do you like it?" she kept responding, with mounting and hilarious frustration, "I don't know!" as she continued to shovel it into her mouth till the plate was empty. She eventually became something of a connoisseur of the cuisine, though.

34. Again, this is all in Hume (1757). For contemporary discussion, see D'Arms (2013).

35. I'll say much more to expand on and defend this point in chapter 6.

36. Hume (1757) discusses most of these, as do D'Arms and Jacobson (2010).

37. Philosophers think they are above this, allegedly adopting beliefs only in virtue of their being thoroughly justified. Recent research shows that they are just as vulnerable to ideological biases as everyone else. For just one example, see Schwitzgebel and Cushman (2012).

38. I know that putting forward this last claim as an "ideological bias" might sound startling, but I strongly suspect that, for most people, belief in the moral equality of all humans really is just an article of faith, and when challenged to provide reasons justifying it, most people would be utterly flummoxed (or give terrible reasons, like that we all are factually equal in our abilities or capacities). Hell, *I'm* flummoxed, and I'm a professional moral philosopher.

39. Isenberg 1977, 163.

40. Thanks to David Pizarro, who is often wrongly amused, for discussion on this point.

41. This is what Hume (1757) calls "blameless disagreement."

CHAPTER TWO

1. Some may think this is no prank; it's an *assault*. Yes it was, but it was also, as we'll see in the next chapter, a prank. Many pranks aim to make people look foolish in order to embarrass or even humiliate them. There's a kind of "We got you!" delight in a successful prank. Pranks that have this form, though, may range wildly in their effects on their targets, from the trivial to the traumatic, and they may well include assaults. Thanks to Elizabeth Brake for discussion.

2. There is serious controversy among philosophers over whether there are only qualified value-wise reasons (a view called normative pluralism), or whether there are, in addition, unqualified normative reasons answering the question, "What should I do all-things-considered?" The former says different kinds of reasons just answer different types of qualified questions, such as "What should I morally do?" or "What should I prudentially or athletically do?" On normative pluralism, there can't be genuine practical conflicts from different value domains; there are just different answers to different questions. However, normative pluralism isn't much borne out by ordinary language (we don't say, "Well, I prudentially ought to stay on first base, but I athletically ought to steal second base"; instead, we just say, "I ought to steal second base" or "Best to get a pinch runner in for me"). The denial of normative pluralism, though, requires that we come up with a clear method for determining how the weight of reasons from different value domains can possibly be weighed (on the same scale?) with each other, and so there seems no clear and coherent basis for coming to all-things-considered verdicts in the face of value conflict. For a nice discussion of the issue (by someone who denies normative pluralism), see Portmore (2021, 8–11). Given the way I've been talking in the text about value conflicts and discerning what we have most reason to do, I seem to be denying normative pluralism, although I'm certainly not resolving the problem of incommensurability I've just noted. But I think wisecracks provide a particularly pressing illustration of both the existence of true value conflicts and a need to figure out how best to respond to these conflicts all things considered ("That was hilarious, but it was really mean, so I'm not sure if I should be amused or upset!").

3. See Frijda (1986), Frank (1988), and Scarantino (2014), among many others.

4. Morreall 2009, 30.

5. Morreall 2009, 31.

6. Roberts 1988, 296.

7. Noel Carroll also tries to defend the view that amusement is an emotion, but he doesn't do so very successfully, I fear. He fends off the objection about motivation by saying that (a) not all emotions have attached motivational tendencies (his counterexample is sorrow), and (b) some instances of amusement do have motivational tendencies (as when amusement at a political satire motivates us to form new political beliefs and do something about it; see Carroll [2014b, 60–61]). The first point isn't supported by the example he gives, as sorrow can be said to motivate a distinctive kind of *inaction* ("I just want to sit here and not do anything."). And the second point is a non sequitur, as it's pointing to motivations caused by amusement, not motivations constituting it.

8. Frijda 2009, 270.

9. See, e.g., Weems (2014) for one relatively recent discussion.

10. See Weems (2014, 12, 20); Hurley, Dennett, and Adams (2011, 290).

11. Vettin and Todt 2005.

12. Hurley, Dennett, and Adams 2011, 292.

13. See Raskin (1984).

14. Hurley, Dennett, and Adams 2011, 293.

15. Hurley, Dennett, and Adams 2011, 290–94.

16. Hurley, Dennett, and Adams 2011, 292.

17. Graham, Papa, and Brooks 1992, 177.

18. See Greengross and Miller (2011), who argue further that greater humor ability predicts mating success and the general ability is greater in males. There are two problems with the study, though. First, their determination of humor ability came from their subjects' (all university students, by the way) ability to write funny captions for three cartoons. This is an extremely limited and specific type of funny-making, however, so it's significantly overstating things to suggest that these results deliver to us the truth about who has a "higher average humor production ability." What relation does a facility with cartoon captioning have to being a funny wisecracker, for instance, or being a dark humor aficionado or an absurdist humor connoisseur, all of which reflect good humor sensibilities too, one would think? In addition, the panel rating what cartoon captions were in fact funnier than others consisted of "four men and two women, all students," so perhaps it's no wonder that the majority rated captions by men funnier on average than those written by women.

19. I'm grateful to Shaun Nichols for extended discussion on this point.

20. Thanks to Rachana Kamtekar for discussion.

21. Nichols 2002 and 2007; Boyd and Richerson 2005; Henrich and Henrich 2007.

22. See Nichols (2007); McGeer (2013, 173–75).

23. For one nice summary and defense of this story, see Lench, Tibbett, and Bench (2016).

24. Maybe they prevent me from getting respect? Goal frustration is about harms, both physical and psychological, whereas disrespect isn't (I can disrespect you without harming you). I'll say more about this point in chapter 5.

25. Whether what I'm about to say implies that we evolved to have two emotional modules with two different functions, or instead we have co-opted a single coarse-grained emotional module into having two different functions is a matter way beyond my pay grade. It doesn't matter what the answer is for my purposes, thankfully.

26. There are philosophical disputes over this point, of course, with some denying that anger (or resentment, as it's put in the philosophical literature) is the correct emotional appraisal of wrongings, rather than something less retributive like disappointment or sadness (see, e.g., Pereboom [2014, chap. 6]). I occasionally use the softer language of "moral upset" to appease these sorts of critics. However, I've spent lots of time arguing for the aptness of anger to wrongings, and I've offered several arguments directed specifically against these critics, in multiple forums (e.g., Shoemaker [2015, chap. 3; 2018b]), and I'm not going to repeat all those arguments here.

27. For example, I may simply write an angry letter to my senator, or quietly (but angrily) shut the door to my room on you when you, my partner, come home late and drunk yet again.

28. Again, see Shoemaker (2015, 2018a, and 2021) for development and defense of these ideas.

29. These are the fundamentals of the view laid out by Strawson (1962/2003), and which I attempted to develop further in Shoemaker (2015 and 2018a).

30. Some of the labels for supposedly competing views include comic moralism, comic immoralism, comic ethicism, and comic amoralism. For just one problem, the

first two are sometimes defined in a way that allows one consistently to hold *both* views in their "moderate" forms, so they aren't really competitors at all. See Carroll (2014b, 86–115).

31. See, e.g., Carroll (2014b, 90); Smuts (2010); Anderson (2020).

32. Carroll 2014b, 90.

33. Sometimes a poem just *is* a joke (or vice versa), so there's not even an analogy needed to bridge them. Think of a dirty limerick, or Strickland Gillilan's poem "Fleas": "Adam / Had 'em."

34. And what's the full recipe for a proper Sazerac? This information will justify the cost of the book alone. Stir a teaspoon of simple syrup together with the three shots of Peychaud's bitters in a cocktail mixing glass. Add two ounces of rye whiskey (preferably Rittenhouse) and a few ice cubes into the mixing glass, then stir till chilled. Coat a frosted cocktail glass with Herbsaint or absinthe. Strain into it the whiskey mixture. Spritz a lemon peel into glass, then add twisted peel. Enjoy! And you're welcome.

35. My brother, Daniel, owner of the great Teardrop Lounge in Portland, Oregon, drew my attention to this great quote about the inviolability of the Sazerac recipe by Charles H. Baker Jr., in his delightful book *The Gentleman's Companion*, a compendium of cocktail recipes from the around the world: "Please, please, never try to vary it; for if you do you'll not be drinking a true Sazerac—just some liquid abortion fit only to pour down drains" (1946 edition, p. 122).

36. From the site "Kazakhstan Jokes," https://upjoke.com/kazakhstan-jokes.

37. Luvell Anderson considers the possibility that it's the creator of the joke whose intentions might matter morally, but he rightly rejects it, noting that in most cases we don't know who the creator of a joke was (so we can't track his or her intentions), and jokes change so much over time, and with each teller, that the creator's intentions are just irrelevant to current instantiations of the joke (Anderson 2020, 5). In the aesthetics literature, there are some who assign authorial intent to a work of art, one that is independent of its actual creator (see, e.g., Nehamas [1986]). I will deal with this possibility later in the chapter.

38. Carroll 2014b, 90–91.

39. In a previous note, I mentioned the aesthetic theory that works of art have authors, and so, in particular, may have authorial intent, where the author is different from the person who actually typed out or painted the work, say. Works of art can contain depths of meaning unbeknownst to their creators, and this meaning could be attributable only to some author who intended it to be that way, if there's any sense to be made of serious aesthetic interpretation. As the primary "author" of this aesthetic view says, "The author is the agent postulated to account for construing a text as an action, as a work" (Nehamas 1986, 688). Actions require intentions. Perhaps, then, when we interpret jokes on their own, we might postulate authors of them too, not referring to any actual person who either made up the joke or told it first, but as an "interpretive construct" (Nehamas 1986, 688) to which we could then attribute intention and motive, and so, importantly, angry blame? No, this is to stretch the metaphor way too far. You can't intelligibly blame an "interpretive construct," which, as Nehamas himself says explicitly, has no actual state of mind, and so has no actual intention or motive (Nehamas 1986, 689–90). (I'm grateful to Daniel Jacobson for discussion of this idea.)

40. I say "typically" in the parentheses because ChatGPT and other AI bots can generate and "tell" jokes, just not very good ones. Indeed, we should focus on the creation of truly funny wisecracks as the best way to pass the Turing test.

41. All of what I say here is of course compatible with some religious people being blaming-angry at the publishers of what they take to be sacrilegious jokes or cartoons.

42. This is the sort of view touted for jokes in Gaut (1998).

43. There may be important asymmetries between blameworthiness and praiseworthiness, and there are some leading theorists in moral psychology who have reported on what they take to be such asymmetries in our actual blaming and praising practices (see, e.g., Doris, Knobe, and Woolfolk [2007]; Knobe and Doris [2010]; and Newman, De Freitas, and Knobe [2015]). This is controversial territory, and I'm simply pushing a burden of proof argument on those who might embrace an asymmetry about these issues as they pertain specifically to humor.

44. Gaut 1998.

45. See, e.g., de Sousa (1987); Bergman (1986).

46. See, e.g., Morreall (2009); Benatar (1999); Smuts (2010); Carroll (2001; 2014b, 92–102).

47. Morreall 2009, 106. Oddly, Carroll later tells a very similar anecdote, offering an example of finding a moron joke directed at "Newfies" funny, despite not knowing who Newfies were: "How do you know a Newfie has been using your computer? There's white-out on the screen" (Carroll 2014b, 99).

48. Carroll 2014b, 100.

49. It's also compatible with another possibility, namely, that moral wronging in a wisecrack just doesn't affect its funniness either way. I think this could be true too, but whether it is or isn't is not really important to my overall argument, and it's also hard to come up with good examples in support of it.

50. See the "benign norm violation" theory of the funny offered by McGraw and Warner (2014).

51. Carroll 2014b, 106–10.

52. Carroll 2014b, 107.

53. Carroll 2014b, 108.

54. Carroll 2014a, 249.

CHAPTER THREE

1. See Dynel (2019, 327–28). I should note that my discussion is focused only on the sort of pranks that people play on each other, not those that are mere clever surprises, as when a group of engineering students manages to place a car emblazoned with the school mascot on top of the tallest building on campus.

2. See Dynel (2019, 330–31). There are exceptions, of course. In the brilliant comic strip *Calvin and Hobbes*, Calvin's father would often pull his leg by offering absurd answers to his questions. For example, when Calvin asks how ATMs work, his dad responds that if you want twenty-five dollars, you punch in that amount, and then the man inside the machine with a printing press makes and ejects the bills. To Calvin's

follow-up question—"Sort of like the guy who lives up in our garage and opens the door?"—Dad replies, "Exactly."

3. See Meibauer (2019b) for discussions of all of these topics and more.

4. My only aim is to articulate the most familiar understanding of lying. There are certainly gray areas at the edges of this formulation, though, for example, half-truths, where the speaker doesn't fully believe that the statement is true *or* false, and there are also cases that don't fit the paradigm very neatly, for example, bald-faced lies, where everyone involved knows the speaker is lying (so there's no deception). These wrinkles aren't relevant to the main aims of this chapter, though, so I'll ignore them.

5. There might be other wisecracks that do so too, including comic exaggeration and transparent falsehoods. To keep things simple, I'll focus just on pranks and leg-pulling, though.

6. Thanks to Rachana Kamtekar for discussion here.

7. I'm grateful to Santiago Amaya for this insightful point.

8. If you're craving philosophical lingo, these descriptions come out of J. L. Austin's speech act theory of language. The first act, in which I communicate information, is called *locutionary*; the second, in which I'm advising, is called *illocutionary*; the third (causing) is called *perlocutionary*. See Austin (1975).

9. Morreall 2009, 36.

10. "On a Supposed Right to Lie from Altruistic Motives."

11. "On a Supposed Right to Lie from Altruistic Motives."

12. There are many sophisticated rejoinders to worries like those I have expressed. Indeed, contemporary Kantianism is a huge cottage industry, both for interpreting Kant and for trying to make his general view more palatable and plausible. I'm not a fan of the enterprise, but that's neither here nor there. I should also note that there's been an entire book published on *Kant's Humorous Writings* (Clewis 2021), which I wouldn't have thought possible. It includes a chapter on "Kant and the Ethics of Humor," for those interested in a more nuanced portrayal.

13. It's not a risk to their autonomy per se, then, which lying and deception can leave perfectly intact. I'm grateful to Eric Cave for discussion here, as well as for the insights provided in Buss (2005).

14. See Fricker (2007).

15. Fricker 2007; Langton 2010.

16. The example, sans headphones, is John Stuart Mill's.

17. Perhaps these are all cases where the parties in question have *tacitly* consented to this treatment? First off, the very notion of tacit consent may be a chimera: It requires some kind of signal, but then, given conventional determinations of which signals will count as consent, why isn't any signaling of tacit consent actually a case of *express* consent? And as the notion of tacit consent has been exploited in the history of political philosophy (e.g., with John Locke), it is a notion riddled with difficulties that I won't go into. Regardless, though, I can't see how, in any of these cases, the individuals in question have in any way, expressly or tacitly, consented to the treatment they've undergone. Perhaps, instead, then, they've all *hypothetically* consented, that is, they would have consented to the treatment in question if asked? While this may be true of the

bridge-crosser, I have a harder time thinking it would be true of the last two. But even if it were, how could hypothetical consent achieve the magic of actual consent? In other words, "consent turns a rape into love-making, a kidnapping into a Sunday drive, a battery into a football tackle, a theft into a gift, and a trespass into a dinner party" (Hurd 1996). How could what these parties would have agreed to under certain conditions if asked enable this transformation? Or, to paraphrase Ronald Dworkin's (1975, 18) famous remarks about John Rawls's hypothetical social contract, "Hypothetical [consent] is not simply a pale form of . . . actual [consent]; it is no [consent] at all."

18. I have focused on cases of deceptive humor where the deception occurs without the consent of the deceived. Something interesting to think about, though, are cases of close friendship in which there is implicit standing consent on both sides to be deceived by the other in leg-pulls at any time. In such relationships, there'd just be no moral reason at all, then, against engaging in this type of humor, and many close friends well know this. But it's just false that we all have implicit standing consent to have our legs pulled by anyone else. Nevertheless, I'm arguing, it could be good for us

19. I'm admittedly stipulating away a very hard problem, namely, what to say about pranks that amuse millions of people when viewed on YouTube. Wouldn't the pleasure of those millions outweigh the moral anger of the pranked party, no matter what, in which case my general "weighing up reasons" strategy would always leave the pranking permissible, no matter how cruel it was? In other words, if enough people (as in the Romans laughing at tortured Christians in the Colosseum?) are amused, then it's fine. As I say, a tough problem, one that has vexed moral philosophers far better than me (for a couple of very sophisticated discussions, see Scanlon [1998, 229–41] and Norcross [1997]). For my part, as I suggest in the text when talking about the second prank, I think there might be certain types of moral reasons—especially those against deliberate cruelty found in some pranks—that are stoppers, nearly absolute constraints on some actions despite the production of any amount of some other value. Perhaps this is the Kantian residue within me. But this is a large issue at which I can only hand-wave here.

CHAPTER FOUR

1. There are several related variants of mockery, including teasing, breaking balls, and taking the piss. I'll treat them all as forms of mockery, at least when they have the conditions I'm about to articulate. But one could delve into their differences in interesting ways. For example, on ten forms of "taking the piss" (and its relation to ball breaking[!]), see Ritchie (2014). Teasing isn't necessarily funny—sometimes it's just brutal bullying—but for an exploration of how intent plays a role in funny (or at least nonserious) teasing, see Haugh (2016).

2. See also Hurley, Dennett, and Adams (2014, 58–59).

3. Paper tickets? What is this, 1979? Were they going to a Foghat concert?

4. I have stolen this comic insult from the interwebs, but the page where I found it no longer exists, so I will claim it as my own.

5. Thanks to Connie Rosati for help with this formulation.

6. I spent a day doing "research" on this question at the hallowed halls of Facebook Library, with many friends participating in a fun and funny conversation. I'm grateful to them all. I went into it with one view and came out of it with a completely different view, the one I'm about to share.

7. Which she did. See Jessica Contrera, "Gloria Steinem Is Apologizing for Insulting Female Bernie Sanders Supporters," *Washington Post*, February 7, 2016.

8. *Philebus* 48–50.

9. *On the Orator*, Book II, Ch. 58.

10. *Leviathan*, Part I, Ch. 6.

11. *Human Nature*, Ch. 8, Section 13.

12. *The Passions of the Soul*, Article 179.

13. Jonson and Siverskog 2012. For other examples of self-mocking humor, see Greengross and Miller (2008).

14. Deploying it also manifests an excellent leadership style. See Hoption et al. (2013). It also seems to give the self-mocker a kind of strategic advantage: "If I make fun of myself for this embarrassing feature, I can control the narrative to some extent, deflating the need for others to make fun of it, and so control how much embarrassment I have to go through for it." Of course, some use self-deprecation as a cudgel, a way of beating themselves up. This is to deploy the humor style known as "self-defeating," and it doesn't correlate very well with well-being. I'll talk explicitly about this humor style and those who tend to deploy it in chapter 6.

Some might think self-mockery isn't real "mockery," though, as perhaps it doesn't involve a sting, and it's often deployed strategically, so as to prevent someone else from mocking you first. I'm not so sure. I think of self-mockery as the almost sheepish presentation of one's own flaw for public consumption and that *ha-ha*! response. Sure, it may be strategic, but as presented in that way, it does sound sting-y to me. In a hoist-with-his-own-petard example of self-mockery on *The Simpsons*, Nelson walks by a mirror and, as a matter of habit, points at the person he sees and says "Ha-ha!" He then realizes who it is and slumps, saying "Hey, that hurts. No wonder no one came to my birthday party." (Thanks to David Pizarro, for both the worry and the Nelson example.)

15. And in families, there doesn't seem to be any gendered division of mockery: both men and women dish out mockery to other family members in more or less equal amounts.

16. From Norrick (1993, 75).

17. Norrick 1993, 77.

18. "Liberal Activist Explains Notion of Tolerance to Man She Just Called a 'Worthless [Expletive],'" *Babylon Bee*, August 19, 2016, https://web.archive.org/web/20160821200919/http://babylonbee.com/news/liberal-activist-explains-notion-tolerance-man-just-called-worthless-expletive/.

19. "Academy Strips 'Schindler's List' of Best Picture Aware Due to Lack of Diversity," *Babylon Bee*, September 11, 2020, https://babylonbee.com/news/academy-strips-schindlers-list-of-best-picture-award-for-not-having-more-lgbtq-characters.

20. *Philebus* 48a–50b; see also Trivigno (2019).

21. Trapp 2019, 159.

22. *Rhetoric* 1389b10; see also Walker (2019).

23. *Human Nature*, Ch. 8, Section 13.

24. *Spinoza's Short Treatise on God, Man, and Human Welfare.*

25. *Reflections on Laughter.*

26. Greengross and Miller 2008.

27. Davies 1991.

28. Hoption et al. 2013.

29. See also Guerin (2019).

30. In Morreall (1987, 39–40).

31. In Morreall (1987, 39). Hutcheson really is the only philosopher in the Western canon who appreciated mockery's sometimes significant positive moral value.

32. Everts 2006, 391.

33. Everts 2006, 384.

34. Everts 2006, 404.

35. Norrick 1993, 78.

36. Norrick 1993, 80.

37. I've got a book manuscript, called "The Architecture of Blame and Praise," that develops and really leans into this idea.

38. Everts 2006, 405.

39. You can see the famous photo as included in the story by Sonam Sheth, "White Supremacist Who Marched in Charlottesville: 'I'm Not the Angry Racist They See in That Photo,'" *Insider*, August 14, 2017, 3:35 p.m., https://www.businessinsider.com/peter-cvjetanovic-White-supremacist-charlottesville-photo-not-angry-racist-2017–8.

40. Some would strongly resist classifying these two online shaming activities together. Collecting and posting publicly available information about White nationalists, they say, is not the same thing as posting private contact information in a provocatively named file that keeps tabs on wounds or deaths. The former is merely a "call for accountability," whereas the latter is a "call for violence." (These are the words of Gordon Coonfield, a communications professor at Vanderbilt, from an article in the *Chicago Tribune* on August 14, 2017, https://www.chicagotribune.com/nation-world/ct-social-media-expose-White-nationalists-20170814-story.html.) This seems an ideologically motivated distinction, though, to say the least. People aren't merely calling Cvjetanovic accountable for his actions; they are instead clearly aiming to get people to *hold* him to account in a way that will *punish* him (for example, get him kicked out of his university). Public shaming is a punishment too. Physical violence against abortion providers is merely one among many ways to punish people. Further, the contact information of abortion providers was also publicly available; it was just harder to find then than it is now. So that's a mere difference in degree, not kind.

41. *The Passions of the Soul*, Article 178; see also Hazlett, in Morreall (1987, 76).

42. This, by the way, is the sort of formulation we call philosophical progress.

43. See Rawls (1971), Rachels (1978), and Sadurski (1985). For discussion, see Feldman and Skow (2019).

44. Everts 2006, 406.

45. I argue at great length in my book manuscript "The Architecture of Blame and Praise" that in fact interpersonal blaming sanctions actually don't require desert either.

46. He now claims to identify as "ex-gay," promoting conversion therapy. See the story by Gina Spocchia, "Milo Yiannopoulos Declares Himself Ex-Gay and Says He's 'Demoted' Husband to Housemate in Bizarre New Interview." *Independent*, March 10, 2021, 19:52, https://www.independent.co.uk/news/world/americas/us-politics/milo-yiannopoulos-ex-gay-b1815296.html.

47. Grasswick 2018.

48. See, e.g., Barnes et al. (2020); Yancy (2018). Specifically, for evidence of actual discrimination against and discriminatory attitudes toward conservatives in philosophy, see Peters et al. (2020). For evidence in social psychology, see Inbar and Lammers (2012). For evidence in legal academia, see Phillips (2016).

49. He now calls dyslexia his "superpower," which, in effect, buttresses my overall point. See "Sir Richard Branson: 'Dyslexia Is My Superpower!'" *Mercury*, April 27, 2023, https://robbreport.com.au/business/dyslexia-is-my-superpower-how-learning-differently-helped-richard-branson/.

50. You can see a still photo of the attack in the story by Paul P. Murphy, "White Nationalist Richard Spencer Punched during Interview," CNN, January 21, 2017, 7:13 a.m., https://www.cnn.com/2017/01/20/politics/White-nationalist-richard-spencer-punched/index.html.

51. I'm grateful to Elizabeth Brake for this succinct way of putting the matter.

52. For excellent philosophical discussion, see Barnes (2016); and Campbell and Stramondo (2017).

53. There's a nice summary in Reid McCarter, "In a Shocking Twist, Everybody's Making Fun of Gal Gadot's Celebrity 'Imagine' Video," *AV Club*, March 20, 2020, https://news.avclub.com/in-a-shocking-twist-everybodys-making-fun-of-gal-gadot-1842425798.

54. See Ronson (2015) for many such examples.

55. See, e.g., Miller (2011); Vanderheiden (2011).

56. For clear and enlightening exposition of the view, see Oliver (1996); Oliver and Barnes (2012); Barnes (2016). For critical discussion, see Wolff (2011); Shakespeare (2013); and Barnes (2016).

57. Quoted in Hamscha (2016).

58. Sutton-Spence and Napoli (2012, 313), drawing from Ladd (2002).

59. As Beyoncé and Lizzo recently found out, this term is now viewed as a no-no. That's part of my point. See Gil Kaufman, "This Is Why Disability Advocates Say It's Not OK to Use 'Spazz' in Lyrics," *Billboard*, August 4, 2022, https://www.billboard.com/music/rb-hip-hop/spazz-lyrics-beyonce-lizzo-disability-experts-opinion-1235121272/.

60. This is a leading theme in the deeply insightful and compassionate work of the philosopher of psychiatry Jonathan Glover, in Glover (2014).

CHAPTER FIVE

1. Rock permanently retired the routine after hearing that some White kids had thought it granted them license to use the term "n——a," albeit probably with more of an "er" ending, when they gleefully repeated the jokes to each other.

2. See the very thoughtful discussion about Rock's routine by Deborah L. Plummer, in *Medium*, September 30, 2020, https://aninjusticemag.com/the-dance-for

-eradicating-racism-3bb09ef65fc4. I draw some of what I say in the next paragraph from it. Interestingly (given what I argued in the last chapter), Ben Schwartz claims that Rock "became a star by punching down" in this routine and wonders who has the moral authority to do so (Schwartz 2016, 143–44).

3. In "Chris Rock's Poisonous Legacy: How to Get Rich and Exalted Chastising 'Bad Blacks'," *Salon*, November 12, 2014, https://www.salon.com/2014/11/12/chris_rocks _poisonous_legacy_how_to_get_rich_and_exalted_chastising_bad_Blacks/.

4. And lest some readers think that Double-A wasn't really wisecracking but was instead delivering some racist "truths," you have to trust me: he really took himself to be making a hilarious crack. He was definitely amused and quite pleased with himself.

5. Although his gifts seemed very rusty in his most recent comedy special, the live-on-Netflix *Selective Outrage*, I'm sorry to say.

6. One exception is the brief article by Bicknell (2007), in which she explores offensive joking, which is mainly about the telling of offensive jokes but is also meant to cover wisecracks in my sense.

7. For the attitude view, see several influential papers by Garcia (1996, 1997, 1999). For the belief view, see Appiah (2002). For the ideology view, see Mills (2003) and Shelby (2003). For the social view, see Ture and Hamilton (1992). For the disrespect view, see Glasgow (2009). For citations and some discussion, see Anderson (2015, 501).

8. Cohen 1999, 77. It has also been discussed in Smuts (2007 and 2010); Carroll (2014b, 111); Anderson (2015); Morreall (2020); and An and Chen (2021).

9. Cohen 1999, 84; emphasis in original.

10. Carroll 2014b, 113.

11. Cohen 1999, 79–84.

12. These first two jokes were provided by a friend.

13. These last two jokes were provided by a different friend.

14. One female friend reported having been harassed in a bar by a man telling this precise joke to her, rendering it impossible for her to find it funny.

15. Thanks to Elizabeth Brake and Olivia Bailey as well for insightful discussion.

16. A friend suggested to me that the funny in this joke might be much easier to find than in the battered woman joke, even though they have similar structures and funny-making properties, because Stevie Wonder, a huge celebrity, is doing just fine in life, so a joke like this couldn't really affect him in any way, and that fact might make it less bitter, and so funnier, than a joke like this would be about a noncelebrity blind Black person who lived in the joke teller's neighborhood. Salt makes tonic water less bitter than it would otherwise be, even though you don't taste the salt in it (the analogy is my friend's).

17. This point resonates with my remarks at the end of the previous chapter about why mocking impersonations aren't funny if they simply apply to a specific impersonated person some features thought to be attributable to that person's group as a whole.

18. Some are found out, of course. For example, investigations revealed that in the six-year period before the Ferguson, Missouri, protests and riots in response to the 2014 police shooting of Michael Brown, several such emails were written between members of the Ferguson police force and court officials. A June 2011 email, for example, said a man wanted to obtain "welfare" for his dogs because they are "mixed in color,

unemployed, lazy, can't speak English and have no frigging clue who their Daddies are." Quoted in German Lopez, "Here Are 7 Racist Jokes Ferguson Police and Court Officials Made over Email," *Vox*, March 4, 2015, https://www.vox.com/2015/3/4/8149699/ferguson-police-racist-jokes. And much more recently, texts between members of the Torrance Police Force in Los Angeles County were discovered that, again, consisted in brutally racist jokes. See James Queally, "Torrance Police Traded Racist, Homophobic Texts," *Los Angeles Times*, December 8, 2021, https://www.latimes.com/california/story/2021-12-08/torrance-police-traded-racist-homophobic-texts-it-could-jeopardize-hundreds-of-cases. Suppose emails like this had never been discovered, though, as is surely true in some other precincts.

19. Feinberg 1985, x.

20. Feinberg 1985, 5.

21. Feinberg 1985, 5.

22. Feinberg 1973.

23. Feinberg 1985.

24. After having been offended by something, you may well determine later that it wasn't offensive after all, but that's not to deny that you were in fact offended; it's just to say that you shouldn't have been.

25. Feinberg (1985) discusses boredom as an offended state, and if you've ever really been bored by someone, as I have by many actual colleagues like the one in the story, that state definitely fits into the offended category.

26. Feinberg 1985.

27. I'm looking at you, Neil Young and Lou Reed.

28. This is not a hypothetical. It has actually happened several times. Here's one incident, reported by Yolanda Woodlee, "Williams Aide Resigns in Language Dispute," *Washington Post*, January 27, 1999, https://www.washingtonpost.com/wp-srv/local/daily/jan99/district27.htm.

29. Examples taken from Shoemaker (2000).

30. See Basu (2019) and Beeghly (2021).

31. In making this rather glib point, I'm simply denying outright one famous theory of well-being, a desire-satisfaction view. According to this theory, people are harmed whenever their informed desires are thwarted, so if a single Swiss person were to have an informed desire that I not think poorly of him, I would be harming him by hating all Swiss people. I find my example to be a powerful reductio ad absurdum of the desire-satisfaction view, but there are others. For example, this view would entail that, were I to form a desire that a stranger I met on a train last year (and will never see again) recover from the illness she told me about during the train ride, then if she fails to recover, I'm harmed, even if I never find out either way (and if she does recover, I'm somehow benefited, on this view) (Parfit 1984, 494). Sophisticated desire-satisfaction theorists (e.g., Heathwood [2006]) have offered solutions, but they all strike me as ad hoc.

32. Benatar 1999, 195–96. See also Carroll (2014b, 110–11).

33. Morreall 2009, 107.

34. Morreall 2009, 108.

35. Ford et al. 2013a, 2013b.

36. See, e.g., Viki et al. (2007); Thomae and Viki (2013).

37. Mallett, Ford, and Woodzicka 2016.

38. Viki et al. 2007.

39. Romero-Sanchez et al. 2009.

40. See Bohner et al. (2005).

41. Saucier et al. 2018.

42. Saucier et al. 2018; Miller et al. 2019.

43. Miller et al. 2019.

44. Ford et al. 2013a, 2013b.

45. It's also important to stress yet again that nearly all of these studies were done on jokes that subjects themselves *read*, not to joke tellings, and certainly not to wisecracks.

46. Thanks to Elizabeth Brake for this point.

47. See, e.g., Prusaczyk and Hodson (2020); Ford and Ferguson (2004); Thomae and Viki (2013).

48. Morreall 2009, 110.

49. Morreall 2009, 108.

50. Anderson 2020, 12. Here he is drawing significantly from Haslanger (2012). See also Leslie (2017).

51. I'm grateful to Olivia Bailey, Justin D'Arms, Simon May, and Connie Rosati for discussion on this point.

52. Boskin 1987.

53. Prusaczyk and Hodson 2020.

54. Ford and Ferguson 2004.

55. Thomae and Viki 2013.

CHAPTER SIX

1. Sprecher and Regan 2002.

2. Kowalski 2000.

3. See Eysenck (1972); Hehl and Ruch (1985); and discussion in Martin (1998, 15–16).

4. True! A symptomatic feature of the neurological disorder Witzelsucht is that patients constantly make puns or tell inappropriate jokes.

5. How many senses we have is actually a source of ongoing disagreement among scientists, but no one doubts that they are, indeed, forms of perceptual experience, and that we have several more than just five.

6. See https://www.sensorytrust.org.uk/information/articles/senses.html.

7. This formulation is essentially taken straight from Aristotle, in the *Nicomachean Ethics*, Book I, Ch. 7.

8. Sometimes we designate only a subset of humans as the relevant comparison class: "You hear pretty well for an old man," I might say to my ninety-year-old grandfather (to which he'll reply, "Huh?").

9. *Nicomachean Ethics* IV, Ch. 10. Aristotle uses a term most often translated as "boor." He was thinking about people with unrefined tastes more generally, though, and that doesn't apply as precisely to the people I have in mind, who might well be highly refined in other areas of evaluative life (they may be able to appreciate fine wines and opera, for instance), but who nevertheless do exhibit an unrefined vice in the humor domain. Thanks to Rachana Kamtekar and John Doris for discussion.

10. Other ways of having a bad sense of humor that I won't discuss might include turning up your nose at so-called unrefined humor, such as slapstick, or refusing to engage in friendly banter because it's "competitive," and competition is "bad."

11. I aim for this way of putting it to be a kind of companion to what's known as the moralistic fallacy, a fallacy coined and explicated in D'Arms and Jacobson (2000). To commit the fallacy is to say that, if it's immoral to feel an emotion, then it's not fitting (not evaluationally correct) to feel it. This is both more general (applying to many emotions besides amusement) and slightly different from the priggish mistake I've articulated in the text, which says instead that, if something has any immoral property in it, then either it can't be funny or it's been made much less funny (independently of whether it's immoral to feel amusement at it, say). When it comes to humor, prigs often commit the moralistic fallacy too, of course, but I've found that the more familiar and natural way of describing their general mistake is to have them shifting from the identification of an immoral property in something to viewing it as less or not funny thereby.

12. *Nicomachean Ethics* IV, Ch. 10.

13. Identified by the Humor Styles Questionnaire, developed by Martin et al. (2003).

14. Martin et al. 2003, 52–53.

15. Martin et al. 2003, 53.

16. Martin et al. 2003, 51–54.

17. A fifty-question self-diagnostic tool, known as the Autism-Spectrum Quotient (AQ), has been available for over twenty years, although it has some outdated questions. It derives from Baron-Cohen et al. (2001).

18. Hans Asperger (1944) himself claimed that an essential feature of (what was then labeled) "autistic psychopathy"—now labeled "Asperger's syndrome"—was "humorlessness," that those with the syndrome didn't "get jokes." See also Samson et al. (2013).

19. "Facts" and theories change, sometimes at a rapid pace, in the study of ASD. I'm trying to capture the most recent state of the art, but what I say here (and about other disorders as well) is happily subject to future empirical refinement or refutation.

20. Or "autistic people," or "autistics." I will go back and forth with the descriptive labels throughout, as there are different views in different camps about how "properly" to refer to members of the group. Count me as adopting the best reasons in favor of whatever usage I adopt at any given time. For more on the ongoing conversation about how to talk about autism, see Joel Abrams, "Watch Your Language When Talking about Autism," *The Conversation*, July 13, 2015, https://theconversation.com/watch-your -language-when-talking-about-autism-44531.

21. Reddy et al. 2002, 228.

22. See Van Bourgondien and Mesibov (1987).

23. https://www.playproject.org/jokes-imagination-and-autism-intervention/.

24. Samson et al. 2013.

25. Cat Damon (@CornOnTheGoblin), "'You promise you didn't get me bees again' / [me from a distance] just open it," Twitter, November 11, 2014, 3:09 a.m., https://twitter.com/CornOnTheGoblin/status/532082657925271552?s=20&fbclid= IwAR1MJm6Bmrg2bIBhaeWzx262KklCEVP90IeQuNpVzsOcTsFg5eCLtOGVcwU.

26. Thomas Frazier, chief science officer of the advocacy group Autism Speaks, in a *New York Times* article on autistic comics, June 18, 2019, https://www.nytimes.com/2019/06/18/well/mind/autism-spectrum-humor-comedy.html.

27. See Nagase and Tanaka (2015). Interestingly, Hannah Gadsby, whose Netflix specials *Nanette* and *Douglas* have garnered lots of attention and controversy, announced in *Douglas* that she had just been diagnosed with autism. This helps to make some sense of her definition in *Nanette* (which I criticized in chapter 1) that comedy involves the creation and then release of tension, a definition that has the most in common with incongruity-resolution and/or relief theories of humor, but that doesn't do well accounting for absurdist, superiority, and other types of humor.

28. Mitchell et al. 1997.

29. Meghan Keneally, "President Obama's Long History of Insulting Donald Trump," *ABC News*, November 10, 2016, https://abcnews.go.com/Politics/president-obamas-long-history-insulting-donald-trump/story?id=43442367.

30. Recent work has demonstrated that the detection of sarcasm can successfully be taught to children with ASD. See Persicke et al. (2013). The training, however, succeeded only with respect to statements that blatantly contradicted what the children could clearly see or knew, e.g., "It's definitely going to snow today" during a warm and sunny day, or "Playing video games is never fun" to a child who enjoys playing video games. In addition, these weren't examples of *funny* sarcasm, and it's unclear how recognizing the reasons to respond with amusement to funny forms of sarcasm could successfully be taught to those with difficulty sussing out intent in others.

31. Reddy et al. 2002.

32. Rieffe et al. 2012.

33. The last two are "subclinical" versions of the disorder.

34. Costa and McCrae 1992; quoted in Furnham et al. (2014, 115).

35. Book et al. 2015, 30.

36. Jones and Paulhus 2010; Baron-Cohen 2011. The other major alternative explanations—low "Big Five" agreeableness, "fast and exploitative life history strategy," and low honesty-humility (Book et al. 2015, 30, 35)—all have difficulty accounting for various features of both the dark triad and other malevolent types and traits.

37. Kidding, kind of. If you want the whole truth, and nothing but the truth, on the actual nature of empathy, see Shoemaker (2015, 126–28; 158–62); as well as Shoemaker (2017).

38. The literature on empathy is vast. For some good discussions of it, I can point you to several of the articles in both Coplan and Goldie (2011) and Maibom (2017).

39. See Mazza et al. (2014), for one of many articles on this topic.

40. Smith 2006, 2009; Markram et al. 2007.

41. See, e.g., Grandin (2006); Dunkin and Rauser (2017).

42. On this point, by pathology, see Decety et al. (2013) about psychopaths; Davies and Stone (2003) about Machiavellians; and Ritter et al. (2011) about narcissists.

43. Jonason and Krause 2013.

44. Wai and Tiliopoulos 2012; de Oliveira-Souza et al. 2008, 156.

45. Porter et al. 2014; James et al. 2014.

46. Martin et al. 2012. There are complications. Narcissists, in addition to favoring aggressive humor, also incline toward affiliative humor, given their desperate craving for self-affirmation and approval every hour of the day (Martin et al. 2012). But it seems the best way "that narcissistic individuals create or boost their exaggerated self-concept may be through sarcasm or aggressive forms of teasing that allow them to enhance the self at the expense of others" (Martin et al. 2012, 181).

47. Proyer et al. 2012.

48. Proyer et al. 2012.

49. Proyer et al. 2012, 266.

50. Proyer et al. 2012, 266.

51. And the greater the misfortunes, the greater the enjoyment; see Porter et al. (2014).

52. Again, there may well be other sources, including being overly literal about language in a way that prevents their "getting" funny sarcasm and irony. See Pexman, Reggin, and Lee (2019).

53. I'm grateful to Justin D'Arms for helpful discussion here.

54. Although there is an "empathy-training" movement, mostly aimed at teachers and health workers, it is actually a movement to expand the range of application of people's already-functional empathic capacities, not help them develop functional, or better-functioning, empathic capacities in the first place. See, e.g., Teding van Berkhout and Malouff (2016) for some discussion.

55. There are many such manifestations, a function of a wide variety of symptoms that may generate numerous combinations. I'm again certainly not talking about all such combinations, only a subset.

56. Thorsen and Powell 1994; Forabosco 1998.

57. O'Connor et al. 2002; Thoma et al. 2011. Indeed, a higher-than-normal degree of empathic sensitivity as a teenager is a significant predictor of later-life depression.

58. O'Connor et al. 2007.

59. Uekermann et al. 2008.

60. Forabosco 1998.

61. Haig 1988, 57.

62. Speaking of control, those with obsessive-compulsive disorder (OCD) tend to have a much-diminished sense of humor, precisely because of humor's qualities of spontaneity, play, and (limited) loss of control (Forabosco 1998, 281).

63. Dutra et al. 2014; see also Gruber et al. (2008).

CHAPTER SEVEN

1. Eric Idle, "Always Look on the Bright Side of Life," *Monty Python's Life of Brian.*

2. Nagel 1971/1979, 13.

3. Nagel 1971/1979, 13.

4. Nagel 1971/1979, 13.

5. Nagel 1971/1979, 13.

6. Nagel 1971/1979, 14–15.

7. Nagel 1971/1979, 23.

8. Nagel 1971/1979, 15; emphasis mine.

9. Randy Newman is perhaps the best purveyor of this dual aspect view of humanity. His songs are often about both features. Listen, for example, to "God's Song (That's Why I Love Mankind)," a bitter song about humanity's foibles and absurdities, written from God's perspective. It does not spare God its poisonously pointed commentary.

10. From Tired Moderate, *The Little Book of Woke Jokes*, n.p., Independently Published (April 19, 2021).

11. Caroline Wharton, Students for Life of America Blog, March 7, 2023, https:// studentsforlife.org/2023/03/07/top-5-grossest-abortion-jokes-chris-rock-made-in -new-netflix-special/.

12. As Franzini (1996, 811) puts it: "The contemporary cliché is that feminists have no sense of humor. Some feminists unapologetically agree, while vigorously pointing out that the cause of feminism is too important to trivialize with expressions of humor."

13. Cann and Collette 2014.

14. Of course, I've been putting this all in fairly stark terms: Either you're engaged or reflective. But obviously, there are degrees here. We can reflect a little or lot, or be engaged a little or a lot. The aim regardless, though, should be to strike the right balance of both.

15. See Christopher (2015); Moran and Massam (1997); Nezu, Nezu, and Blissett (1998); Rosenberg (1991); Sultanoff (1995); van Wormer and Boes (1997). See also the fascinating literature on Jewish humor coping strategies during the Holocaust. A particularly nice discussion can be found in John Morreall's 1997 lecture at the Annual Scholars' Conference on the Holocaust and the Church, "Humor and the Holocaust: Its Critical, Cohesive, and Coping Functions," published here: http://www.holocaust-trc .org/humor-in-the-holocaust/.

16. Lefcourt and Martin 1986; Porterfield 1987; Nezu, Nezu, and Blissett 1998; Capps 2006.

17. Szabo 2003.

18. Papousek et al. 2019; Samson et al. 2014.

19. Prerost 1989; Frankenfield 1996; Weisenberg et al. 1995.

20. Thorson et al. 1997.

21. Cann and Collette 2014.

22. Strick et al. 2009.

23. I'm old. These are references to, respectively, *Raiders of the Lost Ark* and *Die Hard*, which are both movies from the eighties. I'd make reference to a nineties "I'll be back" Schwarzenegger quip, but that probably wouldn't help the cause.

24. An anecdote told by John Doris, who also coined the great word, "tragilarious," to describe it.

25. Henry 2016.

26. Schilling et al. 2018; Schilling et al. 2019.

27. Bergson 1911.

28. Takamatsu 2018.

29. Ferguson, Cameron, and Inzlicht 2020.

30. Zaki 2020; Cameron and Inzlicht 2020.

31. Nick Sars has a moving passage in his 2020 dissertation (Tulane University) in which he discusses a kind of empathic toggling back and forth that General Eisenhower underwent as he planned the D-day attack.

32. Cameron, et al. 2019; see also Cameron, Harris, and Keith (2016).

33. The stress on this as our special "resource" is drawn from Hieronymi (2020), but it is language taken from Strawson 1962/2003, 80).

34. Zaki 2020.

35. Strawson (1962/2003, 79). This is how P. F. Strawson described what he called the "objective attitude" we tend to take up toward those deemed incapable of responsible and interpersonal agency, but it's also what we can take up to avoid what he calls the "strains of involvement" (80).

36. On the album *Parental Advisory: Explicit Lyrics*.

37. See the joke and a complaint about it by Hannah Joslin, "I went to a comedy show about how society takes things too personally, and I took everything personally," *Medium*, June 12, 2018, https://medium.com/@hannahjoslin/hi-ricky-gervais-2282b854e6be.

38. See Nussbaum (2015).

39. "And why include such a thing in this book?" as several concerned friends have asked me. The answer will, I hope, become clear soon enough.

40. Not funny? You haven't heard me tell it.

41. For one powerful presentation of this idea, see Goffman (1959). See also Velleman (1996).

42. Tannen 1989.

43. Norrick 1993, 46–47.

44. Norrick 1993, 47.

45. Norrick 1993, 55; emphasis in original.

46. Kylie Cheung, "This Survivor Comedy Duo Wants You to Know 'Rape Victims Are Horny Too,'" *Jezebel*, December 2, 2021, https://jezebel.com/this-survivor-comedy-duo-wants-to-know-rape-victim-1848150185.

47. Sarah Ellis, "The Women Who Confronted Harvey Weinstein Held a Comedy

Show by Rape Survivors, *Elite Daily*, November 12, 2019, https://www.elitedaily.com/
p/kelly-bachmans-rape-jokes-by-survivors-comedy-show-addressed-trauma-with
-humor-19313668.

48. Emer O'Toole, "Survivors Use Humour to Challenge Rape Culture," *The Conversation*, September 28, 2017, https://theconversation.com/survivors-use-humour-to
-challenge-rape-culture-84671.

49. O'Toole.

50. O'Toole.

51. Of course, there are some people who can and do find pure victimization funny.
"I like people who weren't captured," smirks Donald Trump about prisoner-of-war
John McCain. "Why should I go to that [military] cemetery? It's filled with losers,"
cracks Donald Trump about dead US soldiers. The 1,800 US Marines who were killed
at Belleau Wood in 1918 are "suckers," as are those who voluntarily sign up for military
service, jokes Donald Trump. See Jeffrey Goldberg, "Trump: Americans Who Died in
War Are 'Losers' and 'Suckers,'" *Atlantic*, September 3, 2020, https://www.theatlantic
.com/politics/archive/2020/09/trump-americans-who-died-at-war-are-losers-and
-suckers/615997/.

52. See, e.g., Happe (1993); Winner et al. (1998); Sullivan et al. (2003).

53. For just a few examples, see "Are You Joking or Serious?," at the blog *The Caf-
feinated Autistic*, December 13, 2012, https://thecaffeinatedautistic.wordpress.com/
2012/12/13/are-you-joking-or-serious/; Ian Stuart-Hamilton, "People with Autism
Spectrum Disorder Take Things Literally," *Psychology Today*, April 7, 2013, https://
www.psychologytoday.com/us/blog/the-gift-aging/201304/people-autism-spectrum
-disorder-take-things-literally; and scholarly work by Winner et al. (1998); Diaz (2010);
Mathersul et al. (2013); and Pexman (2018).

54. For just a few examples, see Proyer et al. (2012); Porter et al. (2014); and Torres-
Marin (2019). Hampes (2010, 41) puts the point about those in the dark triad nicely:

> Those who use aggressive humor not only don't want to help someone who's
> feeling badly, but have difficulty experiencing both emotionally and cognitively
> the person's negative feelings. . . . Those who use aggressive humor on a regular
> basis may set up a vicious cycle in which the targets of this style of humor
> withdraw from those who use it, which makes it even harder for those who use
> aggressive humor to get closer to other people, which in turn makes it harder for
> them to develop empathy.

55. I wrote a song about it. The opening line, sung in a country twang, is this:
"There's a hole in my heart where my prostate used to be." For the rest, go here:
https://soundcloud.com/david-shoemaker/what-i-did-on-my-summer-break?utm
_source=clipboard&utm_medium=text&utm_campaign=social_sharing.

References

An, Dong, and Chen, Kaiyuan. 2021. "Jokes Can Fail to Be Funny Because They Are Immoral: The Incompatibility of Emotions." *Philosophical Psychology* 34:374–96.

Anderson, Luvell. 2015. "Racist Humor." *Philosophy Compass* 10:501–9.

Anderson, Luvell. 2020. "Why So Serious? An Inquiry on Racist Jokes." *Journal of Social Philosophy*. https://doi.org/10.1111/josp.12384.

Appiah, Kwame Anthony. 2002. "Racisms." In *Anatomy of Racism*, edited by David Goldberg, 3–17. Minneapolis: University of Minnesota Press.

Asperger, Hans. 1944. "Die 'Autistischen Psychopathen' im Kindesalter" [The autistic psychopaths in childhood]. *Archiv für Psychiatrie und Nervenkrankheiten* 117:76–136.

Austin, J. L. 1975. *How to Do Things with Words*. Oxford: Oxford University Press.

Bain, Alexander. 1859. *The Emotions and the Will*. London: J. W. Parker.

Barnes, Elizabeth. 2016. *The Minority Body*. Oxford: Oxford University Press.

Barnes, M. Elizabeth, et al. 2020. "Are Scientists Biased against Christians? Exploring Real and Perceived Bias against Christians in Academic Biology." *PloS One* 15:e0226826.

Baron-Cohen, Simon. 2011. *The Science of Evil: On Empathy and the Origins of Cruelty*. New York: Basic Books.

Baron-Cohen, Simon, Sally Wheelwright, Richard Skinner, Joanne Martin, and Emma Clubley. 2001. "The Autism-Spectrum Quotient (AQ): Evidence from Asperger Syndrome/High-Functioning Autism, Males and Females, Scientists and Mathematicians." *Journal of Autism and Developmental Disorders* 31:5–17.

Basu, Rima. 2019. "The Wrongs of Racist Beliefs." *Philosophical Studies* 176:2497–515.

Beeghly, Erin. 2021. "Stereotyping as Discrimination: Why Thoughts Can Be Discriminatory." *Social Epistemology* 35:1–17.

Benatar, David. 1999. "Prejudice in Jest: When Racial and Gender Humor Harms." *Public Affairs Quarterly* 13:191–203.

Bergman, Merrie. 1986. "How Many Feminists Does It Take to Make a Joke? Sexist Humor and What's Wrong with It." *Hypatia* 1:63–82.

Bergson, Henri. 1911. *Laughter: An Essay on the Meaning of the Comic*. Oxford: Macmillan.

Bicknell, Jeanette. 2007. "What Is Offensive about Offensive Jokes?" *Philosophy Today* 51:458–65.

Bohner, Gerd, et al. 2005. "The Causal Impact of Rape Myth Acceptance on Men's Rape Proclivity: Comparing Sexually Coercive and Noncoercive Men." *European Journal of Social Psychology* 35:819–28.

Book, A. S., V. L. Quinsey, and D. Langford. 2007. "Psychopathy and the Perception of Affect and Vulnerability." *Criminal Justice and Behavior* 34:531–44.

Book, Angela, Beth A. Visser, and Anthony A. Volk. 2015. "Unpacking 'Evil': Claiming the Core of the Dark Triad." *Personality and Individual Differences* 73:29–38.

Boskin, Joseph. 1987. "The Complicity of Humor: The Life and Death of Sambo." In *The Philosophy of Laughter and Humor*, edited by John Morreall, 250–63 (Albany: State University of New York Press).

Boyd, Robert, and Peter J. Richerson. 2005. *The Origin and Evolution of Cultures.* New York: Oxford University Press.

Buss, Sarah. 2005. "Valuing Autonomy and Respecting Persons: Manipulation, Seduction and the Basis of Moral Constraints." *Ethics* 115:195–235.

Cameron, C. Daryl, Lasana T. Harris, and B. Keith Payne. 2016. "The Emotional Cost of Humanity: Anticipated Exhaustion Motivates Dehumanization of Stigmatized Targets." *Social Psychological and Personality Science* 7:105–12.

Cameron, C. Daryl, and Michael Inzlicht. 2020. "Empathy Choice in Physicians and Non-Physicians." *British Journal of Social Psychology* 59:715–32.

Cameron, C. Daryl, et al. 2019. "Empathy Is Hard Work: People Choose to Avoid Empathy Because of Its Cognitive Costs." *Journal of Experimental Psychology: General* 148:962–76.

Campbell, Stephen M., and Joseph A. Stramondo. 2017. "The Complicated Relationship of Disability and Well-Being." *Kennedy Institute of Ethics Journal* 27:151–84.

Cann, Arnie, and Chantal Collette. 2014. "Sense of Humor, Stable Affect, and Psychological Well-Being." *Europe's Journal of Psychology* 10:213–35.

Capps, Donald. 2006. "The Psychological Benefits of Humor." *Pastoral Psychology* 54:393–411.

Carroll, Noel. 2001. "On Jokes." In Noel Carroll, *Beyond Aesthetics: Philosophical Essays.* New York: Cambridge University Press.

Carroll, Noel. 2014a. "Ethics and Comic Amusement." *British Journal of Aesthetics* 54:241–53.

Carroll, Noel. 2014b. *Humour: A Very Short Introduction.* Oxford: Oxford University Press.

Christopher, Sarah. 2015. "An Introduction to Black Humour as a Coping Mechanism for Student Paramedics." *Journal of Paramedic Practice* 7:610–17.

Clarke, Michael. 1987. "Humor and Incongruity." In Morreall 1987, 139–55.

Cleckley, Hervey. 1976. *The Mask of Sanity.* 5th ed. Saint Louis: C. V. Mosley.

Clewis, Robert R. 2021. *Kant's Humorous Writings.* London: Bloomsbury.

Cohen, Ted. 1999. *Jokes: Philosophical Thoughts on Joking Matters.* Chicago: University of Chicago Press.

Coplan, Amy, and Peter Goldie, eds. 2011. *Empathy: Philosophical and Psychological Perspectives.* Oxford: Oxford University Press.

Coser, Rose. 1959. "Some Social Functions of Laughter: A Study of Humor in a Hospital Setting." *Human Relations* 12:171–82.

Costa, P., and R. McCrae. 1992. *Revised NEO Personality Inventory (NEO-PI-R) and NEO Five-Factor Inventory (NEO-FFI): Professional Manual.* Odessa, FL: Psychological Assessment Resources.

D'Arms, Justin. 2013. "Value and the Regulation of the Sentiments." *Philosophical Studies* 163:3–13.

D'Arms, Justin, and Daniel Jacobson. 2000. "The Moralistic Fallacy: On the 'Appropriateness' of the Emotions." *Philosophy & Phenomenological Research* 61:65–90.

D'Arms, Justin, and Daniel Jacobson. 2010. "Demystifying Sensibilities and the Instability of Affect." In *The Oxford Handbook of Philosophy of Emotion*, edited by Peter Goldie, 585–613. Oxford: Oxford University Press.

D'Arms, Justin, and Daniel Jacobson. 2023. *Rational Sentimentalism*. Oxford: Oxford University Press.

Davies, Christie. 1991. "Exploring the Thesis of the Self-Deprecating Jewish Sense of Humor." *Humor: International Journal of Humor Research* 4:189–209.

Davies, M., and T. Stone 2003. "Synthesis: Psychological Understanding and Social Skills." In *Individual Differences in Theory of Mind*, edited by B. Repacholi and V. Slaughter, 305–53. New York: Psychology Press.

Decety, Jean, Chenyi Chen, Carla Harenski, and Kent A. Kiehl. 2013. "An fMRI Study of Affective Perspective Taking in Individuals with Psychopathy: Imagining Another in Pain Does Not Evoke Empathy." *Frontiers in Human Neuroscience* 7:489.

De Oliveira-Souza, Ricardo, et al. 2008. "The Antisocials amid Us." In *Moral Psychology*, vol. 3, *The Neuroscience of Morality: Emotion, Brain Disorders, and Development*, edited by Walter Sinnott-Armstrong, 151–58. Cambridge, MA: MIT Press.

De Sousa, Ronald. 1987. "When Is It Wrong to Laugh?" In *The Rationality of Emotion*, edited by Ronald de Sousa. Cambridge, MA: MIT Press.

Diaz, Stacy. 2010. *Understanding Metaphors, Irony, and Sarcasm in High Functioning Children with Autism Spectrum Disorders: Its Relationship to Theory of Mind*. Dissertation, Smith College.

Doris, John, Joshua Knobe, and Robert L. Woolfolk. 2007. "Variantism about Responsibility." *Philosophical Perspectives* 21:183–214.

Douglass, Sara, et al. 2016. "'They Were Just Making Jokes': Ethnic/Racial Teasing and Discrimination among Adolescents." *Cultural Diversity and Ethnic Minority Psychology* 22:69–82.

Dunbar, Norah E., et al. 2012. "Humor Use in Power-Differentiated Interactions." *Humor* 25:469–89.

Dunkin, Sandra, and Cheri Rauser. 2017. "Memory as Records Management System." *Sagesse: Journal of Canadian Records and Information Management II*.

Dutra, Sunny J., et al. 2014. "Rose-Colored Glasses Gone Too Far? Mania Symptoms Predict Biased Emotion Experience and Perception in Couples." *Motivation and Emotion* 38:157–65.

Dworkin, Ronald. 1975. "The Original Position." In *Reading Rawls*, edited by Norman Daniels. New York: Basic Books, 1975.

Dwyer, Tom. 1991. "Humor, Power, and Change in Organizations." *Human Relations* 44:1–19.

Dynel, Marta. 2019. "Lying and Humour." In Meibauer 2019b, 326–39.

Eriksson, Kimmo. 2013. "Autism-Spectrum Traits Predict Humor Styles in the General Population." *Humor: An International Journal of Humor Research* 26:461–75.

Eslinger, Paul J., et al. 2011. "Social Cognition, Executive Functioning, and Neuro-imaging Correlates of Empathic Deficits in Frontotemporal Dementia." *Journal of Neuropsychiatry and Clinical Neurosciences* 23:74–82.

Everts, Elisa. 2006. "Identifying a Particular Family Humor Style: A Sociolinguistic Discourse Analysis." *Humor* 16:369–412.

Eysenck, Hans-Jurgen. 1972. "Foreword." In *The Psychology of Humor: Theoretical Per-

spectives and Empirical Issues, edited by Jeffrey H. Goldstein and Paul E. McGhee, xiii–xvii New York: Academic Press, .

Fallis, Don. 2009. "What Is Lying?" *Journal of Philosophy* 106:29–56.

Fallis, Don. 2012. "Lying as a Violation of Grice's First Maxim of Quality." *Dialectica* 66:563–81.

Fallis, Don. 2019. "Lying and Omissions." In Meibauer 2019b, 183–92.

Feinberg, Joel. 1973. "'Harmless Immoralities' and Offensive Nuisances." In *Issues in Law and Morality: Proceedings of the 1971 Oberlin Colloquium in Philosophy*, edited by Norman S. Care and Thomas K. Trelogan, 111–26. Cleveland: The Press of Case Western Reserve University.

Feinberg, Joel. 1985. *Offense to Others*. Vol. 2 of *The Moral Limits of the Criminal Law*. Oxford: Oxford University Press.

Feldman, Fred, and Brad Skow. 2019. "Desert." In *The Stanford Encyclopedia of Philosophy*, edited by Edward N. Zalta. Winter ed. https://plato.stanford.edu/archives/win2019/entries/desert/.

Ferguson, Amanda, C. Daryl Cameron, and Michael Inzlicht. 2020. "Motivational Effects on Empathic Choices." *Journal of Experimental Social Psychology* 90:104010.

Fischer, John, and Mark Ravizza. 1998. *Responsibility and Control*. Cambridge: Cambridge University Press.

Forabosco, Giovannantonio. 1998. "The Ill Side of Humor: Pathological Conditions and Sense of Humor." In Ruch 1998, 271–92.

Ford, Thomas E., and Mark A. Ferguson. 2004. "Social Consequences of Disparagement Humor: A Prejudiced Norm Theory." *Personality and Social Psychology Review* 8:79–94.

Ford, Thomas E., et al. 2013a. "Not All Groups Are Equal: Differential Vulnerability of Social Groups to the Prejudice-Releasing Effects of Disparagement Humor." *Group Processes & Intergroup Relations* 17:178–99.

Ford, Thomas E., et al. 2013b. "Sexist Humor and Beliefs That Justify Societal Sexism." *Current Research in Social Psychology* 21:64–81.

Ford, Thomas E., et al. 2020. "Diminished Self-Concept and Social Exclusion: Disparagement Humor from the Target's Perspective." *Self and Identity* 19:698–718.

Frank, Robert H. 1988. *Passions with Reason*. New York: W. W. Norton & Company.

Frankenfield, Pamela K. 1996. "The Power of Humor and Play as Nursing Interventions for a Child with Cancer: A Case Report." *Journal of Pediatric Oncology Nursing* 13:15–20.

Frankfurt, Harry. 1988. *The Importance of What We Care About*. Cambridge: Cambridge University Press.

Franzini, L. R. 1996. "Feminism and Women's Sense of Humor." *Sex Roles* 35:811–19.

Fricker, Miranda. 2007. *Epistemic Injustice: Power and the Ethics of Knowing*. Oxford: Oxford University Press.

Frijda, Nico. 1986. *The Emotions*. Cambridge: Cambridge University Press.

Frijda, Nico. 2009. "Emotion Experience and Its Varieties." *Emotion Review* 1:264–71.

Furnham, Adrian, et al. 2014. "Measuring Malevolence: Quantitative Issues Surrounding the Dark Triad of Personality." *Personality and Individual Differences* 67:114–21.

Garcia, J. L. A. 1996. "The Heart of Racism." *Journal of Social Philosophy* 27:5–45.

Garcia, J. L. A. 1997. "Current Conceptions of Racism." *Journal of Social Philosophy* 28:5–42.

Garcia, J. L. A. 1999. "Philosophical Analysis and the Moral Concept of Racism." *Philosophy & Social Criticism* 25:1–32.

Gaut, Berys. 1998. "Just Joking: The Ethics and Aesthetics of Humor." In "Jane Austen's Darwinian Gambit." Special issue, *Philosophy and Literature*, suppl. 22:51–68.

Glasgow, Joshua. 2009. "Racism as Disrespect." *Ethics* 120:64–93.

Glover, Jonathan. 2014. *Alien Landscapes? Interpreting Disordered Minds*. Cambridge, MA: Belknap Press of Harvard University Press.

Goffman, Erving. 1959. *The Presentation of Self in Everyday Life*. Garden City, NJ: Anchor Books.

Graham, Elizabeth E. 1995. "The Involvement of Sense of Humor in the Development of Social Relationships." *Communication Reports* 8:158–69.

Graham, Elizabeth E., Michael J. Papa, and Gordon P. Brooks. 1992. "Functions of Humor in Conversation: Conceptualization and Measurement." *Western Journal of Communication* 56:161–83.

Graham, J., B. A. Hosek, J. Haidt, R. Iyer, S. Koleva, and P. H. Ditto. 2011. "Mapping the Moral Domain." *Journal of Personality and Social Psychology* 101:366–85.

Grandin, Temple. 2006. *Thinking in Pictures: And Other Reports from My Life with Autism*. New York: Vintage.

Grasswick, Heidi. 2018. "Feminist Social Epistemology." In *The Stanford Encyclopedia of Philosophy*, edited by Edward N. Zalta. Fall ed. https://plato.stanford.edu/archives/fall2018/entries/feminist-social-epistemology/.

Greengross, Gil, and Geoffrey F. Miller. 2008. "Dissing Oneself versus Dissing Rivals: Effects of Status, Personality, and Sex on the Short-Term and Long-Term Attractiveness of Self-Deprecating and Other-Deprecating Humor." *Evolutionary Psychology* 6:147470490800600303.

Greengross, Gil, and Geoffrey Miller. 2011. "Humor Ability Reveals Intelligence, Predicts Mating Success, and Is Higher in Males." *Intelligence* 39:188–92.

Grice, Paul. 1989. *Studies in the Way of Words*. Cambridge, MA: Harvard University Press.

Gruber, J., S. L. Johnson, C. Oveis, and D. Keltner. 2008. "Risk for Mania and Positive Emotional Responding: Too Much of a Good Thing?" *Emotion* 8:23–33.

Guerin, Charles. 2019. "Laughter, Social Norms, and Ethics in Cicero's Works." In *Laughter, Humor, and Comedy in Ancient Philosophy*, edited by Pierre Destree and Franco V. Trivigno, 122–44. Oxford: Oxford University Press.

Haig, Robin A. 1988. *The Anatomy of Humor: Biopsychosocial and Therapeutic Perspectives*. Springfield, IL: Thomas.

Hampes, William P. 2010. "The Relation between Humor Styles and Empathy." *Europe's Journal of Psychology* 6:34–45.

Hamscha, Susanne. 2016. "Crip Humor." In *Gender: Macmillan Interdisciplinary Handbooks. Sources, Perspectives, and Methodologies*, edited by Reneé Hoogland, 349–62. London: Macmillan, 2016.

Happe, F. G. E. 1993. "Communicative Competence and Theory of Mind in Autism: A Test of Relevance Theory. *Cognition* 48:101–19.

Harman, Gilbert. 1977. *The Nature of Morality*. Oxford: Oxford University Press.

Haslanger, Sally. 2012. *Resisting Reality: Social Construction and Social Critique*. Oxford: Oxford University Press.

Haugh, Michael. 2016. "'Just Kidding': Teasing and Claims to Non-Serious Intent." *Journal of Pragmatics* 95:120–36.

Hay, Jennifer. 1999. "Functions of Humor in the Conversations of Men and Women." *Journal of Pragmatics* 32:709–42.

Heathwood, Chris. 2006. "Desire Satisfactionism and Hedonism." *Philosophical Studies* 128:539–63.

Hehl, Franz-Josef, and Willibald Ruch. 1985. "The Location of Sense of Humor within Comprehensive Personality Spaces: An Exploratory Study." *Personality and Individual Differences* 6:703–15.

Henrich, Joseph, and Natalie Henrich. 2007. *Why Humans Cooperate: A Cultural and Evolutionary Perspective.* New York: Oxford University Press.

Henry, M. 2016. *What They Didn't Teach You in American History Class: The Second Encounter.* Lanham, MD: Rowman and Littlefield Publishers.

Hieronymi, Pamela. 2004. "The Force and Fairness of Blame." *Philosophical Perspectives* 18:115–48.

Hieronymi, Pamela. 2020. *Freedom, Resentment, and the Metaphysics of Morals.* Princeton, NJ: Princeton University Press.

Hoption, Colette, Julian Barling, and Nick Turner. 2013. "'It's Not You, It's Me': Transformational Leadership and Self-Deprecating Humor." *Leadership & Organizational Development Journal* 34:4–19.

Hume, David. 1757. "Of the Standard of Taste." https://sourcebooks.fordham.edu/mod/1760hume-taste.asp.

Hurd, Heidi. 1996. "The Moral Magic of Consent." *Legal Theory* 2:121–46.

Hurley, Matthew M., Daniel Dennett, and Reginald B. Adams Jr. 2011. *Inside Jokes: Using Humor to Reverse-Engineer the Mind.* Cambridge, MA: MIT Press.

Inbar, Yoel, and Joris Lammers. 2012. "Political Diversity in Social and Personality Psychology." *Perspectives on Psychological Science* 7:496–503.

Isenberg, Arnold. 1977. *Aesthetics and the Theory of Criticism.* Chicago: University of Chicago Press.

Jacobson, Daniel. 1997. "In Praise of Immoral Art." *Philosophical Topics* 25:155–99.

James, Samantha, et al. 2014: "The Dark Triad, Schadenfreude, and Sensational Interests: Dark Personalities, Dark Emotions, and Dark Behaviors." *Personality and Individual Differences* 68:211–16.

Jonason, Peter K., and Laura Krause. 2013. "The Emotional Deficits Associated with the Dark Triad Traits: Cognitive Empathy, Affective Empathy, and Alexithymia." *Personality and Individual Differences* 55:532–37.

Jones, D. N., and D. L. Paulhus. 2010. "Differentiating the Dark Triad within the Interpersonal Circumplex." In *Handbook of Interpersonal Psychology: Theory, Research, Assessment, and Therapeutic Interventions*, edited by L. M. Horowitz and S. Strack, 249–68. New York: Wiley, .

Jonson, Hakan, and Anna Siverskog. 2012. "Humorous Self-Presentations among Older GLBTQ Online Daters." *Journal of Aging Studies* 26:55–64.

Kennett, Jeanette. 2002. "Autism, Empathy, and Moral Agency." *Philosophical Quarterly* 52:340–57.

Knobe, Joshua, and John Doris. 2010. "Strawsonian Variations: Folk Morality and the Search for a Unified Theory." In *The Moral Psychology Handbook*, edited by John Doris and the Moral Psychology Research Group. Oxford: Oxford University Press.

Kowalski, R. M. 2000. "'I Was Only Kidding': Victims' and Perpetrators' Perceptions of Teasing." *Personality and Social Psychology Bulletin* 26:231–41.

Ladd, Paddy. 2002. *Understanding Deaf Culture: In Search of Deafhood*. Clevedon, England: Multilingual Matters.

Lampert, Martin D., and Susan M. Ervin-Tripp. 2006. "Risky Laughter: Teasing and Self-Directed Joking among Male and Female Friends." *Journal of Pragmatics* 38:51–72.

Langton, Rae. 2010. "Review of Miranda Fricker, *Epistemic Injustice: Power and the Ethics of Knowing*." *Hypatia* 25:459–64.

Lee, K., and M. Ashton. 2008. "The HEXACO Personality Factors in the Indigenous Personality Lexicons of English and 11 Other Languages." *Journal of Personality* 76:1001–54.

Lefcourt, H. M., and R. A. Martin. 1986. *Humor and Life Stress: Antidote to Adversity*. New York: Springer-Verlag.

Lench, Heather C., Thomas P. Tibbett, and Shane W. Bench. 2016. "Exploring the Toolkit of Emotion: What Do Sadness and Anger Do for Us?" *Social and Personality Psychology Compass* 10:11–25.

Lengbeyer, Lawrence. 2005. "Humor, Context, and Divided Cognition." *Social Theory and Practice* 31:309–36.

Leslie, Sarah-Jane. 2017. "The Original Sin of Cognition: Fear, Prejudice, and Generalization." *Journal of Philosophy* 114:393–421.

Levinson, Jerrold. 1998. "Humour." In *The Routledge Encyclopedia of Philosophy*, edited by E. Craig, 562–67. London: Routledge.

Mahon, James Edwin. 2019. "Contemporary Approaches to the Philosophy of Lying." In Meibauer 2019b, 32–55.

Maibom, Heidi L. 2014. "Introduction: (Almost) Everything You Ever Wanted to Know about Empathy." In *Empathy and Morality*, edited by Heidi Maibom, 1–40. New York: Oxford University Press.

Maibom, Heidi L., ed. 2017. *The Routledge Handbook of Philosophy of Empathy*. London: Routledge.

Mallett, Robyn K., Thomas E. Ford, and Julie A. Woodzicka. 2016. "What Did He Mean by That? Humor Decreases Attributions of Sexism and Confrontation of Sexist Jokes." *Sex Roles* 75:272–84.

Markram, H., T. Rinaldi, and K. Markram. 2007. "The Intense World Syndrome: An Alternative Hypothesis for Autism." *Frontiers in Neuroscience* 1:77–96.

Martin, Mike W. 1987. "Humor and Aesthetic Enjoyment of Incongruities." In Morreall 1987, 172–86.

Martin, Rod A. 1998. "Approaches to the Sense of Humor: A Historical Review." In Ruch 1998, 14–60.

Martin, Rod A. 2007. *The Psychology of Humor: An Integrative Approach*. San Diego, CA: Elsevier Academic Press.

Martin, Rod A., et al. 2003. "Individual Differences in Uses of Humor and Their Relation to Psychological Well-Being: Development of the Humor Styles Questionnaire." *Journal of Research in Personality* 37:48–75.

Martin, Rod A., et al. 2012. "Relationships between the Dark Triad and Humor Styles: A Replication and Extension." *Personality and Individual Differences* 52:178–82.

Martineau, W. H. 1972. "A Model of the Social Functions of Humor." In *The Psychology of Humor: Theoretical Perspectives and Empirical Issues*, edited by J. H. Goldstein and P. E. McGhee, 101–25. New York: Academic.

Martinotti, Giovanni, et al. 2009. "Empathy Ability Is Impaired in Alcohol-Dependent Patients." *American Journal on Addictions* 18:157–61.

Mathersul, Danielle, Skye McDonald, and Jacqueline A. Rushby. 2013. "Understanding Advanced Theory of Mind and Empathy in High-Functioning Adults with Autism Spectrum Disorder." *Journal of Clinical and Experimental Neuropsychology* 35:655–68.

Mazza, Monica, et al. 2014. "Affective and Cognitive Empathy in Adolescents with Autism Spectrum Disorder." *Frontiers in Human Neuroscience* 8:791.

McGeer, Victoria. 2013. "Civilizing Blame." In *Blame: Its Nature and Norms*, edited by D. Justin Coates and Neal Tognazzini, 162–88. New York: Oxford University Press.

McGraw, Peter, and Joel Warner. 2014. *The Humor Code*. New York: Simon & Schuster.

Mcilwain, D., et al. 2012. "Strange Moralities: Vicarious Emotion and Moral Emotions in Machiavellian and Psychopathic Personality Styles." In *Emotions, Imagination, and Moral Reasoning*, edited by R. Langdon and C. Mackenzie, 199–48. New York: Taylor & Francis.

McKenna, Michael. 2012. *Conversation and Responsibility*. New York: Oxford University Press.

Meibauer, Jorg. 2019a. "Bald-Faced Lies." In Meibauer 2019b, 252–63.

Meibauer, Jorg, ed. 2019b. *The Oxford Handbook of Lying*. Oxford: Oxford University Press.

Miller, Seumas. 2011. "Collective Responsibility, Epistemic Action and Climate Change." In *Moral Responsibility beyond Free Will and Determinism*, edited by Nicole A. Vincent, Ibo van de Poel, and Jeroen Hoven, 219–45. Dordrecht: Springer.

Miller, Stuart, et al. 2019. "Savage or Satire: Individual Differences in Perceptions of Disparaging and Subversive Racial Humor." *Personality and Individual Differences* 142:28–41.

Mills, Charles W. 2003. "'Heart' Attack: A Critique of Jorge Garcia's Volitional Conception of Racism." *Journal of Ethics* 7:29–62.

Mitchell, Peter, Rebecca Saltmarsh, and Helen Russell. 1997. "Overly Literal Interpretations of Speech in Autism: Understanding That Messages Arise from Minds." *Journal of Child Psychology and Psychiatry* 38:685–91.

Moran, C., and M. Massam. 1997. "An Evaluation of Humour in Emergency Work." *Australasian Journal of Disaster and Trauma Studies* 3.

Morreall, John. 1983. *Taking Laughter Seriously*. Albany: State University of New York Press.

Morreall, John, ed. 1987. *The Philosophy of Laughter and Humor*. Albany: State University of New York Press.

Morreall, John. 2009. *Comic Relief: A Comprehensive Philosophy of Humor*. West Sussex, UK: Wiley-Blackwell.

Morreall, John. 2020. "The Good, the Bad, and the Funny: An Ethics of Humor." *Southern Journal of Philosophy*. https://doi.org/10.1111/sjp.12390.

Nagase, K., and M. Tanaka. 2015. "Cognitive Processes in Humor Appreciation among Individuals with Autism Spectrum Disorder: Causal Inference and Stimulus Elaboration." *Japanese Journal of Developmental Psychology* 26:123–34.

Nagel, Thomas. 1971. "The Absurd." *Journal of Philosophy* 68:716–27. Reprinted in Thomas Nagel. *Mortal Questions*, 11–23. Cambridge: Cambridge University Press, 1979. Page references are to the 1979 reprint.

Nehamas, Alexander. 1986. "What an Author Is." *Journal of Philosophy* 83:685–91.

Newman, George E., Julian De Freitas, and Joshua Knobe. 2015. "Beliefs about the True Self Explain Asymmetries Based on Moral Judgment." *Cognitive Science* 39:96–125.

Nezu, A. M., C. M. Nezu, and S. E. Blissett. 1988. "Sense of Humor as a Moderator of the Relation between Stressful Events and Psychological Distress: A Perospective Analysis." *Journal of Personality and Social Psychology* 54:520–25.

Nichols, Shaun. 2002. "Norms with Feeling: Towards a Psychological Account of Moral Judgment." *Cognition* 84:221–35.

Nichols, Shaun. 2007. "After Compatibilism: A Naturalistic Defense of the Reactive Attitudes." *Philosophical Perspectives* 21:405–28.

Norcross, Alastair. 1997. "Comparing Harms: Headaches and Human Lives." *Philosophy & Public Affairs* 26:135–67.

Norrick, Neal R. 1993. *Conversational Joking: Humor in Everyday Talk*. Bloomington: Indiana University Press.

Nussbaum, Emily. 2015. "Last Girl in Larchmont." *New Yorker*, February 23, 6.

Obrdlik, A. J. 1942. "Gallows Humor: A Sociological Phenomenon." *American Journal of Sociology* 47:709–16.

O'Connor, Lynn E., et al. 2002. "Guilt, Fear, Submission, and Empathy in Depression." *Journal of Affective Disorders* 71:19–27.

O'Connor, Lynn E., et al. 2007. "Empathy and Depression: The Moral System on Overdrive." In *Empathy in Mental Illness*, edited by Tom F. D. Farrow and Peter W. R. Woodruff, 49–75. Cambridge: Cambridge University Press.

Olin, Lauren. 2016. "Questions for a Theory of Humor." *Philosophy Compass* 11:338–50.

Oliver, Mike. 1996. *Understanding Disability: From Theory to Practice*. London and Basingstoke: Palgrave Macmillan.

Oliver, Mike, and Colin Barnes. 2012. *The New Politics of Disablement*. London and Basingstoke: Palgrave Macmillan.

Papousek, Ilona, et al. 2019. "Humor Creation during Efforts to Find Humorous Cognitive Reappraisals of Threatening Situations." *Current Psychology*, 1–15.

Parfit, Derek. 1984. *Reasons and Persons*. Oxford: Oxford University Press.

Paulhus, D. L., and K. M. Williams. 2002. "The Dark Triad of Personality: Narcissism, Machiavellianism, and Psychopathy." *Journal of Research in Personality* 36:556–63.

Persicke, Angela, Jonathan Tarbox, Jennifer Ranick, and Megan St Clair. 2013. "Teaching Children with Autism to Detect and Respond to Sarcasm." *Research in Autism Spectrum Disorders* 7:193–98.

Peters, Uwe, et al. 2020. "Ideological Diversity, Hostility, and Discrimination in Philosophy." *Philosophical Psychology* 33:511–48.

Pexman, Pamela. 2018. "Do We Understand Sarcasm?" *Frontiers for Young Mind* 6.

Pexman, Penny, Lorraine Reggin, and Kate Lee. 2019. "Addressing the Challenge of Verbal Irony: Getting Serious about Sarcasm Training." *Languages* 4:23. https://doi.org/10.3390/languages4020023.

Phillips, James C. 2016. "Why Are There So Few Conservatives and Libertarians in Legal Academia: An Empirical Exploration of Three Hypotheses." *Harvard Journal of Law & Public Policy* 39:153–208.

Pollio, Howard R., and Rodney W. Mers. 1974. "Predictability and the Appreciation of Comedy." *Bulletin of the Psychonomic Society* 4:229–32.

Porter, Stephen, et al. 2014. "Soldiers of Misfortune: An Examination of the Dark Triad and the Experience of Schadenfreude." *Personality and Individual Differences* 67:64–68.

Porterfield, A. L. 1987. "Does Sense of Humor Moderate the Impact of Life Stress on Psychological and Physical Well-Being?" *Journal of Research in Personality* 21:307–17.

Portmore, Douglas W. 2011. *Commonsense Consequentialism*. Oxford: Oxford University Press.

Portmore, Douglas. 2021. *Morality and Practical Reasons*. Cambridge Elements. Cambridge: Cambridge University Press.

Prerost, Frank J. 1989. "Humor as an Intervention Strategy during Psychological Treatment: Imagery and Incongruity." *Psychology: A Journal of Human Behavior* 26:34–40.

Proyer, Rene T., et al. 2012. "How Does Psychopathy Relate to Humor and Laughter? Dispositions toward Ridicule and Being Laughed At, the Sense of Humor, and Psychopathic Personality Traits." *International Journal of Law and Psychiatry* 35:263–268.

Prusaczyk, Elvira, and Gordon Hodson. 2020. "'To the Moon, Alice': Cavalier Humor Beliefs and Women's Reaction to Aggressive and Belittling Sexist Jokes." *Journal of Experimental Social Psychology* 88:1–11.

Puthillam, Arathy, Sampada Karandikar, and Hansika Kapoor. 2019. "I See How You Feel: How the Dark Triad Recognizes Emotions." *Current Psychology*, 1–8.

Rachels, James. 1978. "What People Deserve." In *Justice and Economic Distribution*, edited by John Arthur and William Shaw, 167–96. Englewood Cliffs, NJ: Prentice-Hall.

Raskin, Victor. 1984. *Semantic Mechanisms of Humor*. Dordrecht: Reidel.

Rawls, John. 1971. *A Theory of Justice*. Cambridge, MA: Belknap Press of Harvard University Press.

Reddy, Vasudevi, Emma Williams, and Amy Vaughan. 2002. "Sharing Humor and Laughter in Autism and Down's Syndrome." *British Journal of Psychology* 93:219–42.

Rentfrow, Peter J., Lewis R. Goldberg, and Daniel J. Levitin. 2011. "The Structure of Musical Preferences: A Five-Factor Model." *Journal of Personality and Social Psychology* 100:1139–57.

Rieffe, Carolien, et al. 2012. "'Don't Anger Me!' Bullying, Victimization, and Emotion Dysregulation in Young Adolescents with ASD." *European Journal of Developmental Psychology* 9:351–70.

Ritchie, Chris. 2014. "'Taking the Piss': Mockery as a Form of Comic Communication." *Comedy Studies* 5:33–40.

Ritter, Kathrin, et al. 2011. "Lack of Empathy in Patients with Narcissistic Personality Disorder." *Psychiatry Research* 187:241–47.

Roberts, Alan. 2019. *A Philosophy of Humour*. Dordrecht: Springer.

Roberts, Robert C. 1988. "Is Amusement an Emotion?" *American Philosophical Quarterly* 25:269–74.

Romero-Sanchez, Monica, et al. 2009. "Exposure to Sexist Humor and Rape Proclivity: The Moderator Effect of Aversiveness Ratings." *Journal of Interpersonal Violence* 25:2339–50.

Ronson, Jon. 2015. *So You've Been Publicly Shamed*. New York: Riverhead Books.

Rosenberg, L. 1991. "A Qualitative Investigation of the Use of Humor by Emergency Personnel as a Strategy for Coping with Stress." *Journal of Emergency Nursing* 17:197–202.

Ruch, Willibald, ed. 1998. *The Sense of Humor: Explorations of a Personality Characteristic*. Berlin: Mouton de Gruyter.

Ruch, Willibald, and Sonja Heintz. 2013. "Humour Styles, Personality and Psychological Well-Being: What's Humour Got to Do with It?" *European Journal of Humour Research* 1:1–24.

Sadurski, Wojceich. 1985. *Giving Desert Its Due*. Dordrecht: D. Reidel Publishing.

Samson, Andrea C., Oswald Huber, and Willibald Ruch. 2011. "Teasing, Ridiculing and the Relation to the Fear of Being Laughed at in Individuals with Asperger's Syndrome." *Journal of Autism and Developmental Disorders* 41:475–83.

Samson, Andrea C., Oswald Huber, and Willibald Ruch. 2013. "Seven Decades after Hans Asperger's Observations: A Comprehensive Study of Humor in Individuals with Autism Spectrum Disorders." *Humor* 26:441–60.

Samson, Andrea Christiane, et al. 2014. "Humorous Coping and Serious Reappraisal: Short-Term and Longer-Term Effects." *Europe's Journal of Psychology* 10:571–81.

Santayana, George. 1896. *The Sense of Beauty*. New York: Scribner's.

Saucier, Donald A., et al. 2018. "'What Do You Call a Black Guy Who Flies a Plane?': The Effects and Understanding of Disparagement and Confrontational Racial Humor." *Humor* 31:105–28.

Scanlon, T. M. 1998. *What We Owe to Each Other*. Cambridge, MA: Belknap Press of Harvard University Press.

Scarantino, Andrea. 2014. "The Motivational Theory of Emotions." In *Moral Psychology and Human Agency*, edited by Justin D'Arms and Daniel Jacobson, 156–85. Oxford: Oxford University Press.

Schiffrin, Deborah. 1984. "Jewish Argument as Sociability." *Language in Society* 13:311–35.

Schilling, Tim, et al. 2018. "Tinted Lenses Affect Our Physiological Responses to Affective Pictures: An EEG/ERP Study." *2nd International Neuroergonomics Conference: The Brain at Work and in Everyday Life*. Frontiers Research Foundation.

Schilling, Tim, et al. 2019. "Looking through 'Rose-Tinted' Glasses: The Influence of Tint on Visual Affective Processing." *Frontiers in Human Neuroscience* 13:187.

Schopenhaur, Arthur. 1987. From *The World as Will and Idea*. In Morreall 1987, 51–64.

Schultz, Thomas R. 1972. "The Role of Incongruity and Resolution in Children's Appreciation of Cartoon Humor." *Journal of Experimental Child Psychology* 13:456–77.

Schulze, Lars, et al. 2013. "Gray Matter Abnormalities in Patients with Narcissistic Personality Disorder." *Journal of Psychiatric Research* 47:1363–69.

Schwartz, Ben. 2016. "Knock Yourselves Out: Punching Up in American Comedy." *Baffler* 31:134–46.

Schwitzgebel, Eric, and Fiery Cushman. 2012. "Expertise in Moral Reasoning? Order Effects on Moral Judgment in Professional Philosophers and Non-Philosophers." *Mind & Language* 27:135–53.

Scruton, Roger. 1987. "Laughter." In Morreall 1987, 156–71.

Shakespeare, Tom. 2013. "The Social Model of Disability." In *The Disability Studies Reader*, edited by Lennard J. Davis, 214–21. 4th ed. London: Routledge.

Shamay-Tsoory, Simone G., et al. 2007. "Neurocognitive Basis of Impaired Empathy in Schizophrenia." *Neuropsychology* 21:431–38.

Shamay-Tsoory, Simone, et al. 2009. "Neuropsychological Evidence of Impaired Cognitive Empathy in Euthymic Bipolar Disorder." *Journal of Neuropsychiatry and Clinical Neurosciences* 21:59–67.

Shelby, Tommie. 2002. "Is Racism in the 'Heart'?" *Journal of Social Philosophy* 33:411–20.

Shelby, Tommie. 2003. "Ideology, Racism, and Critical Social Theory." *Philosophical Forum* 34:153–88.

Shoemaker, David. 2000. "'Dirty Words' and the Offense Principle." *Law and Philosophy* 19:545–84.

Shoemaker, David. 2015. *Responsibility from the Margins*. Oxford: Oxford University Press.

Shoemaker, David. 2017. "Empathy and Moral Responsibility." In Maibom 2017, 242–52.

Shoemaker, David. 2018a. "Cruel Jokes and Normative Competence." *Social Policy and Philosophy* 35:173–95.

Shoemaker, David. 2018b. "You Oughta Know! Defending Angry Blame." In *The Moral Psychology of Anger*, edited by Myisha Cherry and Owen Flanagan, 67–88. London: Rowman & Littlefield.

Shoemaker, David. 2021. "The Forgiven." In *Forgiveness and Its Moral Dimensions*, edited by Brandon Warmke, Dana Kay Nelkin, and Michael McKenna, 29–56. New York: Oxford University Press.

Singer, Peter. 2011. *Practical Ethics*. Cambridge: Cambridge University Press.

Smith, Adam. 2006. "Cognitive Empathy and Emotional Empathy in Human Behavior and Evolution." *Psychological Record* 56:3–21.

Smith, Adam. 2009. "The Empathy Imbalance Hypothesis of Autism: A Theoretical Approach to Cognitive and Emotional Empathy in Autistic Development." *Psychological Record* 59:273–94.

Smith, Angela M. 2005. "Responsibility for Attitudes: Activity and Passivity in Mental Life." *Ethics* 115:236–71.

Smuts, Aaron. 2007. "The Joke Is the Thing: *In the Company of Men* and the Ethics of Humor." *Film and Philosophy* 11:49–65.

Smuts, Aaron. 2010. "The Ethics of Humor: Can Your Sense of Humor Be Wrong?" *Ethical Theory and Moral Practice* 13 (3): 333–47.

Sondergaard, Bent. 1991. "Switching between Seven Codes within One Family—A Linguistic Resource." *Journal of Multilingual & Multicultural Development* 12 (1/2): 85–92.

Sorenson, Roy. 2007. "Bald-Faced Lies! Lying without the Intent to Deceive." *Pacific Philosophical Quarterly* 88:251–64.

Sprecher, S., and P. C. Regan. 2002. "Liking Some Things (in Some People) More Than Others: Partner Preferences in Romantic Relationships and Friendships." *Journal of Social and Personal Relationships* 19:463–81.

Stalnaker, Robert. 2002. "Common Ground." *Linguistics and Philosophy* 25:701–21.

Stokke, Andreas. 2013. "Lying and Asserting." *Journal of Philosophy* 110:33–60.

Strawson, P. F. 1962. "Freedom and Resentment." *Proceedings of the British Academy* 48:1–25. Reprinted in *Free Will*, edited by Gary Watson, 72–93. 2nd ed. Oxford: Oxford University Press, 2003. Page references are to the 2003 reprint.

Strick, Madelijn, et al. 2009. "Finding Comfort in a Joke: Consolatory Effects of Humor through Cognitive Distraction." *Emotion* 9:574–78.

Sullivan, Kate, Ellen Winner, and Helen Tager-Flusberg. 2003. "Can Adolescents with Williams Syndrome Tell the Difference between Lies and Jokes?" *Developmental Neuropsychology* 23:85–103.

Sultanoff, S. 1995. "Levity Defies Gravity; Using Humor in Crisis Situations." *Therapeutic Humor* 9:1–2.

Sutton-Spence, Rachel, and Donna Jo Napoli. 2012. "Deaf Jokes and Sign Language Humor." *Humor* 25:311–37.

Szabo, Attila. 2003. "The Acute Effects of Humor and Exercise on Mood and Anxiety." *Journal of Leisure Research* 2:152–62.

Takamatsu, Reina. 2018. "Turning Off the Empathy Switch: Lower Empathic Concern for the Victim Leads to Utilitarian Choices of Action." *PloS One* 13:e0203826.

Tannen, Deborah. 1984. *Conversational Style*. Norwood, NJ: Ablex.

Tannen, Deborah. 1989. *Talking Voices: Repetition, Dialogue, and Imagery in Conversational Discourse*. Cambridge: Cambridge University Press.

Teding van Berkhout, Emily, and John M. Malouff. 2016. "The Efficacy of Empathy Training: A Meta-Analysis of Randomized Controlled Trials." *Journal of Counseling Psychology* 63:32–41.

Telfer, Elizabeth. 1995. "Hutcheson's Reflections upon Laughter." *Journal of Aesthetics and Art Criticism* 53:359–69.

Thoma, Patrizia, et al. 2011. "Cognitive and Affective Empathy in Depression Linked to Executive Control." *Psychiatry Research* 189:373–78.

Thomae, Manuela, and G. Tendayi Viki. 2013. "Why Did the Woman Cross the Road? The Effect of Sexist Humor on Men's Rape Proclivity." *Journal of Evolutionary, and Cultural Psychology* 7:250–69.

Thorson, J. A., F. C. Powell, I. Sarmany-Schuller, and W. P. Hampes. 1997. "Psychological Health and Sense of Humor." *Journal of Clinical Psychology* 53:605–19.

Thorson, James A., and F. C. Powell. 1994. "Depression and Sense of Humor." *Psychological Reports* 75 (suppl.): 1473–74.

Torres-Marin, Jorge, René T. Proyer, Raúl Lopez-Benítez, Kay Brauer, and Hugo Carretero-Dios. 2019. "Beyond the Big Five as Predictors of Dispositions toward Ridicule and Being Laughed At: The HEXACO Model and the Dark Triad." *Scandinavian Journal of Psychology* 60:473–83.

Trapp, Michael. 2019. "Laughter and the Moral Guide: Dio Chrysostom and Plutarch." In *Laughter, Humor, and Comedy in Ancient Philosophy*, edited by Pierre Destree and Franco V. Trivigno, 145–62. Oxford: Oxford University Press.

Trivigno, Franco V. 2019. "Plato on Laughter and Moral Harm." In *Laughter, Humor, and Comedy in Ancient Philosophy*, edited by Pierre Destree and Franco V. Trivigno, 13–34. Oxford: Oxford University Press.

Ture, Kwame, and Charles V. Hamilton. 1992. *Black Power: The Politics of Liberation*. New York: Vintage.

Uekermann, Jennifer, et al. 2008. "Executive Function, Mentalizing and Humor in Major Depression." *Journal of the International Neuropsychological Society* 14:55–62.

Van Bourgondien, Mary E., and Gary B. Mesibov. 1987. "Humor in High Functioning Autistic Adults." *Journal of Autism and Developmental Disorders* 17:417–24.

Vanderheiden, Steve. 2011. "Climate Change and Collective Responsibility." In *Moral Responsibility: Beyond Free Will and Determinism*, edited by Nicole A. Vincent, Ibo van de Poel, and Jeroen Hoven, 201–18. Dordrecht: Springer.

van Wormer, K., and M. Boes. 1997. "Humor in the Emergency Room: A Social Work Perspective." *Health and Social Work* 22:87–92.

Velleman, J. David. 1996. "Self to Self." *Philosophical Review* 105:39–76.

Vettin, Julia, and Dietmar Todt. 2005. "Human Laughter, Social Play, and Play Vocalizations of Non-Human Primates: An Evolutionary Approach." *Behavior* 142:217–40.

Viki, G. Tendayi, et al. 2007. "The Effect of Sexist Humor and Type of Rape on Men's

Self-Reported Rape Proclivity and Victim Blame." *Current Research in Social Psychology* 13:122–32.

Wai, Michael, and Niko Tiliopoulos. 2012. "The Affective and Cognitive Empathic Nature of the Dark Triad of Personality." *Personality and Individual Differences* 52:794–99.

Walker, Matthew D. 2019. "Aristotle on Wittiness." In *Laughter, Humor, and Comedy in Ancient Philosophy*, edited by Pierre Destree and Franco V. Trivigno, 103–21. Oxford: Oxford University Press.

Wallace, R. Jay. 1994. *Responsibility and the Moral Sentiments*. Cambridge, MA: Harvard University Press.

Wastell, Colin, and Alexandra Booth. 2003. "Machiavellianism: An Alexithymic Perspective." *Journal of Social and Clinical Psychology* 22:730–44.

Watson, Gary. 2013. "Psychopathy and Prudential Deficits." *Proceedings of the Aristotelian Society* 113:269–92.

Weems, Scott. 2014. *Ha! The Science of When and Why We Laugh*. New York: Basic Books.

Weisenberg, Matisyohu, Inbal Tepper, and Joseph Schwarzwald. 1995. "Humor as a Cognitive Technique for Increasing Pain Tolerance." *PAIN* 63:207–12.

Winner, E., et al. 1998. "Distinguishing Lies from Jokes: Theory of Mind Deficits and Discourse Interpretation in Right Hemisphere Brain-Damaged Patients." *Brain and Language* 62:89–106.

Wolf, Susan. 1982. "Moral Saints." *Journal of Philosophy* 79:419–39.

Wolff, Jonathan. 2011. *Ethics and Public Policy*. London: Routledge.

Wu, Ching-Lin, et al. 2014. "Do Individuals with Autism Lack a Sense of Humor? A Study of Humor Comprehension, Appreciation, and Styles among High School Students with Autism." *Research in Autism Spectrum Disorders* 8:1386–93.

Yancy, George. 2018. "Yes Academic Bias Is a Problem and We Need to Address it: A Response to Larregue." *American Sociologist* 49:336–43.

Yip, Jeremy A., and Rod A. Martin. 2006. "Sense of Humor, Emotional Intelligence, and Social Competence." *Journal of Research in Personality* 40:1202–08.

Zaki, Jamil. 2020. "The Caregiver's Dilemma: In Search of Sustainable Medical Empathy." *Lancet* 396:458–59.

Index

Page numbers followed by "f" refer to figures.